THE SEVEN DEADLY SINS OF CAPITALISM

REINVENTING A MODEL FOR THE ECONOMY, SOCIETY AND WELFARE

Published under licence 2012 by Searching Finance Ltd.

ISBN: 978-1-907720-68-0

Typeset by Deirdré Gyenes

THE SEVEN DEADLY SINS OF CAPITALISM

REINVENTING A MODEL FOR THE ECONOMY, SOCIETY AND WELFARE

Mike Guillaume

About the author

Mike Guillaume is the co-founder and manager of e.com-ReportWatch, an American-headquartered, London-based company that specializes in listed company reports' assessment and benchmarking. Mike has a wide knowledge of corporate and financial reporting and has been the editor of the "*Annual Report on Annual Reports*" since 1996 (go to www.reportwatch.net). Prior to that, his track record includes extensive entrepreneurial and international management consulting experience. He worked first as an organizational consultant for a U.S. firm. Then he created and managed the Enterprise Group; first focused on business planning for startups and local enterprises; then on strategies for international SMEs, global firms and public institutions. He has consulted extensively across a wide range of industries in Europe, North and South America, and Southeast Asia, with a good grasp of the financial and energy sectors among others. Parallel to his career path in markets, he did stints in the public sector (as a part-time economy minister cabinet advisor, public-private partnerships (as program manager and consultant), and academia (as visiting professor in international strategy). That blend gives him good vantage points for watching economics and economies.

Mike has a degree in political science and international economics, and a background in financial management and analysis. He has authored many articles and contributed to various publications, analyses and seminars. Born in Charleroi (Wallonia, Belgium), Mike has lived, worked and consulted in twenty-five countries on four continents. He now splits his work and life between London ("*a city founded by the Romans and I'm not tired of it*"), a former Roman village, and "*other less Roman-influenced places.*"

More about Mike and views on economics, capitalism and change on www.mikeconomics.net.

About Searching Finance

Searching Finance Ltd is a dynamic new voice in knowledge provision for the financial services and related professional sectors. Our mission is to provide expert, highly relevant and actionable information and analysis, written by professionals, for professionals. For more information, please visit www.searchingfinance.com

CONTENTS

INTRODUCTION
– ON SINS, VIRTUES, LIBERALISM, AND CAPITALISM

Sometimes it looks wonderful - look at entrepreneurship, innovation, new drugs and other inventions; sometimes it is really awful - consider unemployment, poverty, environmental damage, among others.

That is capitalism.

For all its failings, flaws and sins, market capitalism still probably represents economically "*the worst system devised by wit of man, except for all the others*," to paraphrase what Winston Churchill said about political democracy. "*Highly imperfect. Yet so are we. But it is still among humanity's most brilliant inventions. It is still a uniquely flexible, responsive and innovative economic system*," writes Martin Wolf.[1]

On a personal note

Those who have met me or read my writings can hardly define me as anti-capitalist. I am a liberal by temperament, by instinct

1 "*Seven ways to fix the system's flaws*" by Martin Wolf (Financial Times, January 23, 2012).

and by upbringing.[2] Therefore, I consider the individual, and not the family, the state, a community, or a nation, as the core of a modern society. Consequently, for any liberal, liberty lies – or should lie – at the heart of the political system – what LIBERALISM is all about – and be the modus operandi of the economy – what free-market CAPITALISM is about. Being a liberal naturally also means being open to other people's ideas, new or old, from left, center or right; as well as looking for pragmatic approaches rather than for ideological solutions. "*When the facts change, I change my mind*," said Keynes. "*A good idea is a good idea, regardless of where it comes from*," states the British liberal think tank Centre Forum, adding that data, not dogma should support liberal aims and values.[3] Reality checks are required as often as the situation demands. Some of them can validate your views, others can make you revise your opinions or judgments, sometimes radically. Contrary to hard-line opponents of capitalism (is there anyone left?) and its most outspoken critics (there are growing numbers here), I have no problem with how to make my bread and butter and make a decent living (up to a point, as life cannot be reduced to economy) within the system and acknowledge its merits. Still, it is important to check the flaws and see the limitations. Nothing is perfect in this brave new world. I also have to admit that writing such a book would have been for me a more

2 To repeat the words of Nick Clegg in his acceptance speech upon winning the British Liberal Democrats' party leadership contest in November 2007. Endorsing such words does not imply any support to the Con-Lib government. See my comment about "*It's time for left-liberals to join Labour*" on Liberal Conspiracy (http://liberalconspiracy.org, May 12, 2010); and "*Cable-nomics: a reader*" on www.leftfootforward.org (September 2010).

3 In the same vein: "*L'événement sera notre maître intérieur*," stated Emmanuel Mounier, a French and Christian philosopher, founder of the Esprit review. This contradicts not only with traditional leftist ideologues, but also with the almost religious assertion of free-market zealots, such as the economist George Stigler: "*When the facts contradict theory, they are wrong and theory is right.*"

difficult exercise some years – or decades – ago.[4] The system was then more entrepreneurial (or Smithian, if you want), more about the real economy and less about finance. It looked less disputable then, especially as representing the most credible, if not sole, alternative to communist and so-called "socialist" regimes (not to mention other models which may return to fashion in the wake of capitalism's troubles). It was mainly viewed as a set of mechanisms and not as an ideology except in the eyes of hard-line opponents inside and enemies outside (how many divisions these days?).

The purpose of this book is not about religion – and certainly not about creating a new one! Using a religious reference as a book title does not mean that the author regards himself as a kind of devotee and evangelist (old-fashioned or newborn) pleading, on economics and in general, for some forms of heavenly or cardinal virtues. Yet these, or at least some, may admittedly come in handy in times of economic, financial, social or moral distress. For those who are not aware, or have forgotten, and for the many more who that live with other beliefs, in Christianity, "*the seven deadly sins*" refer to objectionable and mortal vices.[5] "*I could've had religion*", as the Irish blues rocker Rory Gallagher sang. "*But...*" As far as I am concerned and as the following pages will show, I have never considered capitalism as a religion and behaved like one of its apostles. However, a loss of faith in the system might have been at work to come up with the criticisms developed in this book. Call it liberal blues or a blues for capitalism? As old bluesmen sometimes put it: "*I'm no sinner, but I ain't no saint.*" I was baptized a Catholic (a useful reminder here: it is

4 To be honest, my first doubts came in the late sixties, when I became increasingly suspicious about the confusion between promoting democracy and exporting capitalism. What was the Cold War really about? Did it have the same meaning to all? The Pinochet and other Latin American monetarist "experiences" played for me as a first wake-up call.

5 The deadly sins were defined as wrath, greed, sloth, pride, lust, envy, and gluttony.

the Catholic Church that splits sins between the DEADLY and other VENIAL sins) then became a "post-Christian agnostic" (or is it atheist, I am not sure), or, more simply put, a free-thinker, with some Protestant leanings and some interest in Buddhism. A number of years spent consulting in Asian countries (mainly Buddhist and Muslim) were a culture shock. I discovered another way of thinking more focused on the long term, and a great emphasis placed by families on education, two issues increasingly neglected in Western societies (particularly in America).[6] From Asia, I came back with the notion that great civilizations exist or have existed in many places, and not only where you were born; and that there is no reason to impose models just because they worked in a particular place. My way or the highway is not my approach.[7] Therefore, I have great respect for any form of individual faith or collective set of beliefs, as long as liberties and secularism are not threatened. I attach great importance to these latter aspects, in a world in which religious fundamentalism is growing. Even if faith is often stronger than reason, for better or worse, as history is teaching us, reason and rationality should prevail as much as possible. "*The truths of religion are never so well understood as by those who have lost the power of reason*," said Voltaire.

My Weltanschauung (a nice German word for view of the world and of life) has strongly been shaped by three sets of thought: the British economists and moral philosophers (Smith, Mill, Locke et al.), the French Enlightenment philosophers and political scientists (Voltaire, Diderot, Montesquieu et al.), and

---

6 Harvard University professor Kenneth Rogoff writes: "*educate, educate, educate. It is really hard to see another way out of the growing sustainability problems that capitalism has given us.*" in "*Our ignorance will yield more crises in capitalism*" (Financial Times, February 2, 2012). Better late than never.

7 This totally contradicts with the bible-and-gun supremacist approach defended among others by George W. Bush's Defense Secretary Donald Rumsfeld who declared seriously that the U.S. intervention would "*bring civilization*" to Irak. He has now enough time to read that the region was civilized when North America was not even yet the map.

the Founding Fathers of the United States (Franklin, Jefferson, Washington et al.). The founders of modern economics were part of my secondary school curriculum: Hume, Cantillon, Smith, Malthus, Ricardo, Mill, Bastiat, and their followers. I found some sense, common sense, and nonsense (the latter was often easier to find in some followers' work) in learning about and from them. That is to say, macroeconomics and political economy have been with me for some time. I was also lucky enough to learn the long and often fascinating history and geography of countries such as Britain, France, the United States, India, and China.[8] This combined with those travels that broaden the mind has given me a less ethnocentric perspective. Running a consulting business (kicked off the hardest way thanks to a Chicago-based company with a number of Texan colleagues) proved to be an invaluable learning process on the way the real economy works – and does not work, at times. There are high and lows arising from that experience in this book. Over the last decade, I have been involved in a more corporate, financial and investor-oriented side of business. This is present in the book too. This book is the distilled product of these years of work and reflection that has developed over time.

Liberalism # capitalism

Though significantly forged by the three movements defined above, liberalism and the word "liberal" itself have evolved into various meanings and practices. The Oxford English Dictionary gives a very good definition of liberal: "*wanting or allowing a lot of political and economic freedom and supporting gradual social, political or religious change.*" A very British definition indeed, which seems natural in the country where it

8 Yes, I know about that insularity. Nevertheless, I keep on enjoying the smell of liberalism that pervades certain places and times on the British Isles and that you cannot find anywhere else.

was invented before being exported, adapted, and sometimes much distorted in other places. Ironically, France and the U.S. stand among the countries where "liberal" is frequently used as an insult, yet for opposite reasons. In the country of Alexis de Tocqueville, left-wingers use the word to indicate dislike for capitalism, liberalism, and the right in general. In Tocqueville's country (once visited by Jefferson), there has never been a real liberal party, and a real modern progressive left has never really emerged. You may chalk this up to the role of the state in French society, whose political pendulum swings from more or less statist right to left. In Benjamin Franklin's country (also visited by Tocqueville), liberal can be in a conservative's eyes a nasty word to talk about "left-wing" state interventionists, who are of course labeled "un-American." To foreigners, the equation between a country, an economic system and, for many, a religious belief, may look weird, especially in the 21st century. Listening to most of the right-wing media, politicians, business people, (neo)conservatives, think tanks, Tea Party goers, and other evangelists, it is clear that economic freedom is more valued than political liberty and social justice. These are sometimes, if not often, regarded as a threat to the sacred market system and other (un)related values. (Public) principles seem to matter less than (private) interests. The U.S. is probably one of the only countries where a minimum tax proposed on millionaires is deemed as a "*war on capital*" by a Republican Party candidate. No wonder even Warren Buffett himself states that his country is leaning towards plutocracy!

There are liberals and… liberals. The progressive liberal camp to which I belong puts the same emphasis on political liberty, social justice and environmental protection as on free markets, and therefore believes in and works with "*liberal means towards progressive ends,*" as Giles Wilkes finely sums it up.[9] Coupling the two words would be a tautology in many

9 Giles Wilkes is the former chief economist of Centre Forum (http://centreforum.org), a British independent liberal think-tank.

U.S. eyes (yet a few conservative or centrist liberals can be met here too), but let us forget American exceptionalism. In the Commonwealth and in most parts of the world there are different kinds of liberalisms – and capitalisms. As opposed to America's mainstream, European liberalism has always been as much about political and social democracy as about free markets. "*Free as we wish unless we harm others*," said John Stuart Mill. At the end of the 19th and the beginning of the 20th century liberal parties were including a significant number of progressive leaders and members whose ideals of social justice made way for new left parties and much needed social reforms. David Lloyd George was among their most prominent figures and may be regarded as a founder of a social-liberal welfare system as opposed to Bismarck-style paternalistic welfare. These last decades (and sometimes further back in time), bar a few rare exceptions, "liberal" parties in Europe have increasingly drifted towards various forms of economic conservatism, in spite of dashes of Thatcherism here and there. Supporting the economic interests (of the middle and upper classes) now prevails over defending liberal principles, though never to the same extent as in America where it is blatant. In some countries, e.g. in Eastern and Northern Europe, ultra-right or populist parties even label themselves as liberal with content that has little to do with Locke, Montesquieu or Jefferson.

Although they often work together, capitalism is not per se synonymous with liberal democracy. Was it not Milton Friedman himself who wrote: "*History suggests that capitalism is a necessary condition for political freedom. Clearly it is not a sufficient condition*."[10] Economic and political liberalism can clash: more power of capital often results in less free markets, usually means increased injustice and inequality, and sometimes seriously harms individual liberties. History teaches us that big business thrived under Hitler's rule (remember

10 Milton Friedman: "*Capitalism and Freedom*" (University of Chicago Press, first published in 1962). By the way, Milton Friedman was an agnostic.

Dr. Porsche, the Krupp family, and... Henry Ford!). All-to-market "neoliberalism" championed by Milton Friedman, Ronald Reagan, Margaret Thatcher and their many disciples – some of them not exactly the most democratic champions (remember a certain General Pinochet) – has brought discredit on the liberal-capitalist mix. The term "liberal" is now at least ambiguous and at worst ideological or negative. If liberal still sounds positive to some ears, neoliberal very often expresses disapproval or discontent.[11] Because of – and thanks to – its quadruple meaning – cultural, political, social and economic – liberalism has been multifaceted since its origins, which are diverse.[12]

Capitalism is not monolithic either. In Europe and Latin America, social-democratic and other progressive parties were needed to make capitalism less wild, implement bold reforms refused or delayed by economic, political and social conservatives (often including religious forces and right-wing liberals), and create new economic and social models allowing redistribution that free markets would NEVER have achieved with their "invisible" hand. Today, we see competing models of capitalism flourish, from American – or, more broadly, Anglo-Saxon – to Rhenish, from Asian to Nordic, from feudal to post-communist (both in oligarchic style), from state-led to development-driven.

Capitalism is no longer what it used to be

The system has always proved able to change, that is one of its great strengths. As Zygmunt Bauman, a very critical observer,

11 Some talk of "neo-liberal nationalism", e.g. to refer to the Dutch right-wing government. See: "*The rise of Dutch neo-liberal nationalism*" on www.opendemocracy.net (April 12, 2012).

12 A definitive account on the history of liberalism has probably been written in the excellent 800-plus-page book by the French Catherine Audard, professor at the London School of Economics: "*Qu'est-ce que le libéralisme? Ethique, politique, société*" (Folio Essais, 2009).

writes: "*capitalism has an in-built wondrous capacity of resurrection and regeneration.*"[13] Somewhat ironically, it is more flexible than many of its rigid and doctrinaire defenders in the books or in the field. With all due respect to Adam Smith, and every economist (liberal or not) owes him a lot, one of the major flaws in a work that remains essential is the metaphor of the invisible hand.[14] This has proved to be an illusion more than once in the history of capitalism, as illusory as the somewhat related principles of perfectly informed and rational economic agents (as defined or analyzed by the French Léon Walras and the English William Jevons, among others).[15] As Joseph Stiglitz puts it: "*the reason that the invisible hand often seems invisible is that it is often not there.*"[16] The invisible hand is very often the heavy hand of dominating firms or the hand taken by financiers in markets. Besides, one thing is certain: for all its VIRTUES – and there are still some real and a few unmatched ones – the market no longer has the answers to all the problems. Saying that capitalism is capable of changing and regulating only by itself is like asking the tobacco industry to tell people not to smoke.

The NATURE of capitalism has changed. Financial markets' side effects far outweigh their benefits to real economies. Corpocrats rule over small entrepreneurs. Risk-betting traders make a much quicker buck than risk-taking businesspeople (except for a few rags-to-riches stories for TV shows). Bankers have switched to short trading at the same time they have lost

13 "*On the Nature of Capitalism*" on www.social-europe.eu (October 17, 2011).

14 Adam Smith: "*The Wealth of Nations*" (1776, republished e.g. by Bantam Classics, 2003). The "invisible hand" is referred to in "*The Theory of Moral Sentiments*" (republished in Penguin Classics, 2010). The Scottish economist may be forgiven, his words must be put in context, and his times were not ours.

15 Léon Walras: "*Elements of Pure Economics, or the theory of social wealth.*" (1874). William Stanley Jevons: "*The Theory of Political Economy*" (1871). A summary of "*The Rationality Principle and Classical Economics*" by the Canadian philosopher Maurice Lagueux goes to the point (go to www.philo.umontreal.ca/textes/).

16 Joseph E. Stiglitz: "*Making Globalization Work*" (W. W. Norton, 2007).

credit (all meanings, bar the cards). Greed fuels large parts of the system. Individual shareholders have no say. Daily share price targets have replaced medium-term strategies. Unrelated derivatives travel buck naked. Speculative bubbles burst regularly. Too many economists are just conformists. Casino finance pays off (much) more than the provision of a good service. Many policymakers are subservient to markets and their latest ratings. Those flaws come on top of other weaknesses – some of them qualifying as original sins: booms and busts, inequities and inequalities, selfishness, the cult of growth, supposed rationality, unfettered globalization, overconsumption, indebtedness, environmental damage… What were once virtues – making profit is not sinful as such – turn into vices: making money with money proves purposeless and value-destructive and can be terribly harmful for those without deep pockets.

Markets are unstable by nature. That has its charms – who needs the stability of the Middle Ages and communism? That comes at a price too, named crisis and recession, and a few other "on"-ending words. The latest crises will not be the last, whatever the short- or long-term economic or business cycle school (Juglar, Schumpeter, Kuznets "swings" and Kondratiev "waves"). "*Once we were satisfied that the cycle was ten years in length and since that was smashed*," said Irving Fisher… in 1946. However, even if upward cycles may occasionally last longer – some even argue that recessions last for not as long as in the past – bubbles burst and crises tend to repeat more often and spread much faster than in the past. There were at least six major crises in the last fifty years compared with two in the previous half-century. Now, "thanks to" globalization, each significant crisis has repercussions almost everywhere, at least to some extent, which was not the case even in the relatively recent past.[17] The logical question that arises from this book's title and content is: if it suffers from "deadly" sins,

17 To give but one example, a deep Eurozone recession could cut China's growth by 50 percent.

will capitalism die from this crisis? Well, the system has gone through many crises and has proved extraordinarily resilient: sometimes stronger, sometimes weaker, sometimes stepping backward, sometimes moving forward. One of the great questions of our times is which forms of economic models will dominate – and are desirable – in the coming years and decades.

The latest crises – some are not over, at least in some parts of the world – are more serious because, in addition to their usual ingredients, they are the result of a conjunction of worrying trends and factors. Those are: too large, too powerful and uncontrolled financial institutions; a tyranny of short-termism; pure irrationality (often disguised as "rational markets"); irresponsible public policies (not everywhere, though); and, last but not least, unprecedented greed. "*We have just witnessed a... phenomenon in the financial markets. A crime has been committed. There is a victim (the helpless retirees, taxpayers funding losses, perhaps even capitalism and free society). There were plenty of bystanders. And there was a robbery (overcompensated bankers who got bonuses for hiding risks, overpaid quantitative risk managers selling patently bogus methods)... Most poignantly, the police may have participated in the murder.*"[18] These lines were written in the middle of the first great financial crisis of the 21st century. They do not come from a bunch of leftists but from a professor of risk engineering and a derivatives consultant! The Madoff gang, the Lehman brothers, the Greenberg solo, Freddie and Fannie, Merrill marauders, Barclays' Libor manipulators, and other champions of greed were and are no exceptions, they were and are still part of a system now extremely dependent on it. To make things worse, regulators are often "captured" by the institutions they are

18 Nassim Nicholas Taleb, professor at New York University; and Pablo Triana, derivatives consultant: "*Bystanders to this financial crime were many*", in the Financial Times (December 8, 2008).

charged with regulating.[19] The net result of the explosive mix of malpractice and a financial system that had run out of control (mostly, yet not only, in Anglo-Saxon economies), was the late-2000s financial turmoil. Although based on credit, it was paid in cash. Year 2008 losses on major stock markets ranged from 34 percent to 65 percent. And the costs and losses, first estimated at $1,000 billion by the IMF in April 2008 (i.e. in the early stages of the crisis), were recalculated by the same IMF at $4,100 billion one year later (with estimated total write-downs on U.S. assets only at $2,700 billion).[20] Over a longer period, an IMF database, which reviews systemic banking crises since 1970, shows that the average fiscal cost of such crises at about 15 percent of GDP.[21] A hell of a lot of money!

Sins?

This book deals with the SINS of capitalism. Logically, it contains much more on the negatives than about the positives. The virtues may still deserve words of praise yet to a lesser extent than in the past. To be fair, one could also write a lot more about the sins of the alternatives to capitalism, such as authoritarianism, communism, fascism, feudalism, nationalism, populism, state socialism, totalitarianism... These are other stories. And stating that all tried alternatives have proved worse is not sufficient to plead not guilty and rest the case.

Why should we not talk of sins when, after all, it was (and still is) about religion – at least for some?[22] Goldman Sachs'

19 "*Reckless Endangerment. How Outsized Ambition, Greed, and Corruption Led to Economic Armageddon*" by Gretchen Morgenson and Joshua Rosner (Times Books, 2011), in which the authors focus on Fannie Mae.

20 See the critical comment by Martin Wolf on "*Why Obama's new Tarp will fail to rescue the banks*", and "*IMF puts financial losses at $4,100bn*", in the Financial Times (February 10, April 21, 2009).

21 In "*The cost of resolving financial crises*" by Luc Laeven, a CEPR Research Fellow, on http://voxeu.org (October 2008).

22 Isn't Mitt Romney, among others, mainly a capitalist preacher, after all?

CEO once said that he was "*doing God's work*"[23] One of the first representatives of Chicago school economics, Frank Knight, thought that professors should "*inculcate*" (sic) the belief that each economic theory is "*a sacred feature, not a debatable hypothesis.*" Furthermore, Friedmanites, Hayekians, and other dedicated followers of the market religion (make) believe that economic and market forces are like the forces of nature.[24] This thinking has turned into a form of "no alternative" determinism applied full steam ahead through the forces of globalization. Ironically, it often borders on a form of intellectual totalitarianism less hard but not less dogmatic than communism – remember "*the end of history*" and the absolute triumph of capitalism? Even many former free-market opponents or skeptics have bought the all-to-market rhetoric. A cult of money and consumption has also replaced, or at least competes with other more traditional and less materialistic faiths (nations, states, communities, religions).

Capitalism is an economic system based on certain mechanisms. Not less, but not more either. It should not be turned into an all-embracing ideology, because "*you simply can't run an economy as complicated as ours on ideology alone.*"[25] Nor should it be viewed as a religion, e.g. by making it synonymous per se with free market or democracy, or, even worse, by mixing up market economy with some form of market society – where everything is bought, sold and traded.

---

23 "*I'm doing 'God's work'. Meet Mr Goldman Sachs*" (Sunday Times, November 8, 2009). A few days later, he declared that his words should not have been taken seriously...

24 Quoted by Naomi Klein in her excellent yet scary "*The Shock Doctrine*" (Penguin Books, 2007).

25 Jared Bernstein, quoted in "*The Free Market: A False Idol After All*" (The New York Times, December 30, 2007). Jared Bernstein is an economist at the Washington-based Economic Policy Institute.

Seven sins – Take two

The first edition of this book was written in a hurry, with a sense of urgency, and quickly self-published when the subprime-based financial crisis was upon us and resulted in the worst economic downturn since the Great Depression. Thanks to Ashwin Rattan, who thought that such a work should develop over time and suggested a new edition, the reader will find here an entirely revised, fully updated, and much expanded yet concise book. The only thing that has not changed is the seven deadly sins, as well as the seven (not so) venial ones. They have all remained intact, many having worsened. Why's that? Because they are HERE TO STAY.

Observing the lack of reactivity at economic and business levels, the use of expedients and piecemeal changes (named plans, programs, packages) by governments and political elites, and the mounting social costs, I had come to the conclusion that, in such changing times, partly created by crazy people at all levels, things should change.[26] Have things changed? Well, on balance, not that much, and certainly not as much as they should have. And some crazy behaviors still rule the game. Some had thought that the days of reckoning had come. One of the rare economists to predict the subprime mortgage crisis, Turkish-born Nouriel Roubini, said early in 2009: "*the problems suggest the system is bankrupt*."[27] A few years on, "*cowardly states*" (to use the words of Richard Murphy) are still footing the debt-laden bills, some of which were significantly caused by financial sector bailouts. Policymakers are still tinkering with banking regulations. They are more than ever bowing

26 Words freely inspired by Bob Dylan ("*Things Have Changed*", from the "*Wonder Boys*" soundtrack album, Columbia, 2000). Hardly an anticapitalist, the famous management consultant Tom Peters wrote more than once that many of the corporate leaders could be considered as crazy, at least at some moments.

27 "*What they said then: And now*", in the Herald Tribune (January 27, 2009). Nouriel Roubini is an economics professor at New York University Stern School of Business.

down to those strange "creatures" named financial markets and rating agencies.[28] Bar a few minor adaptations, the system has remained much the same, with many of its flaws not fixed and most sins not atoned for.

Still, David Rothkopf states that "*Free-market evangelists face a lonely fate*" and sees as likely the shift toward an "*Asian model of capitalism*" with "*a more active role for government*."[29] Do not bet your bottom dollar. One debt crisis and recession later, it is back to business as usual, or not far. As Philip Stephens wrote in the Financial Times: "*the markets are masters again*."[30] In China, India and elsewhere, there are some signs of a more short-term-driven system now gaining ground to the detriment of the more long-term oriented Asian models.

Unless you are one-sided or blind to the faults and problems (sometimes due to power position or ideology, or both), it is now relatively easy, also for non-dogmatic free-market partisans, to go on a fault-finding exercise and identify major flaws in the system.[31] (One should nevertheless pay a tribute to long-time market skeptics who saw the bad times coming years before others – the list includes my old amico Walter Coscia.) It is a moral duty if we want the system to adapt, transform, change, and (re)invent something else that works more efficiently, more fairly, more justly, and more freely. Thousands of pages have been written on the subject. Still, I thought a recap – with a bit of value added, I hope – could do no harm. After

28 Richard Murphy: "*The Courageous State: Rethinking Economics, Society and the Role of Government*" (Searching Finance, 2011). At long last daring proposals from the left, which had run short of ideas for a while, to boldly defend the role of the State in modern economies.

29 David Rothkopf: "*Free-market evangelists face a lonely fate*" in the Financial Times, February 1, 2012.

30 "*Three years on –and the markets are masters again*" (Financial Times, July 30, 2010).

31 Forbes magazine attributed "*The Worst Economic Recovery Since The Great Depression*" to… Obama's "*Keynesian economics*." (January 12, 2012). Who the hell started the crisis? You have to be Forbes to forget that! Only in America.

reviewing the seven deadly sins plus seven other not so venial ones – some at the heart of capitalism, some having developed more recently – the last part of the book proposes a TOOLBOX made up of more than one hundred principles, suggestions, ideas and possible actions and reinvention policies towards a new model for the economy, society, and welfare.

Notes for the reader

Nowadays in many books, footnotes are printed at the end of a chapter or at the end of the book. I find it frustrating to have to flip pages to read the endnotes. Consequently, in many cases nobody reads them. Considering that footnotes are sources of information that add significant value to the texts, the reader will find them placed on each page.

To travel across the array of examples, names, places, abbreviations and acronyms, use the index placed at the end of the book. From there, you can journey through capitalism past, present, and future.

PART 1
SEVEN DEADLY SINS OF CAPITALISM

"Capital as such is not evil; it is its wrong use that is evil."
MOHANDAS GANDHI

"Capitalism is the astounding belief that the most wickedest of men will do the most wickedest of things for the greatest good of everyone."
JOHN MAYNARD KEYNES

SIN NO. 1: TOO BIG

"Man is small, and, therefore, small is beautiful."
ERNST FRIEDRICH SCHUMACHER,
economic thinker, in the 1970s

"Sometimes I have to admit that our company is so gigantic and the inertia of the system is so big that it is for us impossible to play our role as managers."
ALFRED P. SLOAN JR.,
CEO of General Motors, in the 1930s

Big pharma (prescription 1)

Early in 2009, Pfizer's CEO told the Financial Times that his company was considering the acquisition of a "large rival" to improve its financial health, adding that "*The real goal is to grow revenues*" and that, naturally, it should (sic) "*meet the criteria of shareholder value.*"[1] FT journalist Andrew Jack pointed out that the CEO's remarks were reflecting a strong need to compensate for a sharp drop in forecast sales of existing patented drugs that had become "*exposed to competition.*" That says much about one of today's worrying trends in the capitalist system: being bigger for the sake of it, and doing this by acquiring competitors instead of trying to grow your own revenues – and innovate – by your own means, products and resources.

The sickness and its (in)direct consequences for companies is perfectly illustrated in the case of Pfizer. Having been conservative (in the positive meaning of this word) for decades with regard to external growth and epitomizing large-scale innovative entrepreneurship with William Steere at the steering wheel, Pfizer then embarked on a frantic buying spree.[2] Numbers matter. In 1990, sales were $4,757 million, ROE (return on equity) was 16.9 percent, EPS (earnings per share, here for continuing operations) were $0.17. In 1999, sales were up to $14,135 million, ROE had more than doubled to 35.9 percent, and EPS reached $0.85. For those who pay more attention to market value, this had jumped from $3.37 per share to $32.44 over the same period.

Then came the 2000s.

The New York-based firm bought, directly or via purchases, Warner-Lambert, Pharmacia, Upjohn, Parke-Davis, Agouron,

1 January 5, 2009.

2 See performance indicators as reported in Pfizer annual reports from 1991 to 2000, from which our figures were sourced. Incidentally, or coincidentally, it is worth noting that the quality of information (and the number of ratios) in annual reports started decreasing in the early 2000s.

Searle, Sugen... Does anybody but the accountants remember the acquisition costs? Unlikely. Many more individuals paid the price and felt the pinch. "Shareholder value," he said. The share price was divided by two between 1999 and 2007, resulting in a $140 billion fall in value. Sure, as an immediate effect of acquisitions, revenues almost tripled in six years. End-2007 EPS (for continuing operations) were at $1.19, i.e. progressing less than over a comparable period based on organic growth. What about the ever-important ROE? After a mysterious surge to 55.2 percent in 2002, it fell back to a 15 percent average for the last five years. Less than one month after Pfizer's announced intention, this led to the planned purchase of rival Wyeth for $68 billion, with $22.5 billion coming from a consortium of banks... and a dividend cut (with that "*shareholder value*" still in mind, we assume!). Has the drug giant learned from its past errors? Hopefully, both the acquirer and the acquired have since then found pills for memory and diet treatments in their pipeline. Never mind! Pfizer CEO promised that this "*takeover will be different*".[3] Heard that tune before? Never mind, you will hear it again! Three years after that huge purchase, Pfizer was considering plans to spin off its animal health division, in which it is still a world market leader. The goal was "*to streamline activities after investor criticism over poor returns*."[4] A euphemism for saying that the company has become too big to be manageable.

To be fair, Pfizer preceded or followed the crowd and is far from being the sole company in its industry to have demonstrated an addiction to size: consider e.g. GlaxoSmithKline (GSK), whose full name should now be, take a breath, Burroughs-Wellcome-Glaxo-Laboratories-Smithkline-Beecham, had imaginative (?) brand experts not shortened the

3 Reports on www.reuters.com, Financial Times, BusinessWeek (January 26, 27, 28, 2009).

4 "*Pfizer talks to banks about unit's $3bn part-flotation*" (Financial Times, February 20, 2012).

company identity after its numerous acquisitions and mergers. Hopefully, also, if not mainly, for their shareholders and employees, pharmaceutical companies will avoid the sleeping pills that make them lethargic and discover weight-watching and anti-obesity prescriptions that apply to themselves and not only to patients. But from what we are seeing and hearing here and there, many in and out the sector have not learned from turning their own labs' know-how into effective medicines which, after all, concern executive and managers' eyes, skills and, er, brains! Instead, they keep on repeating the same mistake and just emulate each other.[5] In the case of Pfizer, is it not just because some on the boards were sick of watching Johnson & Johnson becoming No. 1 in the American pharma industry?[6] The answer here might be a simple yes. A few weeks after Wyeth's takeover by Pfizer, the rival Merck announced, in a move that looks a bit like a response, its plan to acquire Schering-Plough. The reasons for the acquisition were very similar to Pfizer's move (patent expirations, etc.). The merger was completed in November 2009. Note the astonishing comment made about this by an analyst: "*It seems somewhat inevitable... There is overcapacity and [the companies] need to take each other's capacity out of the market.*"[7] In other words, it is about growing fat to get fit! A strange prescription, isn't it?

---

5 According to Dealogic (www.dealogic.com) and as reported by the New York Times (January 5, 2009), the combined global volume of M&As announced in 2008 amounted to $3.3 trillion. That was down 28 percent from 2007, but still the fourth-highest yearly total ever. In 2010, M&A activity rose by 23 percent in the U.S.

6 Johnson & Johnson overtook Pfizer in the n° 1 position in pharmaceuticals in the 2007 and 2008 Fortune 500 rankings. Pfizer came back to n° 1 in 2009.

7 Information and analyst's quotation on www.reuters.com (March 9, 2009). About Merck and Schering-Plough: "*Merck, Schering-Plough set to complete merger*" (Reuters, November 3, 2009).

Bigger in Detroit -and then?

General Motors (GM) management was probably angry at watching Toyota overtaking it.

Playing by the rules of free markets seems increasingly replaced for large corporations by searching for market domination. Before considering a merger with Chrysler and then dropping it, GM had first turned to Ford for a possible deal. What for? Piling up losses? With hindsight GM's attitude looks even more disgraceful, as it shifted from almost all possible merger options to announcing the sale (or something else) of some of its biggest brands. This proved, if it was still necessary, that the company had become unmanageable, mainly owing to size. Many industry experts and management specialists had pointed at those problems for years, but the Detroit giant was as blind to them as it was to the performance of leaner and meaner Japanese automakers.[8] After those failed attempts to grow bigger than big, GM begged shamelessly for taxpayers' money (just call it a bailout); not only in the U.S., but also in Sweden (for Saab, an ailing division that GM had never managed to reignite after having bought it), and in Germany (for Opel, that would probably have fared better without Detroit's bureaucratic management). The style came close to blackmailing, before finally being parked at No. 11 garage (we mean Chapter). If the Detroit giant is faring a bit better again - to hell and then back as the world's top vehicle manufacturer in 2011 - it is certainly not because of external growth and organic fat, on the contrary![9] Now, compare how other (smaller) manufacturers are driving the global motorway.

8 In one of his first books ("*The Concept of the Corporation*"), Peter Drucker advised GM's Alfred Sloan to decentralize. This was dismissed as a betrayal. That was in 1946...

9 After such failures, the news that GM would take a stake in Peugeot sounded a bit surprising while, at the same time, Opel was still in trouble ("*GM poised to take 7% stake in Peugeot*", Financial Times, February 29, 2012), and discussions were held to secure the future of its Australian division ("*Holden rescue deal likely soon...*" on www.news.com.au/business (January 10, 2012).

Mergers: (some) good motives and (often) bad results

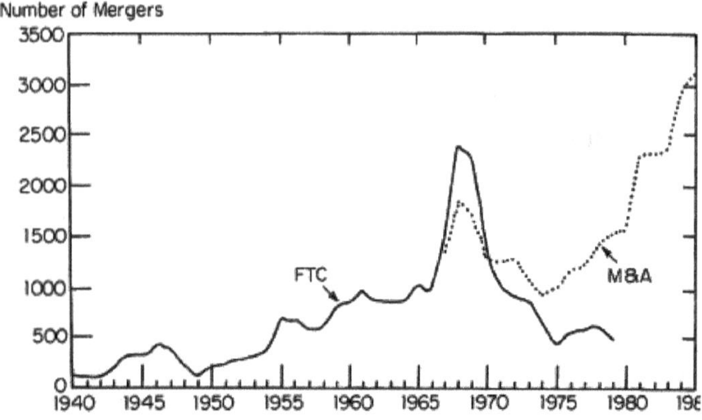

Number of mergers and acquisitions in the U.S. (Source: NBER, 1987).[10]

As the above chart shows, for the 50 years after World War II in the U.S. economy, mergers and acquisitions are not something new, but they have, bar a few contractions, continued to rise, especially since the 60s in America, the 80s and 90s in Europe, and over the last two decades on a global scale. In the first half of the 1990s there were more than 1,500 mergers in the U.S. financial sector alone. There can be good motives behind mergers, acquisitions, or other more flexible forms of joint ventures: increased revenues, larger market share, economies of scale or of scope, critical size (essential or inevitable in some industries), access to new markets, diversification, synergies, vertical integration, etc. However, too many M&As (mergers and acquisitions) seem to be driven by that fear of being left behind, or by a bad desire, or a clear design, to choke off rivals; or even by a runaway solution to internal problems. In their (too?) quick discovery process of capitalism, the Russians, among

10 "*Mergers and Acquisitions in the U.S. Economy: An Aggregate and Historical Overview*" by Devra L. Golbe and Lawrence J. White for the National Bureau of Economic Research (NBER) (University of Chicago Press, 1987). FTC series stopped in 1979 and were picked up by M&A periodical (dotted line).

others, seem to have learned bad lessons on this subject too: announcing a possible mega-merger of metals groups including Norilsk Nickel, the Financial Times mentioned "*easing debt*" as a primary motive.[11] Easing debt! Frequently M&As are inspired by glory-seeking or pure megalomania packaged as "strategic thinking" in the name of good old "shareholder value". In this hunter-and-hunted world, we have even seen sillier things, such as buying a competitor in order to avoid being purchased by that competitor or another. This has been obvious in the maneuvers in the aluminum and mining industries, among others.

More examples? We have witnessed the cases of companies buying others just "with" ("because of" would be a more suitable word) their – current or most recent – market value: Time Warner was much bigger in sales than AOL when the latter took the former over. Since then, a market (value) correction came, the company was renamed and the acquirer has become a division of the acquired. Ryanair has bid more than once for a complete takeover of older and once bigger Irish rival Aer Lingus. The low-cost carrier already has a stake in the latter and now generates three times more revenues, but a major underlying factor to help or justify (?) the purchase is the much bigger market cap. What is the point in buying "*a small, peripheral regional airline with declining traffic*", as Ryanair's boss named it?[12]

According to the maverick management guru Tom Peters: "*Bigger is almost never better. Big mergers are stupid. (They) spring naturally from big egos. At times of market uncertainty, the biggies, even the so-called "good" biggies, bulk up to defend themselves... And yet we do "it" again and again...*"[13]

11 "*Norilsk tycoons eye mega-merger with metals groups to ease debt*" (Financial Times, January 20, 2009).

12 "*Ryanair loses European court battle over Aer Lingus takeover*" (The Independent, July 7, 2010).

13 Tom Peters: "*26 Rules for Recessions*", posted on June 30, 2008 on www.tompeters.com.

Summarizing the reasons why M&As are, on the whole, less successful, would take an entire book. It boils down to at least six explanations, at work alone or together:

- An ill-conceived business model;
- A wrong fit (between products, cultures, et al.);
- Embedded problems in the acquired company;
- An ill-advised financial structure (mind the investment bankers here, too!);
- A decrease in market responsiveness (internal or "digestion" concerns being put first and slowing down reactive capabilities);
- A wrong timing – or sudden or unplanned change – in the business, industry or economic environment that make the "best" plan go down – or makes things worse.

Three other bad examples (and related disorders)

Everybody (well, almost) admits that the so-called "merger of equals" between Daimler and Chrysler, the one "*driving mergers to a new level*"[14], was indeed a real lie driven (here literally) by the ego of the then Daimler CEO Jürgen Schrempp.[15] For those who have forgotten, three years after the merger, which was indeed an acquisition, pure and simple, market value stood roughly equal to the value of... the sole acquirer before the merger. In parallel, the company's share value had declined by one-third. Less than ten years after merging two companies

14 As put in IR Magazine (October 1998), among many other laudatory comments at that time. To be honest, our first impression was not bad either. But it took me less time than other analysts, e.g. when watching the company reports (from were figures were sourced), to see that the merger was not "equal" at all - which one is? - and was doomed to fail, for at least four of the six reasons listed above.

15 Talking about egos in the same industry, it is well known that Volkswagen's acquisition spree owes much to its chairman's megalomaniac ego.

that were never capable of working together, DaimlerChrysler together went back to Daimler and Chrysler separate. Despite this, just a few years after the failure, Daimler dared to declare an interest in buying the Volvo car division from Ford Motor, before the (not so) Swedish carmaker was finally sold to the Chinese Zhejiang Geely group. Would it have done better than Ford, and that it did itself with Chrysler? Oh, what happened to the latter? It was finally sold off to Fiat, for reasons that are still strongly debated.

What inspired the failed attempt of Belgo-Dutch bank and insurance group Fortis to buy its old rival ABN Amro, in a joint bid with Banco Santander and Royal Bank of Scotland? Apart from flattering the ego of a bunch of then almost retired Belgian aristocrats, the acquisition looked very much like a revenge sought for the failed Amsterdam bank's bid on the Fortis banking division (formerly known as Generale Bank, a part of what Belgians dubbed "The Old Lady") a few years before. The fact is that two capital increases were needed in the six months following the announcement and the first stages of the acquisition. This left an impression of poor evaluation, miscalculation, misjudgment, and lies, pure and simple. The failed marriage did not result in a happy ending. To avoid bankruptcy, Fortis (that can translate as "strong" in Latin) the 20th largest company by revenue in 2007, was bailed out and then broken up by the Belgian and Dutch governments at the end of September 2008. Fortis was just another example of financiers' "bigness" folly.

How many financial sector executives have read the literature about M&As in their industry? In April 1991 (ninety one!) BusinessWeek published a special report titled: "*If mergers were simple, banking troubles might be over.*" Five years later, a thorough review conducted at Wharton School reported "*the value gains that are alleged (from consolidation) have not been verified.*"[16] Ten years later, in January 2001, a G10 study concluded that mergers in the financial sector were "*raising the risk*" of a banking crisis.[17] Despite all those results and cautionary statements, another ten years later, Citigroup went from acquiring to selling, from merging to demerging. In January 2009, The Economist noted that it would be CEO's role "*to slim the bank further and faster.*"[18] Slim? What a slam for the U.S. financial group's strategy, after years of cheers and claps from analysts and media (investors were less cheerful, though). Recently, a consultant noted that the M&A flow in the financial sector has dried up because of "*the poor track record of integration… Many of the mergers of the past 15 years have been forced to unscramble.*"[19]

In February 2012, the merger of the two mining companies Glencore and Xstrata was announced as a "*unique model for the industry although it would be difficult to replicate by others*" (to quote an industry analyst). Another unique merger! Heard that one before. In fact, the two companies followed the example of BHP and Billiton, which had merged more a decade before.

"*One of the benefits of this deal is that it liberalises both companies. The combined group would have more strategic flexibility,*" added another industry observer.

Mergers making groups more flexible? Um. A shareholder in both companies said that "*a combined entity offers a lot more*

16 "*The Value Effects of Bank Mergers and Acquisitions*": a remarkable review conducted by Steven J. Pilloff and Anthony M. Santomero for the Wharton Financial Institutions Center (October 29, 1996).

17 Quoted by The Independent (January 26, 2001).

18 "*Citigroup. A house built on Sandy*" (The Economist, January 17, 2009). Reading annual reports can be a worthwhile experience, e.g. when Citigroup and Fortis CEO statements were justifying Travelers and ABN Amro's acquisition, respectively. One could add similar comments in the banking sector about UniCredit, HypoVereinsbank, Royal Bank of Scotland, and many others.

19 Amin Rajan, chief executive of Create Research, quoted in "*Industry cautious about M&A recovery*" (Financial Times FTfm supplement, March 12, 2012).

than on a standalone basis."[20] Mergers bringing more value to shareholders? Check the statistics!

However, analysts still buy - and sell - them to investors who are often forced to swallow it whole (looking at the long-term figures and a few key ratios of BHP Billiton does not make the most convincing case).[21] Market reactions to mergers should deserve as much psychological (or psychiatric) research as economic analysis and management books, especially for corporate leaders and the analysts and investors who follow them (or is it vice versa?).

The sequence is almost invariably repeated:

- A merger or acquisition is presented as necessary or indispensable;
- The merger is hailed as a success for the acquirer, the acquired, and of course shareholders, both by company executives and analysts;
- After a (usually short) while, cost savings and "synergies" are announced (and applauded by bankers, investors and of course analysts. Usually, shareholders have already become less enthusiastic at this stage);
- Parts of the group are sold (as recommended by bankers and analysts);
- Key financial performance indicators improve (other indicators, such as products, service, innovation seem to matter less), which sometimes mean they get back to previous levels (in percentage but with more volume)

20 All quotations come from the Financial Times: "*Glencore and Xtrata would be 'unique' model*" (February 2, 2012). FT commentators added a few days later that the "*Integrated model* (would) *break new ground*," yet a successful merger "*is no mean feat*" (February 8, 2012).

21 Check e.g. EBIT (only "*underlying*" is highlighted, which may imply something), ROCE (ROE is not highlighted in Annual Report 2010) and earnings over more than 5 years (not easy to grasp historical data, which might also mean something).

and bankers start lending again, while markets are pleased;

- The company plans new acquisitions (back to square one with the same cheers).

Big in pharma (prescription 2)

What is at least destructive (the often told 1 + 1 = 3 equation to justify M&As is just laughable), at worst sinful, and in between pointless, is to focus on mergers and acquisitions as a main growth factor and to (make) believe that it is size that matters. A company is not great per se because it is big. Take innovation, for example. A lot of examples in history prove exactly the opposite. Small can be beautiful, and often delivers better results.[22] Returning to the pharmaceutical industry, consider the example of Novo Nordisk, a world leader in diabetes care, based in Denmark. With sales of $8,262 million (2007 figures used for comparability), the company "weighed" between 2.5 and 6 times less than the top ten health care groups, such as Pfizer. Sales and net income grew from DKK23,385 million and DKK3,620 million respectively in 2001 to DKK41,831 million and DKK8,522 million in 2007.[23] Over the same period, the equity ratio has proved very stable too, being maintained in the 65-70 percent range. Compared with the above-mentioned Pfizer performance over the same period, and with many big shots in the industry, the Bagsvaerd-based company should certainly not blush, not least with its sustained and more focused R&D expenses.

---

22 See the article written by Catherine Armst on www.businessweek.com: "*Drug Mergers: Killers for Research*" (March 9, 2009). What has the complete acquisition of the smaller Genentech by its larger parent Roche brought to both parties? And so on...

23 Figures for and before 2007 to make comparisons with Pfizer (cited above) meaningful. Data were sourced from Novo Nordisk annual reports. DKK (Danish krone) has been used to avoid currency impact in comparisons.

The lessons (or prescription?) from the Novo Nordisk way are clear – and should be for many in any industry. Even in a business where R&D costs are high, and where economies of scale or scope are claimed to be critical, a medium-sized player that is focused and growing mainly organically, can stay more entrepreneurial, be more innovative, and more responsive to customers – and meet patients' needs. Some of the makers of generic drugs (e.g. in Japan and India) provide more evidence of this. Empirical evidence (strangely overlooked in the economic literature) shows that spinoffs, buyouts (by management and employees) and IPOs from larger companies are more flexible and often fare much better than as internal divisions, whatever the industry.

Should the readers – and practitioners – infer from the above that being big is always bad? Certainly not, as in a number of industries, size can be a critical success factor, like in mining, oil, gas, cars, steel (yet some smaller players can still prove more successful here and there).[24] In addition, growing externally is not inherently doomed. Still, one would recommend caution and to care about the side effects.. Then to use the M&A technique – or "art", as some authors call it – cautiously and sparingly, instead of buying for the sake of it, and having to digest and be on a diet.[25] Research by Campa and Hernando about shareholder value creation in European M&As showed that "*Acquirers' cumulative abnormal returns are null on average.*"[26] According to Professor Sudi Sudarsanam, a noted expert on acquisitions: "*The odds of positive and*

---

24 Reflect on this statement made by Nick Butler, former group vice-president for strategy at BP: "*The era of global oil giants is over. A new model is emerging in which smaller national and larger international companies must work in new partnerships.*" (Financial Times, July 27, 2010).

25 "*The Art of M&A*" by Stanley Foster Reed, Alexandra Reed Lajoux, H. Peter Nesvold (McGraw-Hill, 4th edition, 2007).

26 "*Shareholder Value Creation in European M&As*" by José Manuel Campa (IESE Business School) and Ignacio Hernando (Banco de Espana), in European Financial Management (Vol. 10, No. 1, 2004).

significant value creation for acquirer shareholders may even be less than 50 percent, which is what one would get with the toss of a fair coin."[27] Multiplying (or is it adding or subtracting?) this 50 percent by (to) the usual estimate of an average 50 percent failure rate of acquisitions, mergers and joint ventures naturally still leaves us a few percentage points of successful business combinations (industry language) or further consolidation (analysts' lingo). Far less than what is usually trumpeted and expected.

GE: market value was too big to be true

Is there any rational explanation to the long-lasting yet inexplicable fascination (since slightly diminished) for the combination of businesses branded General Electric (GE)? Is it once again the "size matters" fashion (a size almost as big as former CEO Jack Welch's retirement package)? Yes, the market value was multiplied by about 30 in twenty-five years, to reach $410 billion at the end of Welch's tenure. How come? It looks as if markets and investors were on automatic pilot, buying and increasing the stock price just because… this was high and went higher. Five years after Welch's departure, market cap was down (or back) to $173 billion (January 2009), i.e. an average decrease of $47 billion per year since "Neutron" Jack's retirement. It has been stable ever since. Call it a market correction, or just another bubble burst? After having grown mainly via

27 Sudi Sudarsanam: "*Creating Value from Mergers and Acquisitions. The Challenges*" (Prentice Hall, 2004). Though this well-documented book (600-plus pages) based on solid conceptual and empirical research still makes recommended reading, one may strongly disagree with some of the author's views, also expressed in a paper titled "*Friend or Foe: securing shareholder value in mergers and acquisitions*" (published by the Cranfield School of Management in 2001, available at www.som.cranfield.ac.uk/som/). Sudarsanam's assertions can be argued: e.g. when he writes that hostile takeovers deliver better than "friendly" ones, and that many acquisitions improve management "monitoring" (sic), mainly via the role of more financial-institutional shareholders. A number of cases and events keep on proving just the contrary, not least on the destructive role of purely financial holdings (not to mention the role of hedge funds).

acquisitions, turned into a conglomerate, and having been excessively praised for its value, GE finally had to "*learn to dance*."[28] On average over the last decade, GE's revenues have been 40 percent higher than Siemens', a real competitor at least in a number of areas. Why has GE's market value been between four times and two times bigger over the same period? It is puzzling that comparable Japanese "sogo shoshas" have never been "awarded" with the same premium and have consistently been undervalued (and not only in terms of market cap). Hitachi, sometimes presented as a "Japanese GE" has revenues less than 50 percent lower than GE, but its market value is more than ten times smaller than its U.S. peer.[29] There is no economic reason for that. GE was clearly overpriced as a whole – and when compared to the sum of its parts. The trouble with market value is that it is often too big to be true, and is thus far from being a good measure of company size, bigness and… real performance.[30] To be fair, GE's post-Welch strategy marked a real – yet often costly – shift from face value to book value and has been more smartly managed so far than at some rivals', putting some flesh – we mean products – where only money was shown under Welch's tenure. Still, to keep on thriving, GE had to prove "lean and mean". Less big, that is. GE is only one example among others.

Too big to fail?

"Too big to fail" was not an expression invented for the late-2000s financial crisis. The concept, used at unprecedented levels at that time, is still ready if necessary. A recent study of the relationships between 43,000 transnational corporations

28 To use Harvard Business School Professor Rosabeth Moss Kanter's words: "*When Giants Learn to Dance*" (Fireside, 1989).

29 Like for most listed Japanese companies, Hitachi's actual free float is much smaller than GE's. But this does not justify such a big gap in company market value.

30 It is a bit surprising that a quality economic daily such as the FT keeps on ranking companies by market value and refers to them as the "*world's largest companies*".

conducted by complex systems theorists at the Zurich-based Swiss Federal Institute of Technology shows a core of 1,318 corporations with interlocking ownerships and 147 "*tightly knit companies*", of which all of their ownership is held by other members. The research showed that one percent of the companies was able to control 40 percent of the total wealth in the network.[31] If one or more of those big companies fail!... we know what comes next.

Among a list of examples that would be long enough to fill a chapter, AIG (American International Group) is certainly a case in point. A top 20 U.S. company that still ranks in the global top 50 by revenues and is among the largest property and casualty insurance groups worldwide, AIG enjoyed the privilege of receiving the largest government bailout in U.S. history (in the good company of Fannie and Freddie).[32] Without public support (amount: $180 billion), then begged for in pure blackmailing style by former chairman Maurice Greenberg (who headed the group for forty years), the company would simply now be out of the Fortune list.[33] We can spare the details that led to the last-minute rescue (lent in four shots, because the first, second and third were not sufficient) of a business filled with (and emptied of) money, and worked out with a lot of ABS, CDS and CDO stuff (naturally rated AAA for most!)[34] The story boils down to a home truth: AIG, among many others, was too big to be managed efficiently.

---

31 "*Revealed – the capitalist network that runs the world*", a summary of that very interesting research published in New Scientist (October 24, 2011: www.newscientist.com). The study was based on a database of 37 million companies and investors.

32 Fortune Global 500 (2011).

33 At the end of 2011, U.S. bailed-out companies were still owing $132.9 billion to the government, with AIG topping the list ($50 billion) (Washington Post, January 26, 2012).

34 Asset-backed securities, credit default swaps, and collateralized debt obligations. Remember how Warren Buffett dubbed CDS (credit default swaps): "*financial weapons of mass destruction*". For AAA, (don't) trust your rating agent!

"*Too big to fail is to dumb to keep*," wrote FT columnist John Kay in 2009.[35] Even so, with a different cast (well, not completely) the scenario for the Eurozone governed by the same "Too big to fail" logic, this time applying to the borrowers (member states) as well as to the lenders (bankers).

Small, beautiful, and more than that

"*Any intelligent fool can make things bigger, more complex, and more violent. It takes a touch of genius – and a lot of courage – to move in the opposite direction*," wrote E.F. Schumacher.[36] A small enterprise can indeed be a beautiful thing. Entrepreneurs often do not regard themselves as "capitalists" – and rightly so, as their primary goal is not to amass money. Lest some forget it, real entrepreneurs pay themselves with (a part of) the bottom line, which says it all. A true entrepreneur, the late Steve Jobs often said he did not want "*to be the richest person in the graveyard.*" That makes a difference, not only in size and style, but also in behavior. As the American psychologist David McClelland says, an entrepreneur's key motivation is the need for achievement and an urge to build. Among others, Peter Drucker saw taking risk as a key characteristic of entrepreneurship.[37] Many big capitalists hardly (still) share the spirit of adventure and the risk appetite of small entrepreneurs. Many forget what they once were. Many (e.g. in the financial sector) do not have the faintest idea of what entrepreneurship means!

---

35 Financial Times (October 28, 2009).

36 Ernst Friedrich Schumacher: "*Small is beautiful. a study of economics as if people mattered*" (Blond & Briggs, 1973).

37 David McClelland: "*The Achieving Society*" (Free Press MacMillan, 1967; Peter F. Drucker: "*Technology, Management and Society*" (HarperCollins, 1970), "*Innovation and Entrepreneurship. Practice and Principles*" (republished by Collins Business, 2006).

Entrepreneurship has its thrills and spills. And the virtues – and competitive advantages – of a small enterprise are real. Let us point to seven key advantages:[38]

- Structure is flatter and less complex;
- Communication is more simple;
- Decision-making process is quicker;
- Customer drive is much stronger;
- Flexibility is higher.
- A number of medium-sized companies also display much greater innovation capabilities than big ones.[39] So much so that an unwritten law of capitalism is that most product and technological breakthroughs comes from outside large corporations and dominating groups. The then relatively small Apple and Microsoft drove a few computer giants out of the market and forced a company like IBM to adapt.[40] They did not succeed because they were big, they became big due to their success (having started in 1975, Microsoft first ranked in the U.S. Fortune 500 only in 1995). To take another example, the leading companies in wind turbines did not appear in the established energy sector.

38 A much too short summary of reports released by OECD and other institutions or research centers. Our five virtues are inspired by a blog post of… a former Microsoft executive: "*The Top 5 Competitive Advantages of Small Businesses*" by Skip Reardon on http://myventurepad.com/.

39 "*Innovation and Entrepreneurship. Practice and Principles*" is the title of a management book written in 1985 by Peter F. Drucker that still makes compelling reading (HarperCollins, 1985). Read also: "*Innovation: The Attacker's Advantage*" by Richard N. Foster (Summit Books, 1986).

40 After years of domination of the computer and software industry (with market shares over 60 percent in some segments, i.e. well behind what Microsoft is holding nowadays...), IBM saw its core business shrink, its then CEO declaring he was "*mad at losing market shares,*" and reported in fiscal year 1992 what was then the biggest loss in U.S. corporate history. It took years to turn the giant around, but it had to shed a large part of its core activities.

- SMEs are the biggest job generators, with 65-75 percent of existing jobs and 80-90 percent of new jobs created by small companies in most economies (in India, half of GDP comes from SMEs). This is not reported widely enough in the media, who talk more about big visible job losses in large firms than invisible job creation in small enterprises. Somewhat strangely, big happens to see smaller as better: the global value of corporate spinoffs has doubled from 2011 to 2012 to reach $400 billion, highlighting an increasing trend for large companies to refocus their business by disposing of non-core assets (often presented as core before…).[41]

Some studies point out the lower productivity of small firms. This may undoubtedly constitute an obstacle to growth in some areas and industries, in many cases the answer is: who cares?[42] The French economist Jean Fourastié often took the classic example of the hairdresser, whose average productivity had not increased over fifty years. Productivity measures the more and not the better, and can sometimes seriously clash with the quality and service provided by smaller enterprises, and harder to find in big ones. Why should the hairdresser cut faster? Why would the grocer not have a chat with his/her customers? Should the plumber work quickly or effectively?

Still, a small enterprise can also turn into a dreadful experience. Small firms shed a large number of jobs that often go unnoticed, and almost nobody sheds a tear. Contrary to popular belief or a certain form of market religion, free enterprise

41 Figures from Deloitte and "*The Spinoff Report*", cited by the Financial Times (February 20, 2012).

42 Read e.g. "*Decline and small. Small firms are a big problem for Europe's periphery*" (The Economist, March 3, 2012). The article refers to interesting papers from Carnegie Mellon University and the London School of Economics available at: www.economist.com/smallfirms12.

is not always entirely synonymous with capitalism.[43] Capitalist economies are not always as enterprise-friendly as they need to be. Enterprise's freedom may be seriously hampered by regulatory burdens: creating and growing a company is often similar to a hurdle race, and is in some places a very difficult process (and not only in African developing countries).[44] To make things worse, "Too small to succeed" is still regarded as a sign of personal failure in some cultures – a legacy of a religious past here, public sector's influence there. Perhaps surprisingly, America's strong religious backdrop deals with the bankruptcy issue – and its consequences – more fairly. Banking conditions hinder enterprises' growth: fundamentally, borrowing has always been much tougher for small companies than for large corporations, and not only in credit crunch days.[45] Thousands of companies go bust for various reasons: mismanagement, tough competition and financing problems to name but a few. As to the latter, the role of the banking sector should not be underestimated. In the UK, five dominant lenders account for more than 90 percent of lending to SMEs, compared with 15,000 institutions capable of providing financial services in the U.S. Creating and growing a small enterprise is more difficult than in the past, owing to the power of large corporations: consider the role played by department stores in retail against the small shop around the corner.

However, millions of enterprises keep on succeeding just because they (want to) stay small and take advantage of that

43 Strangely (is it?), typing "*free enterprise*" on Wikipedia directs to "*Capitalism*" as if it was equivalent. Was it penned in Chicago?

44 It takes twice as many days to start a business in Sub-Saharan Africa as in... Eastern Europe, which is not yet itself a benchmark long after the demise of communism (source: World Bank "*Doing Business*" database, 2012).

45 On January 7, 2009, three months after the October 2008 crash, BusinessWeek website published two articles titled: "*Why Banks Still Won't Lend*" and "*Loans to Companies in Bankruptcy Dry Up*". In the U.S., the four biggest commercial banks control two thirds of the total assets of commercial banks. We have observed the same trends during the long-lasting Eurozone crisis.

– think of your butcher, baker, plumber, electrician, computer troubleshooter, and so many others. Small-scale production, distribution and services are the key to a renewed economic model.

The "Size does matter" economic model that prevails today often means internal forces of inertia become stronger than healthy external market pressure. Becoming too big, too slow, too fat, less flexible, less responsive, less agile are risks faced by many firms, and a cause of failure of fall for some. "*Pardon me for asking, but if a company is too big to fail, maybe – just maybe – it's too big, period*," wrote Robert Reich.[46] An old Vietnamese proverb says: "*The fattest pig is the first to be killed*."

46 Robert Reich, on his blog http://robertreich.org/ (October 21, 2008).

SIN NO. 2:
TOO FAR

"The universe as we know it is a joint product of the observer and the observed."
PIERRE TEILHARD DE CHARDIN

"There are two lasting bequests we can give our children: one is roots, the other is wings."
HODDING CARTER, American journalist

Beer buddies

Leuven (Flanders), anno 1366: the Artois brewery is founded. Almost 650 years later, what has become the No. 1 beer-maker in the world is still officially headquartered at the same Brouwerijplein (Brewery square) in Leuven and now boasts over 150 brands sold in 30 countries. A flashback: in January 2009, two months after the merger between the (less and less) Belgian Inbev and the (then very) American Anheuser-Busch, the renamed Anheuser-Busch InBev released a string of communiqués. These announced: a price increase for lager beers (the third in one year in its country of origin, i.e. Belgium, for the few who are still aware); job-cutting plans (needed (sic) "*to conserve cash and repay debt*"); another round of debt repayment; and the opening of an office in New York, where some managers from its Belgian base would be moved "*to implement cost cuts following the $52 billion merger that formed the company.*" As a first step, the CEO and CFO "*will split their time between New York and... Leuven*" (apparently, a brewer now cares more about "responsible drinking" than about its carbon footprint.) A company spokesperson added that the company "*remains fully committed to its other offices and breweries in Belgium.*"[1]

For the 620 years between 1366 and 1986 Artois remained a modest and hard-working local brewer with drinkers enjoying a glass (or more) of Stella. Investors and analysts mocked it as a parochial enterprise, without ever getting much reaction from the publicity-shy Leuven brewer. In 1987, the Flemish Artois and the Walloon Piedboeuf joined together to form the truly Belgian Interbrew. In 1995, the group made its first move far from its roots and acquired Toronto-based and Canadian second brewer Labatt. In 2000, Interbrew bought the British

1 All quotes in italics come from Andrew Cleary on www.bloomberg.com (January 15, 2009) and from company press releases. Information and comments from the Financial Times, Reuters, De Tijd, BusinessWeek, and company annual reports (when and where data were available).

brewer Bass, established in 1777. That, added to other smaller purchases, almost doubled volume figures. The 2001 annual report was displaying 100-plus brands with operations in 20 countries. The annual report for 2003 – which boasted about a portfolio of 200 brands – yet paradoxically still stressing "*organic growth*" in its "*Letter to Shareholders*", announced the "combination" with the Brazilian Ambev, naming it InterbrewAmbev, and then (re)branding it InBev in the 2004 annuals. In 2006, InBev announced the move of its white-beer brewery from Hoegaarden to the Piedboeuf location. In 2007, volume brewed was 6.5 bigger (in hl) than ten years before; and the annual report highlighted a few premium and local brands distributed in 80 countries. In 2008, InBev bought the U.S. producer of Budweiser Anheuser-Busch in an all-cash agreement of $52 billion, and sold off Labatt, bought only a few years before. In 2009, the combined group was again renamed, this time as Anheuser-Busch InBev (aka AB Inbev), and has become the world's largest brewer, with more than 20 percent market share worldwide and 50 percent in the U.S. This thanks to its Stella brand of origin, plus Bud, Beck's and Leffe beers, as well as large interests in the makers of Corona and Tsingtao. No wonder many people, including investors, are not sure anymore where decisions are taken and what nationality the company has.

Eating others' lunch: chocolate, mustard, olive oil

Remember the chocolate saga of Côte d'Or?

With beer, chocolate still represents one of the rare economic assets of Belgium. But its best-known brand Côte d'Or – of which Belgians consume more than 500 million products a year – founded in 1883 by Mr. Neuhaus (whose name is now associated with a top-end praline maker) has long gone. It passed from Swiss hands to U.S. ones (Kraft Foods) in a few years. In another famous business saga, in 2010 Kraft

Foods (again) took over the iconic British confectionery-maker Cadbury. The then Business Secretary Peter Mandelson warned the U.S. food giant not to try to "*make a quick buck*" and the then Prime Minister Gordon Brown said it was "*very important to the British economy*." Founded in Birmingham in 1824, Cadbury had already started transferring some production plants to other parts of the country, as well as to Eastern Europe. Naturally, Kraft Foods has not changed this course and is doing the same for Côte d'Or, whose Mignonette small chocolate bars' manufacturing has now been moved to Central Europe.[2] Of the many other stories of products – sometimes products that made history – moving far from their roots, we could also take the example of Dijon's mustard, whose well-known brands Amora and Maille date back to 1919 and… 1747, and were bought by Unilever in 2000. They have been moved from their place of origin by a decision taken at HQ level in November 2008.3 The same Unilever acquired olive oil producer Bertolli – created in 1865 in Tuscany – in 2004 to sell it in 2008 to a Spanish group.

Our "eat others' lunch" list could include more small beer, blue chips, and much food for thought. Are these those not success stories of enterprises going from local rags to global riches, after all? Are they not the logical consequences of globalization, in which one has to move production and other factors closer to customers and markets? Perhaps, but those examples chosen at random from a very long list tell us about how far capitalism has moved from grass-roots economies.

---

2 About Côte d'Or: "*Chocotoff gaat mogelijk uit België*" (De Tijd, 16 juni 2011). Among the many articles published about the Cadbury takeover: "*Don't try to make a quick buck from Cadbury, Mandelson tells Kraft*" (Guardian, December 4, 2009); "*Get your hands off our sweets*" (Guardian, January 16, 2010); "*Cadbury deal near end, Kraft CEO sees sleep*" (Reuters, February 2, 2010); and "*RBS kept client Cadbury in the dark as it prepared to back Kraft's hostile bid*" (Guardian, April 28, 2010). Adding insult to injury, the takeover was funded by RBS, a British bank then partly owned by the government.

3 "*Amora va fermer son usine de Dijon*" (Le Monde, 20 novembre 2008).

How this may have an impact on product or service quality, and yes, financial performance – the "quick buck" is not always on the other side of the fence. And how faraway control is difficult to manage (as the above examples illustrate it, what was bought sometimes ends up on the for sale list).

Another round of beers

Let us get back to beer. The brew often turns less potent than it smells and tastes in the first round. In the case of Anheuser-Busch InBev, a bit of semantics and semiotics may help –or not. Three (and a half?) changes of corporate brand in ten years reflect... the lack of a clear sense of origins and direction. The latest formula – we would not swear it will be the last – does not do the best job. The ID is so complicated that it must abbreviated to AB Inbev to be remembered – or simply pronounced. That certainly means something about an increasingly uncertain DNA. "*Een Stella*" was easier to remember in the Flemish-French dialect still spoken at Brouwerijplein....

So much for the "soft" branding issues. Now to the "hard" financials. Both the recurring number of acquisitions and divestments and the poor quality of the Belgian group's financial reports do not help when making comparisons. As a result of multiple acquisitions, volume metrics and market shares have naturally moved up. How about real performance indicators? The least one can say is that ROE, ROA (total assets have increased, not the return), EBIT (which resumed growth only after huge cost savings, these due to the negative of faraway moves), SG&A margin, and debt-to-equity ($35 billion indebtedness, or one-third of its market value as of March 2012) would not outshine most competitors' ones. Far from that. Against its close – and often more focused – rivals, such as Asahi, Carlsberg and Heineken, indicators would show size as one of the only main decisive advantages for the Belgo-

American-Brazilian player.[4] No small beer, of course, but was it worth swallowing so much to digest so slowly?

Not tipsy after bottom-line matters?

Let us get back to the top line. Like (too) many multinationals, AB Inbev is moving from a product-based company to a financial portfolio management group. This has some consequences for the core business – and the consumer. According to the (not so) average beer drinker, many draft beers or lagers are becoming interchangeable, while beer experts now find the group's special beers less, er, special. In Belgium, AB Inbev's home (?) country, it is increasingly difficult to find pubs and cafés with more than a dozen beers (it is Jupiler everywhere), all or most from three or four large brewers. In other countries, one-taste-fits-all (on tap or in bottles) is often becoming the "choice". Pessimists even consider that after taste uniformity brand dilution will follow. It looks as if the running global brands would be hardly compatible with managing local roots and tastes. Had smaller breweries survived independently to produce local beers closer to customer taste, then Hoegaarden would probably have kept its locally-brewed "Witte" and Jumet its own brew (or "Cuvée"), markets and distribution channels permitting.[5] Fortunately, there are still many independent breweries. Yet far behind the early 20th century peak of more than 3,000 beer-makers, Belgium still hosts more independent breweries and special beers than any other country. In Britain

---

4 Check historical performance in company's annual reports over the last decade, provided figures are (made) comparable.

5 Another beer-gulping story: "Cuvée de l'Ermitage" was created and brewed in Jumet - a section of Charleroi, Belgium, within walking distance from the place where I was brought up- by the then privately owned Brasserie de l'Union. This was then acquired by Alken-Maes, which was in turn acquired by Scottish and Newcastle (McEwan's maker), who stopped production before being jointly acquired by Carlsberg and Heineken in April 2008.

too, recent reports talked of 50 new microbreweries opening yearly.[6] More diversity is tastier than uniformity.

Faraway shareholders

Many contemporary corporations go and stand back too far. From their origins, their core businesses, their products and processes, their markets and consumers, their employees, their shareowners. Adam Smith already noted in the 18th century: "*The greater part of proprietors seldom pretend to understand anything of the business of the company...*"[7] A recent book argues that shareholders' attitudes have not changed much since. In an FT column, Michael Skapinker points to one of the developments that "*have made matters worse*" in the latest financial crises: "*the growing distance of shareholders from the business they invest in.*"[8] Some may still have in mind that the (failed) ABN Amro acquisition originally came from the tough demands of one of its small key but nevertheless remote stockholders, a London-based pension fund that did not care much about the strong Dutch roots (even if these had been blended with a long-lasting international presence). From that perspective, sovereign funds may bring a better answer than excessively short-term driven hedge or other funds. They often invest with a long-term view (the fact that they belong to a place can be a pertinent explanation), have a stabilizing effect both in host countries and in investments, and do not interfere

6 Read e.g.: "*Brewed force*" (The Economist, December 17, 2011), "*Real ale revival led by small breweries*" (The Guardian, August 2, 2011).

7 Adam Smith: "*The Wealth of Nations*" (1776, republished e.g. in Bantam Classics, 2003).

8 "*Corporate Ownership and Control: British Business Transformed*", by Cambridge Professor Brian R. Cheffins (Oxford University Press, 2008); Financial Times (November 18, 2008).

in day-to-day management.[9] However, mind out for sovereigns' mind changes and whims as an uncertainty factor.

The listing and almost subsequently inevitable takeover of stock exchanges makes Adam Smith's concern even more true. Should a merger between Deutsche Börse and NYSE take place, the biggest part of continental Europe's stock exchanges would be in American hands: Euronext is already controlled by NYSE and the Nordic OMX was acquired through an odd Dubai-Nasdaq montage. The benefit for retail shareholders is far from obvious. If bigger bourses allow large corporations more access to capital, it certainly increases the costs for smaller and midcap companies, for which there are hardly alternatives to the classic and more expensive borrowing mechanisms. Raising local equity has become mission impossible in most developed (?) economies, except where venture capital is available, and this is a serious hindrance to SMEs' growth. Then there are the bondholders: what has made Greece, Ireland and Portugal particularly vulnerable in the Eurozone crisis is not only the scale of their indebtedness but the fact that a large portion is held too far away.

When Iceland melted…

Cross-border holdings are indeed one of the main features of that distance factor. And they often play more for the worse than for the better. In 2005, Iceland was showcased as a model of a stable and prosperous society.[10] The "model" melted (down) in a few weeks in the last quarter of 2008. From that moment on, "Icelandization" will probably stand in economic textbooks as

9 For investment figures, check: "*Sovereign Wealth Funds Assets Under Management*" by Monitor (www.monitor.com). For analysis, read: "*The impact of Sovereign Wealth Funds on economic success*" (PricewaterhouseCoopers UK, October 2011).

10 The "*2nd Conference on Gross National Happiness*" (sic) organized at a Canadian university was referring to Iceland as a model in "*Local Pathways to Global Wellbeing*". That was in June 2005 (available from www.gpiatlantic.org/conference/reports).

a trademark for the destructive mix of financialization, disconnection, delocalization, dematerialization and destabilization. All flaws which fall under the "too far" heading – in addition to the occasionally related short-termism, irresponsibility and greed. A few numbers sum up the mess:

- Banking sector (visible) debts were six times higher than the country's GDP.
- Major components of debt were short-term ones.
- Private households' indebtedness was on average at 250 percent of personal income.
- Half a million foreigners had deposits in Icelandic banks.
- In a couple of weeks the stock exchange market value dropped by 90 percent.
- The total cost of the crisis was estimated early in 2009 at 75 percent of GDP as a minimum.[11]

The great Iceland financial disaster illustrates perfectly how far today's capitalist financial virtuality lies from economic realities.

… and London felt the cold…

Though Iceland might have been the biggest in proportion, it is not the only case in point. The fact that the City of London's financial revenues account for an estimated 30 percent of UK's GDP, i.e. much more than any financial center in any developed economy, is an explanation of the heavy toll taken on the British economy in the late-2000s financial crisis. Those who argue for an even stronger City should think twice. By

11 The reasons why some institutions and individuals made deposits while having so little information is baffling: see e.g. "*Councils were negligent in making Icelandic deposits, rules watchdog*" (The Guardian, March 26, 2009).

comparison, Wall Street accounts for 12 percent of New York employment (but 30 percent of earnings); while Luxembourg and Zurich have 10 to 15 percent of their workforce in the financial sector.[12] To make things worse, significant flows are going to and coming from places far away from the banks of River Thames. One third of listed companies' equity is in the hands of foreign investors, and huge portions of the property sector are held by Middle-East investors.[13] This means the City depends much more on the outside world than in its glory days, no matter what David Cameron's efforts in defense of its interests in Brussels are. That gives an explanation for the heavy toll taken on the British economy in the latest financial crisis. Not as serious as in Iceland, but worrying nevertheless. The excessive weight – and influence – of a far-flung banking sector does the rest, if we can say so, turning Britain's financial comparative advantage in good times into a bigger weakness on stormy weather.[14] The magnitude of RBS's problems – and bailout-came after a string of other falls and rescues (which almost appear minor in retrospect): Northern Rock, HBOS, Lloyds, Bradford & Bingley, etc. These should have rung the alarm bell. Still, after the hangover the City returns to financial business as usual. Lest some have not noticed, RBS's 2008 astronomical £28 billion loss (the equivalent of Luxembourg's GDP!) was largely

12 Luxembourg is home to 1,300 investment funds and about 200 banks and 14,000 domiciled holding companies.

13 Why was the Shard tower erected so far from Qatar? As opposed to the Empire State Building for the Americans, and except for building capabilities, it can hardly be regarded as an example of British pride, and not only because St Paul's Cathedral is now dwarfed by the new tower.

14 It was a London-born economist, David Ricardo, whose "*On the Principles of Political Economy and Taxation*" laid out the theory of comparative advantage (1817, republished in 2004 by Dover Publications). Let us not forget to travel northbound and forget the Square Mile for a while. Ten years ago, Edinburgh and Scotland could boast about being home for two of the major UK banks. Except, up to a point, for HQs, these moved further away from their roots, were knocked down in the 2008 turmoil, and were, rather ironically, bailed out by a Prime Minister born in Scotland, Gordon Brown. Should Scotland return to independence, it would be with significantly diminished financial powerhouses.

made up of write-downs for goodwill impairments "*on past acquisitions*," "*a legacy of RBS's seven-year acquisition spree*" embarked on by a chief executive dubbed a "*deal junkie.*"[15] In other words, like so many of its sector peers, and in more than one meaning, the bank went too far. Saying that Britain is a global leader in banking is much exaggerated, as large parts of the sector (e.g. investment banking) now excessively depend on foreigners. Building a competitive advantage upon that is perhaps illusory, and partly out of control. If another property, Eurozone, Middle-East or Far-East bubble bursts the consequences would be as disastrous as in the late-2000s financial crisis.

... in a chocolate-box economy

Why is London's financial sector more fragile and the surrounding British economy more exposed than, say, New York and the U.S., Tokyo and Japan, Frankfurt and Germany, Paris and France? The economic answer is quite simple. The manufacturing, industrial and technological "hinterland" of those four countries still weighs enough to make up in good days and pick up when times get hard, at least when the worst is over. UK manufacturing output went down from over 30 percent of total gross value added in the early seventies to less than 15 percent in the first years of the 21st century, while manufacturing employment fell from 30 percent to about 10 percent over the same period.[16]

To be sure, the trend has been the same in many industrialized countries (the U.S. economy lost 4 million manufacturing jobs during the last decade), it hast just been worse in Britain.

15 "*RBS counts £28bn cost of past ambition*", by Jane Croft, in the Financial Times (January 20, 2009).

16 Source: Thomson Datastream, Financial Times (February 9, 2009). U.S. manufacturing sector now accounts for 12 percent of GDP, less than half its percentage in the 1950s. By comparison, Germany has kept steady around 25 percent.

Who among policymakers cared about the manufacturing decline? If Labour was not working (sic), the Thatcher years did not work better for manufacturing, far from it, and New Labour just followed in those footsteps of an all-to-service economic model. This, combined with private sector poor management and financial sector preference for easy money, has helped turn Britain into a chocolate-box economy. The automobile industry is a case in point. Once a champion in automotive and mechanical engineering, the UK is now a small part in the global assembly line.[17] In 2010, a Times article was still referring to Jaguar Land Rover as "*the UK's largest carmaker.*" What an illusion! For years, a Vauxhall has consisted of a German engine, an American in the driver's seat, and a British logo on the grill. John Bull or any City trader buying a Bentley or an Aston Martin do not seem to care if the former is now designed in Deutschland (and powered by Volkswagen) and the latter is controlled from Kuwait. He or she should. And it's not just about cars. BOC for gases, Pilkington for glass, Corus for steel, Scottish and Newcastle in beverages, ICI for chemicals, BAA for airports, Scottish Power in energy, Cadbury for confectionery, Body Shop in cosmetics… And bacon! 80 percent of the bacon eaten in the UK is imported.[18] Where and when the plants or stores remain, decisions are made remotely and value added goes elsewhere. As another sign, the top five richest persons in Britain in the Sunday Times "*Rich List 2012*" are… not British and run foreign conglomerates.[19] "Deindustrialization" is a

17 In February 2012 the UK government promised to "*leave no stone unturned*" to keep GM's two British plants open when the carmaker announced more cuts at its European divisions (Financial Times, February 15, 2012).

18 Bacon data reminded by Tony Jackson in his column in the Financial Times: "*We need new thinking to bring home the UK bacon*" (February 27, 2012).

19 "*UK's Rich List: Sunday Times Rich List 2012*" (April 29, 2012).

political theme in the U.S. and France.[20] In the UK, it has been a reality for the last thirty years.[21]

Banks go too far from home

The RBS disaster also illustrates another dimension of today's capitalism. As Lord Turner, chairman of the UK Financial Services Authority, declared, banks have grown "*beyond a socially reasonable size*."[22] Moreover, because of their obsession with size and their me-tooism (see other chapters), many, if not most of the banks have now moved far from their local origins and branches. These are now replaced with ATMs and faceless online operations. The financial sector has also moved from its traditional core business (deposits and loans, remember these basics?) and, simultaneously or subsequently, from its balance sheets. According to New York University professor Nouriel Roubini, half of the estimated $3,600 billion losses on U.S.-generated assets having resulted from the financial crisis have been incurred abroad![23] Ireland is another case in point. In 2010, the net exposure of banks to central and local government debt showed the German Hypo Real Estate as most exposed (€10.3 billion), followed by RBS (4.2 billion), Allied Irish Bank, Bank of Ireland, as well as Crédit Agricole and BNP Paribas (both from France), Danske Bank (Denmark), et al.[24]

---

20 See e.g. "*19 Facts About The Deindustrialization of America That Will Make You Weep*" by Michael Snyder (September 27, 2010) on www.businessinsider.com. Centrist candidate François Bayrou made it a key theme in the French 2012 presidential campaign, and it was endorsed by the main contenders.

21 Read my blog post on the subject matter on Lib Dem Voice: "*From shipyards to wind turbines -Britain needs BETS*" (www.libdemvoice.org, February 15, 2010).

22 Read e.g. "*FSA chairman Lord Turner sparks debate on tougher punishments for bailout bankers*" (The Independent, December 13, 2011).

23 Source: www.rgemonitor.com (February 2009). It can go both ways: end-February 2009, the Dutch ING weighed up the possibility of applying for U.S. bailout funds because of the importance of operations in the country.

24 "*Ireland debt crisis: European banks' exposure*" (Daily Telegraph, November 15, 2010). See also: "*Goldman Sachs publishes list of banks exposed to PIIGS*" on www.investmenteurope.net (July 14, 2011).

What are the real economic benefits of having all those banks operating in Dublin?

Why did Dexia, a Belgian-French bank (still ranked 49th in Fortune Global 500 in 2010) having specialized in financing public institutions and municipalities announced a €3.3 billion loss in February 2009, and another €11.6 billion loss three years later? Mostly because the financial group had moved too far from its shores instead of staying focused on its core business (some "communes" and "municipalities" in France and Belgium badly need infrastructure and social projects). Fiscal year 2008 losses were attributable to the sale of the U.S. FSA (acquired in 2000 and in which millions were still injected a few months prior to the sale due to subprime mortgage-related affairs), and other counterparty operations involving Lehman Brothers and... Icelandic banks (here we are again). Year 2011 losses still owed to the aftermath of the previous U.S. crisis, with Greece-related loans coming on top. What a waste of money! Imagine what could have been done for local and regional economies in the U.S., Belgium, France and elsewhere with just a small portion of those amounts! Fortunately, not all the banks follow the same money flows, but the exceptions are a rare species. Yet naturally not totally immune – who can be in this globalized economy? – the relative stability or even good performance of Canadian and Swedish banks amid the latest financial turmoil may be explained by at least four factors: more conservative management, more effective regulatory schemes, more on-balance-sheet activity, and more locally driven operations, with more calculated risks abroad. In other words, not going far for the sake of it.[25]

When everything is too far and out of reach, one should not be surprised to fall victim to distant events. Apparently,

25 A higher degree of disclosure and reporting transparency should be added as a plus point for Canadian banks. Check the sustained annual report rating and ranking of top Canadian banks BMO, Scotiabank, CIBC, RBC, Toronto-Dominion in the "*Annual Report on Annual Reports*" on www.reportwatch.net.

analysts, economists, media and politicians have short memories: think back to the long Japan's depression, 1987's "Black Monday" (Dow Jones' largest one-day fall), the 1997 Asian turmoil, the burst of the "Internet Bubble", Argentina's crying, etc.[26] In most cases, the crises were made worse due to incoming and outgoing international capital flows that inflated and then destabilized local economies. By the way, with the exception of Joseph Stiglitz, Naomi Klein and a few others, not that many commentators (and certainly not IMF ones) mention that some Asian economies, e.g. Malaysia and Thailand, recovered more quickly from the late-1990s financial crisis thanks to the role of public initiatives, the insulation of some parts of their economies, and more protected financial sectors. Speak softly, or you are labeled a protectionist! What else than "protecting" national – and banking – interests have most governments in Japan, Asia, America, Europe done in the latest financial crises? Do as I say…

How national can a company be today?

"*How national is a company today?*" asks a prominent group of French economists.[27] For all its limits, AB InBev (simplified ID) also stands as a showcase for company internationalization. Like others, and more than many, it has succeeded in transforming a local manufacturer into a global player – and market leader. Many other companies and their managers have shown great capabilities for moving far from home while at the same time staying close to their roots (with subsequent financial flows for the country of origin), and sometimes even close

26 The mix of country and corporate crises could be traced in CDS (credit default swaps) well before the Eurozone crisis: a top five of credit derivatives outstanding published in the Flemish business daily De Tijd (November 6, 2008) was showing Italy as riskiest, followed by Spain, Deutsche Bank, Brazil, and General Electric Capital. At that time, Greece was not yet at the top of the list…

27 "*L'entreprise a-t-elle encore une nationalité?*", by Patrick Artus and the French Cercle des économistes, in "*La guerre des capitalismes aura lieu*" (Perrin, 2008).

to remote customers. With fewer inhabitants than Belgium, Sweden has a bigger roster of truly international firms who have grown abroad than modern Britain has, for example. Assa Abloy, Atlas Copco, Electrolux, Ericsson, H&M, IKEA, SCA, SKF, Trelleborg, Volvo, to name but a few, hold strong or leadership positions in their respective industries (from compressors to appliances to packaging to trucks and hundreds of other products). That may be explained by excellence at striking a good balance between a "yellow-and-blue" pride (Swedish companies remain proud to be Swedish) and a high adaptability to any local environment where they operate. An explanatory factor may also be found more than incidentally in the Swedish model of capital structure, based on a balanced mix of strong national family-derived investment groups, thousands of local shareholders, and foreign ones. Although on a smaller scale than the Swedes, the traveling Dutch, perhaps because their "naam is klein" and their land and home market too (but not their self-regard, also for the better, as the ABN Amro-Fortis story has shown) are often rightly reckoned as born exporters, yet they remain Dutch without any doubt.[28] The Swedish and Dutch examples certainly fit what the Canadian essayist J.R. Saul calls "*positive nationalism*."[29] Strong at home, and perhaps paradoxically, close to markets and customer needs everywhere explains the success of large Japanese corporations, which, nonetheless, remain very Japanese in their heart and

28 When the Belgian, Dutch and Luxembourg governments jointly bailed out the virtually bankrupt bank and insurance group Fortis in September 2008, the Dutch government's attitude attracted criticism from Belgium because it would have paid too much attention to their self-interest, also by drawing ABN Amro back to Holland. What's the problem? Pride? Was it so appropriate to sell off at a discounted price, the way the Belgian government did it in an awkward deal with the French BNP Paribas, letting another decision center drift away? Well, as a consolation, at least the two Belgian communities (the Flemings and the Walloons) could reunite against the old Northern enemy! The net result was the loss of one more Belgian controlled banking group, but the Dutch parts back to Holland.

29 John Ralston Saul: "*The Collapse of Globalism and the Reinvention of the World*" (Penguin Books, 2005).

soul. The distance factor does not seem to have been such a hindrance and loss of identity (compare with Inbev above) for Canon, Fujifilm, Honda, Nikon, Pioneer, Sharp, Sony, Toyota, which were more attentive to changing customer needs than the Detroit big wheels, American and European electronic manufacturers, etc. The net results of that national and global mix were most visible in our living rooms and on the roads over the last decades.

Post-World War II saw "Made in USA" capitalism triumph almost everywhere outside Communist or developing countries, with Americanization then almost synonymous with globalization. But the "Buy it" and "My way" attitudes of a very nationally branded U.S. capitalism - Coca-Cola and McDonald's for food, Fordism for production, as well as the Harvard Business School and myriads of consultants for management thinking - have turned from strength to weaknesses in a more competitive and less American-centric environment. Today's U.S. capitalism must look - and act - less "national" to compete against both global rivals and local brands. GM was too big to succeed, and then to fail, whereas its archrival Chrysler was probably too American and Ford Motor had gone too far with an unmanageable stable of brands. At the beginning of the 21st century, the Dearborn-based giant was "*running down a dream*", being the owner of Ford, Mercury, Mazda, Volvo, Jaguar, Aston Martin and Land Rover.[30] Managing remotely such Japanese, Swedish and English-style carmakers proved too difficult from Detroit, and, despite a true international experience, stretched too much the company's core business.[31] Ford had to get rid of all its "premium" brands in less time than it had taken to build them up.

The thing is, as Warren Keegan, Gary Hamel, C.K. Prahalad, Michael Porter, and other noted specialists in global strategy

30 "*Runnin' down a dream*" freely taken from Tom Petty's song title (MCA Records, 1989).

31 Moving too far from a company's core business may certainly fall under this sin.

have consistently pointed out, to think global and act local, or to balance local demands with a global vision.[32] Note that in some cases, staying where you are works much better to meet some needs – and perform economically. Almost 40 percent of China's new luxury goods consumers do not mind purchasing global brands but prefer products designed specifically for (and in) China. This trend is perceptible in other countries and industries. As Sony's chairman Akio Morita once put it, the challenge is to be able to "glocalize".[33]

The well and the ocean

For the sake of clarity, our viewpoint does not in any case imply that growing international and thus moving far is bad as such.34 On the contrary. Whether you see the world as "*flat*", you view it as "*borderless*", or you want to "*make globalization work*", "*Competing with Everyone from Everywhere for Everything*" has become our common fate.[35] David Ricardo may have been

32 While often attributed to a number of marketing authors or globalization advocates, the expression "*Think global, act local*" seems to have been coined by David Brower, the Californian founder of the environmentalist Friends of the Earth. The term "Globalization" would have been used first by Harvard professor Theodore Levitt (in 1983?).

33 Warren J. Keegan: "*Multinational Marketing Management*" (Prentice Hall, 1984), "*Global Marketing Management*" (7th Edition, Prentice Hall, 2001). Gary Hamel and C.K. Prahalad: "*Competing for the Future*" (Harvard Business School Press, 1996). Michael E. Porter (Editor): "*Competition in Global Industries*" (Harvard Business School Press, 1986). George Yip: "*Total Global Strategy: Managing for Worldwide Competitive Advantage*" (2nd edition, Prentice Hall, 2002).

34 In a previous life, I taught international management to young execs and advised companies on their globalization strategies and have no regrets about that! Those were the days of "happy" globalization at best, or globalization as a necessary evil at worst.

35 The words refer to the titles of inspiring books published these last decades: "*The World Is Flat*", by Thomas L. Friedman (Farrar, Straus and Giroux, 2005); "*The Borderless World*", by Kenichi Ohmae (Fontana, HarperCollins, 1991); "*Making Globalization Work*", by Joseph E. Stiglitz (W. W. Norton, 2007); "*Globality: Competing with Everyone from Everywhere for Everything*", by Harold L. Sirkin, James W. Hemerling, and Arindam K. Bhattacharya (from the Boston Consulting Group) (Business Plus, 2008).

buried some time ago, his free-trade legacy remains, as well as the message that trade contributes to exchange between civilizations. Moreover, an international mindset is praised more than to go for any form of "splendid isolation" (not always so splendid), or worse, for nationalistic jingoism, which have proved harmful more than once in history.[36] "*Travel broadens the mind*" or, as a Chinese proverb goes, "*The frog in the well knows nothing of the ocean.*"

Why would it necessarily be good just because it is far? Forget exoticism for a while and enjoy the taste of those fruits, vegetables, etc. bought only in season on the local market square (a smell of Rousseau's daydreams here). One man's local beer is another man's regional wine. The grass is not always greener on the other side... Why might it not be good just because it is not made nearby? Discover something from somewhere else and enjoy the flavor of those exotic fruits, vegetables, etc. traded off-season in the global marketplace (distant echo from David Ricardo here). One woman's black coffee is another woman's green tea. The grass is always greener...

36 Used to name the British policy in the late 19th century, U.S. ones now and then, and also the title of a song by Warren Zevon (on "*Transverse City*", Virgin, 1989).

SIN NO. 3:
TOO SHORT

"See the wind, turn the rudder."
CHINESE PROVERB

"We now have a serious financial problem caused largely by short-termism, which is far and away the single most destructive business impulse today."
DON PEPPERS, management consultant

Enronitis, or share price at the top

Enron stock price 1991-2001 (Source: Candlestick Trading Forum)[1]

There are a few definitions of "Enronitis":

- The sickness of companies which artificially fabricated millions (or billions) in revenues and/or profits to pump up their stock prices and shareholder value – and, lest we forget, to pay subsequent executive compensation for "market performance";
- The shockwaves sent through stock markets after the 2001 collapse of the Houston, Texas-based energy trader (followed by other fake revenue-makers' failures);
- "*Nervousness over a company because of suspected accounting problems*,"[2] or just excesses of "*creative accounting*" as Alan Greenspan himself dubbed it;

1 Source: "*Don't Get Enron'd*", at www.candlestickforum.com/PPF/Parameters/12_66_/candlestick.asp.

2 Definition from www.yourdictionary.com.

- Or, more simply and more broadly, as entirely short-term driven corporate and financial management. Actually, it was (having witnessed what has happened since, we are not sure that past simple should apply) the most perfect (or imperfect) example of all the excesses of short-termism.

In fifteen years, the company grew from a few to 21,000 employees and ranked as the U.S.'s seventh largest company by revenue. In 2000, the year before its fall, Enron's stock grew almost 300 percent faster than the average S&P 500. Enron's management obsession with hitting a weekly, daily, or even hourly stock price high may look crazy in hindsight but was considered by many or most as good practice in the company's glory days. Days when, to quote former CEO Jeff Skilling, "*in every business we've been in, we're the good guys*", and when Fortune was comparing Enron's hipness to Elvis Presley's, for bringing a "*new model*" to the energy sector![3] It might have been a new model – although a highly disputable one: fossil fuels being finite resources, these should not be treated under short-term market considerations – but besides the crass dishonesty of top executives, the model was defined mainly, if not only, by short-term price considerations.

The share price illness is affecting thousands of listed companies. Looking at the above chart, and bar the unhappy ending, do many companies not show similar price trends over a certain period – or dream of them? Likewise, many stock-holders would not mind enjoying a higher price when they sell some shares. Today, the CEO's job often seems to consist of making (mainly big) shareholders as rich as possible as quickly

3 CEO's quote and other information recapitulated in a good article by Thomas Frank on www.salon.com: "*The Enron outrage*" (December 15, 2001). Fortune magazine named Enron "*America's Most Innovative Company*" for six consecutive years from 1996 to 2001. The article also points to admiring notes from famous consultants and business analysts (Enron's annual reports were not worst packaged, either).

as possible, as opposed to managing companies to sell products and generate long-term income. Still, is it a company objective to have its stock sold by (some of) its owners (to whom?) at a high price, instead of keeping shareholders inside? Should share price (highs), earnings per share (EPS), market value, and other so-called "market fundamentals" – which are for most economically and businesswise not fundamental at all – be the objectives of financial and corporate management? The answer is a straight no. Those are signals, results – and not objectives – of good management among other performance indicators that have to be watched regularly, but mostly by and towards investors. Talking about these, too many investors cannot resist the temptation to check their portfolio value on one of their mobile devices whenever they get a chance, even though they know that most short-term share price movements "*are only the noise of rustling underground.*"[4] Those signals should not distract executives, management and employees from other major goals of a business. Earnings and dividend-based share ownership are a good thing, price-driven stock options are not. In a review of "*The Speculation Economy,*" a book written by Lawrence E. Mitchell, BusinessWeek magazine commented:

> "*Over time, the expectations of the investor class brought a radical switch in how managers of public corporations operated. No longer could they solely focus on maximizing plant efficiency or besting competitors. Instead, investors' lust for ever-higher share prices meant the stock market ceased being a mere financing vehicle and became an institution 'whose insatiable desire for profit demanded satisfaction from even the most powerful corporations.' By spawning this culture of 'short-termism,' finance had trumped industry, and U.S. business would never be the same.*"[5]

---

4 As John Kay wrote in "*Investors should resist the tyranny of quarterly earnings*" (Financial Times, February 29, 2012).

5 "*The Speculation Economy. How Finance Triumphed Over Industry*", by Lawrence E. Mitchell (Berrett-Koehler, 2007); reviewed in BusinessWeek under the mean-

Financial reporting is the place to check this.

Ewold de Bruijne, a Dutch financial communication specialist, sums it up: "*In reports, the discussion of share performance based on the stock price movement makes a lousy investment case, for two reasons: it's about the past and it's about a metric that is the competence of investors, not of management.*"[6]

Market cap: what goes up…

Market capitalization is calculated by multiplying company shares by the current market price for one share.[7] It is therefore not only a very narrow measure of company size and performance but also a very short-term indicator, as the value changes every day, hour, minute, and second.[8] Too many people, investors included, have short memories, and therefore repeat the same mistakes. Enron's market cap exceeded $60 billion in December 2000, i.e. 70 times its profit. In the same period, remember the acquisition of Time Warner by the much smaller AOL in the early 2000s. The only things that were bigger at AOL than at the New York-based media group were the AOL founder's ego and the firm's market value. That was judged sufficient to make a deal! "Equipped" with such a high market cap, AOL purchased Time Warner for $164 billion and struck a deal giving the acquirer, small by all measures, a majority stake. A bit less than two years later, a goodwill write-off resulted in a loss of about $100 billion, i.e. 60 percent of the price paid for the purchase! A bit more than two years later,

ingful heading: "*The Making of a Stock Market Society*" (November 27, 2007).

6 Cited on www.reportwatch.net. Ewold de Bruijne is also a regular member of the rating panel for the "*Annual Report on Annual Reports*".

7 Both market value and market cap are used to define "capitalization". The term should not be confused with company or enterprise capitalization (sum of equity plus long-term debt) and with market value as the higher estimated price that a buyer would pay or the replacement cost.

8 Surprisingly (or not?), the Financial Times has kept on publishing a Global 500 based on market value, which is much more volatile than revenues.

the AOL acronym was dropped from the corporate identity and became a division of the... acquired company. Leaving its specifics – and the huge amounts – aside, this is just one example among many showing where share price fetishism can lead: overvalued market caps, overpriced stocks and companies, overpaid acquisitions, and underperformance and value destruction for investors – sometimes recorded only months or weeks after the peak (in price, value…).

The gap between market value and other key indicators should at least be worth a check. Not to mention the required close watch on the fundamental medium-term figures and ratios. Who can really (make) believe that Apple market cap was suddenly worth twice as much as Microsoft, or more than Google, Goldman Sachs, GM, Ford, Starbucks and Boeing combined in mid-February 2012?[9] Does it generate so much more economic value than each or all of those? How could Facebook be worth up to $100 billion based on $3.7 billion revenues and a stunning $1 billion profit (really?), questionable user figures (even before 83 million fake accounts were uncovered), and its own homepage as most visited one?[10] How long before another Internet or other bubble bursts? What goes up….

Shareholder value: yes, but for whom?

"*The virtuous cycle of shareholder value creation*" was the title of an article published in 1997 in the McKinsey Quarterly, but also the implicit or explicit words used in thousands of annual reports (especially in CEO messages) published since the mid-

9 "Apple Stock's Lofty Heights, in Context" in the Economix blog (New York Times, February 9, 2012).

10 Not all comments about the IPO were as ecstatic as in the Huffington Post ("*Facebook IPO Reveals Its Stunning Size*", February 1, 2012). Read e.g. Barry Ritholtz's column in The Washington Post: "*What Is Facebook Really Worth?*" (February 12, 2012), where the way to count (active) users is much questioned.

1990s.[11] One of the most trumpeted buzzwords from the last decade, "managing for shareholder value" is at best a tautology - which company would dare to say it does not have to give a decent return to its owners? - and at worst a spin put on company information - and results that are sometimes not heading at all toward value creation. The simplest way to define it would be through the "profit cycle" based on income statement figures:

- Revenue > Net profit > ROE > EPS > Dividend paid (stable at worst, increased at best).

More sophisticated mathematical calculations are discussed in economic literature. A "neutral" definition of shareholder value creation is given by IESE professor Pablo Fernandez:

- Created shareholder value creation = Equity market value x (Shareholder return - Required return to equity).[12]

Whatever the definition, these last decades' burst bubbles and boom busts have cost a lot in shareholder value, except for the savviest investors and... stock-option beneficiaries. Having added the word "sustained" to shareholder value does not much change the hard realities. Especially for individual

investors, who now own less than 50 percent of equity shares in the U.S., down from 90 percent in the 1950s. Actually, the Enron chart profile shown above looks very much like a number of other price graphs, e.g. for financial institutions' stocks before and after the late-2000s financial crisis.

11 "*The virtuous cycle of shareholder value creation*" by Jacques Bughin and Thomas E. Copeland (McKinsey Quarterly, May 1997), which states that "*shareholders and job seekers have a common interest: high returns on capital.*" Another example of high-return but nevertheless near-sighted and highly ideological business economics.

12 "*A definition of Shareholder Value Creation*" by Pablo Fernandez, IESE Business School (April 2001). Paper available at http://papers.ssrn.com.

Following a few other analysts, FT commentator Michael Skapinker has also pointed to "*the short-term nature of [shareholder] holdings*", increasingly held by institutional investors, often operating under the influence of short-term driven analysts.[13] Whether they are private or institutional, investors tend to buy, trade and sell more shares in less time than in the past. "*In the old days finance was treated as a modest helper of production,*" wrote Paul Sweezy, who added: "*It tended to take on a life of its own and generate speculative excesses in the late stages of business cycle expansions.*"[14] Now, some refer to the system as "financialized" or as a "speculation-based" economy.[15] Lawrence E. Mitchell sums up the metamorphosis: "*Previously, a small number of equity investors had treated stocks much like bonds, preferring those with hard assets backing each share... The new form of speculation [is] based on a growing willingness to own stock issued not on the basis of productive assets or past profits but on the possibility of profits to come,*" preferably in the short term.[16] Exactly what Enron was all about.

"*Shareholder value is a result, not a strategy... Your main constituencies are your employees, your customers and your products.*" Who said that? Jack Welch! Yes, the legendary

ex-CEO of GE, made famous as one of the leaders of the share holder value movement, "*a man who ruthlessly downsized and restructured in pursuit of... shareholder value.*" Words of (late) contrition? As Toronto University's professor Roger Martin

13 "*Every fool knows it is a job for governments*", in the Financial Times (November 18, 2008). Read also: "*Economic Implications of Changing Share Ownership*" by Benjamin M. Friedman (Harvard University, October 1996), available at http://papers.ssrn.com.

14 Paul M. Sweezy: "*Economic Reminiscences*", in the Monthly Review (May 1995).

15 Including Paul Sweezy, or John Bellamy Foster (see "*The Financialization of Capital and the Crisis*", on www.monthlyreview.org, April 2008).

16 In "*The Speculation Economy. How Finance Triumphed Over Industry*", by Lawrence E. Mitchell (Berrett-Koehler, 2007).

puts it: "*The pursuit of shareholder value simply fails as a unifying theory to produce value in business.*"[17]

"Making the quarter" (and short expectations)

A few blips on the screens of analysts, followed by traders, investors and fund managers too often stand as the major or only signals emitted by and received from (stock) markets. Sometimes they look and sound as the be-all and end-all of CFOs or IR officers. In his message in the annual report 2002, Porsche's chief executive wrote that:

"*short-term performance has acquired more importance recently, based on quarterly balance-sheet figures and therefore on hectic value assessment of at best limited value.*"[18]

Although the tyranny of short-termism remains most prevalent in the Anglo-American model, it has spread across the global economy. Because markets are now virtually working round-the-clock, follow the same standards, and, to make things worse, are increasingly based on automated or "algo" trading.

When India-based Satyam's founder confessed a $1.4 billion fraud early in 2009, he said that: "*he had inflated profits and cash while understating liabilities and became addicted to the lies to keep up with analysts' expectations.*"[19]

---

17 Jack Welch's quotation and journalist comment from India's Economic Times: "*Shareholder's value's not the issue*" (March 19, 2009). Roger Martin: "*Fixing the Game: Bubbles, Crashes, and What Capitalism Can Learn from the NFL*" (Harvard Business Press, 2011). Roger Martin is dean of the Rotman School of Management at the University of Toronto.

18 Annual report 2002. Though with slight shifts now and then, Porsche has not much changed course, and delivered better strategically, on products, and on financial performance than on other aspects of its management (e.g. reporting transparency and governance).

19 Quoted by Sandeep Parekh (Financial Times, January 12, 2009). Satyam was a leading Indian IT services group and the scandal had the magnitude of a local

Got this? Analysts' expectations!

This should not come as a surprise as "beating expectations" seems to have become many officers (including at the highest level) and reporters' major concern and favorite sport in recent years. Even professional commentators often confuse improving results with beating analysts' expectations. The trend is most obvious in quarterly reporting and may mislead investors. In October 2007 the Swedish group Ericsson issued a "profit warning" (another strange expression in modern market vocabulary) implying that operating profit would go down for the last two quarters. Net result: a quarter of the market cap wiped out in one single day! One month later, the company lost another 11 percent in market value because current quarterly earnings "*would come in at the lower end of expectations.*" Here we go again: short expectations. This is not to say that interim reporting is pointless. Quarterly reporting is most necessary (as a minimum) inside any business of a significant size (not least to get a grasp of cycles). The problem lies in making it a duty and turning subservient to analysts and short-term investors who can, sometimes, if not often, unfairly penalize companies, just because they are being short of a number or market expectations. "*Short-termism refers to the excessive focus... on short-term earnings guidance, coupled with a lack of attention to the strategy, fundamentals, and conventional approaches to long-term value creation.*" Who states that? A bunch of anti-capitalists? No, the CFA Institute Centre, which gathers 90,000 certified financial analysts worldwide.[20]

In the above-mentioned message, Porsche's CEO also stated that:

Enron ("*Accounting scandal at Satyam could be India's Enron*" on www.reuters.com, January 7, 2009). The ailing company was acquired by Mahindra group a few months after the troubles.

20 On www.cfainstitute.org/centre/topics.

> "*many companies still give priority to the long-term increase in their value... which may require patience and persistence for many years...*".

Whew! Indeed, short-term supposed share(holder)-driven management is often conducted at the expense of long-term product quality and/or customer service and/or medium-term strategy. In the case of Porsche, a longer-term commitment also translated into... shareholder value: from 1993 to 2003, shareholders' equity was multiplied by 7.5. A result of a medium-term strategy more than an obsession with short-term signals. Not many carmakers could boast about such an increase at that time. Let alone these days?

Nothing ventured, something lost

Long-term loans have for long been harder to obtain for thousands of SMEs, except in countries such as Germany, where the Mittelstand and small or larger banks have worked hand in hand for decades, with a strong family-controlled and SME-based export machine. In Italy or for Overseas Chinese, family connections work as a substitute for banks. In the U.S., many startups are primarily funded by... credit cards (which is of course financially unhealthy). Banks have switched to more profitable (?) and less risky (??) mortgage, trading, dealing, hedging, and other related operations. In France, the share of loans in bank assets fell to 38 percent in 2003 from 84 percent in 1980, while the share of deposits in liabilities went down from 73 percent to 27 percent over the same period. In parallel, the percentage of securities in assets and liabilities surged from 5 percent to about 50 percent. Other economies show similar trends.

Midcap markets are unattractive, too expensive, or just non-existent, which is a real hindrance for medium-sized companies with high-growth potential. The impact is clear: there are fewer listed companies in the UK now than there were after the late-

2000s financial crisis; and, at a global scale, thousands of SEs are not capable of turning into MEs due to the lack of financing sources. Microcredit solutions in developing and emerging economies are insufficiently used. Another noticeable trend is the diminishing role of long-term venture capital, in Europe and elsewhere, increasingly replaced by shorter-term "investment" strategies.[21] The mission statement in the annual report 2002 of 3i referred to "*Europe's leading venture capital company*", adding: "*We invest in ambitious unquoted companies with high growth potential.*" In 2004, the mission slightly changed to "*a world leader in private equity and venture capital.*" The 2007 annual report mentioned "*high-return assets*" as the first strategic priority. The annual report 2008 introduced "*a world leader in private equity,*" leaving the term venture capital out. IPOs, a critical part of venture capitalists' exit strategies averaged 150 to 200 a year in the U.S. in the nineties. They fell to half those figures in recent years.[22] As a recent survey by Deloitte concluded: "*among venture capitalists, there's China and there's everyone else.*"[23] Follow the money…

The increased share of stock trading robots, algorithmic and high-frequency trading (55 percent of exchanges in America, 40 percent in Europe) has added another short-termist pressure on real economies and business executives. The role played by derivative instruments of various forms (forward, swap, equity, foreign exchange, credit…) should also be mentioned as a short-term disequilibrium and destabilizing factor for companies and economies, especially when they are used for speculative purpose. Today, derivatives amount to an equivalent of five times the total stock and bond market value

21 Research done in the U.S. by HIS Global Insight showed in 2005 that companies once backed by venture capital accounted for 17 percent of GDP (cited in The Economist, March 14, 2009).

22 Cited in the Financial Times (April 30, 2009), where the author of the article Richard Waters noted that "*Risk aversion put paid to the glory days when start-ups were desirable.*"

23 "*Global trends in venture capital - 2009 global report*" (Deloitte, 2009).

worldwide. Incidentally (is it?), derivatives provide another illustration of how capitalism has moved from the real to the financial economy: while Jack the entrepreneur has to undergo a full-asset striptease to obtain a credit from a bank, Nick the trader can sell e.g. an option contract which is "naked", i.e. not covered by any security ownership.

The long and short (in) reports

Annual reports remain a place where investors can check if companies – and their investments – delivered not only the last year but also on a longer-term period. Here again, an emphasis on short-term performance has gained ground, especially among U.S. listed corporations.[24] Key figures rarely span over more than two years; "selected" financial data usually select a limited number of indicators, often buried in a tedious Form 10-K, and a five-year span is becoming rare; long-term ratios are scarce; quarterly figures focus on share price and dividends and overlook other fundamentals. Reflecting the trends analyzed above, quarterly releases, "profit warnings" and analysts' briefings now receive more attention than longer-term annuals. Blue chips have been no exceptions to the rule: under Welch's tenure General Electric was mainly highlighting market value; Ford Motor has dropped its results' fulfillment check from its operating highlights since 2002's poor performance; and Sara Lee, among the first annuals setting forth a CFO summary deleted this in bad times and cut performance indicators down to a few. En passant, Sarbanes-Oxley (or Sox), a bill enacted in the wake of Enron and other scandals, has hardly improved anything on those matters. There is more tyranny of short-termism today than before Enron's case.

Behind reporting lies the choice of relevant indicators, effectively measuring medium-term performance and putting

24 Read "*The rise and fall of American annual reports*", by Mike Guillaume, in the "*Annual Report on Annual Reports 2006*". Things have worsened ever since.

short-term highs and lows in a broader perspective. What does matter?

- ROE or ROCE? These indicators supplement each other, but the good old return on equity certainly remains a primary measure both for management and for shareholders and a perfect medium-term performance metric. Under the pressure of financial analysts, too many reports or presentations tend to divert the attention by overemphasizing a higher return on capital employed (which adds funded debt to company equity) that can hide lower equity performance… and result in more indebtedness.

- Total assets or ROA? These last years, a large majority of annual and periodic reports have stopped calculating the return on assets.[25] The size of assets (or "fat") often seems to matter more than their efficient use (or "muscle").

- Market value or revenues? A perfect sign of short-termism (based on the latest share price), the former has tended to become something that overdrives investors, analysts, and… managers' behavior in their judgments.

- Before or after exceptionals? Well, both should be set forth, but including or excluding exceptionals sometimes lead to a biased grasp of the real operating performance, when it is not pure window dressing. Not to mention the recurring exceptional items!

- Quick payback or medium-term ROI? These last years, the former has clearly outweighed the latter. Charles H. Green identifies three main reasons for that: first, investment owners are turning over faster; uncertainty feeds the "*get rich quick*" mentality ("*Why tie your money*

25 According to the "*Annual Report on Annual Reports,*" these last years, on average, around 10 percent of annuals set forth ROA.

up because, hey, you never know!"); lastly, uncertainty also feeds perceived risk (investments are assessed at "*increasing hurdle rates*" for "*farther-out timeframes*").[26]

- Short-term earnings and dividends or medium-term shareholder return? A research about ten-year returns from world's largest companies (ranked by market cap…) showed five financial institutions as worst performing. All of them had posted big quarterly profits and paid decent dividends for at least half of the period, but then…[27]
- Price or earnings? Again, think twice. How to interpret a recent study showing that, when American P/E (price-earnings) ratios are low, ROE (return on equity) over the next decade is an average 8 percent; while when they are (too) high, the average return is down to 3 percent?[28]

Short-termism has gone to such an extreme that these last ten years, bar some Japanese groups, top Canadian banks, and a few blue chips or smaller firms, many more listed companies have provided quarterly "guidance" (another strange word) than disclosed detailed targets in figures for the next one to three years, which would give real indications about the strategic course.[29] Fortunately, not all companies have followed the short-termist fashion. Let us have a quick look across the board. Even in downturn contexts, Philips' president has kept on comparing achieved results with the management board's

26 "*Short-termism, ROI and Green Economics*" (Business Week, October 24, 2007). Charles H. Green is the founder and CEO of New Jersey-based Trusted Advisor Associates.

27 "*Best and worst returns from large companies*" over February 2002-2012 period (Bloomberg, The Economist, February 18, 2012).

28 Cited in The Economist: "*Where have all your savings gone?*" (December 6, 2008).

29 Based on the assessment of 500 to 1,000 annual reports on yearly average, the "*Annual Report on Annual Reports*" has showed that a maximum of 15 percent of annual reports disclose meaningful outlook and one- to three-year target figures.

agenda. Finnish paper manufacturer Stora Enso has always extensively reported medium-term share indicators, whatever the operating environment. In the same industry, Sappi (South Africa) checks out target fulfillment, even if they are not positive. Scandinavian airliner SAS has remained a high-flying reporting exercise full of figures, despite continuing losses and turbulences. Some reports – and corporations – go the extra mile. Asahi Breweries (Japan) puts market positions and results in perspective, and a majority of Japanese firms are showing a sustained commitment to reporting medium-term strategy and indicators, and checking out these annually for their stockholders. Adidas (Germany) has consistently reported past objectives, compared results, and future targets in the first pages of its annuals. In the telecoms, a sector where overall reporting has often been poorly transparent and accurate, the Canadian Telus has been a consistent model for its bold display of targets and results, followed by thorough explanations about their (non-)fulfillment in the financial review. That is good news! Some do not lose sight of their strategy, their business, and their long-term financial purpose.

Product myopia – again

In 1960, Theodore Levitt published his influential paper "*Marketing Myopia*" in the Harvard Business Review. The author was referring to companies excessively focusing on their products and overlooking customer needs and market changes. That is another form of short-termism, more benign but with potential internal and external in the long run. Levitt's paper already pointed out the oil sector as a bad example, and its impact was so big that some redefined their business as "energy" rather than just "petroleum". More than fifty years on, besides having added gas and more downstream operations to their portfolio, the oil giants are behaving exactly the same as… before Levitt's article, especially in America, China, and India. Although groups such as BP and Royal Dutch Shell are spending hundreds of millions on renewable energies, do not expect them to shift to these on a sustainable basis. Like in most cases in capitalism's history, innovation will come from outsiders, as we are already seeing for wind turbines or small-scale cogeneration systems, for example.

Apart from rereading Levitt's article, oil and gas giants should draw some inspiration from two examples. First, in the 1970s, after a failed attempt to take over its rival Saint-Gobain in the glass industry, BSN's boss Antoine Riboud decided to leave the sector and to turn the company into a food group (food and beverages were at that time just a small division at BSN). A couple of years later, it merged with Gervais Danone and has now become a world leader in dairy products. Second, in the 1980s, the then Volvo chief executive said that the group's business was not to produce cars, but to meet transportation needs. That probably explained why, many years later, the Swedish company did not have many problems selling its auto division – even though it was still its largest business unit – and then merging its truck division with Renault's. Recent statements from Ford's chairman Bill Ford mark a step (or drive) in a less short-termist direction, e.g. by pointing to the… short-term risk of permanent traffic congestion.[30] Those are very good examples of a strategic visions that depart from the prevailing short-sightedness.

Harvard's professor Michael Porter stated that since the mid 1990s "*strategy had lost its intellectual currency. It was losing adherents. People were being tricked and misled by other ideas... Strategy has suffered... from the emergence of the notion that in a world of change, you really shouldn't have one... things were moving so fast, you couldn't afford to pause.*"[31] There is no short-

30 "*Ford head warns rise to 4bn cars risks world gridlock*" and "*Drive to keep the industry moving*" (Financial Times, February 27, 2012). But naturally all car manufacturers keep on producing more vehicles.

31 "*Michael Porter's Big Ideas*" (Fast Company, February 2001).

age of "short" things in today's capitalism. Without stretching that much, why should a company invest in employees, since, after all, they might leave someday? And why investing in customers if the payback takes more years than investors' expectations? Etc. The negative effects of short-termism outweigh the positive ones, and by far. Despite those, long-term strategy is often lost in short-term market translation.

SIN NO. 4: TOO SELFISH

"It is not from the benevolence of the butcher, the brewer or the baker that we expect our dinner, but from their regard to their own interest."
ADAM SMITH

"Egotism is an alphabet of one letter."
OLD SCOTTISH PROVERB

The butcher and the baker are not alone – or are gone

The butcher, brewer and baker story (note the absence of a banker) told by Adam Smith made economic history.[1] Even outside the circle of classical liberals, many now recognize that acting out of self-interest can result in the common interest. If not all, which would be costly and illusory, at least of a broader group: buyers, consumers, shareholders, investors, suppliers, tax collectors, and other forms of individuals and groups now often referred to as "stakeholders". Self-interest makes the business work, it fuels the economy, and, up to a certain point, benefits the whole society and the environment. Up to a point. Peter Drucker got it right in repeating that "*the purpose of a business is to create and keep a customer*." Does he capture it all? Not completely.

What if things tumble, around the corner and further down the road? "*There goes the neighborhood*" is an expression used in a variety of contexts, such as the impact of a big mortgage crisis, which is also "*harming the neighbors of people in foreclosure, even those who aren't having trouble making loan payments.*"[2] Being surrounded by houses for sale, emptier streets, dirty sidewalks, etc. does not make life very enjoyable. The environment in its broadest sense can affect any enterprise, small or big, and hits self-interest. "Business in the Community" is one of the Prince's Charities, and aims at mobilizing "*business for good*", among others "*to address key social issues and the needs of local communities*", that is, to make British business more aware of what is happening in the wider

---

1 Adam Smith: "*The Wealth of Nations*" (1776, republished e.g. by Bantam Classics, 2003).

2 "*There Goes the Neighborhood*" was the title of an article published in Boston-based The Atlantic (January-February 2008) and describing the impact of foreclosures on the neighborhoods in the U.S. It is also a song by Sheryl Crow (A&M, 1998).

surroundings.[3] Perhaps not a coincidence in a country that was home to great utilitarians. According to this school of thought (of which Jeremy Bentham, John Locke and John Stuart Mill are the main representatives), the greatest good for the greatest number should be the major economic and political goal. Human beings are free to do anything unless they harm others, and governments should therefore interfere when "others", i.e. the society, is threatened or harmed.

Some background information helps explain my concern. I was born in a "Black Country", not the one north of Birmingham, UK, but the "Pays Noir" still surrounding Charleroi, Belgium. Once a rich area at the heart of the industrial revolution, with coal mines, steel, glass and textile factories, and "*smokestacks reaching like the arms of God into a beautiful sky of soot and clay,*" it has experienced stagnation in recent decades.[4] Tens of thousands of employees lost their jobs, thousands of (self-) employers lost their businesses. Then it spiraled downward. Butchers, bakers, and others (as to brewers' fate, check under another sin in this essay) saw fewer customers coming less often and with less and less money. Those were and are still living in less maintained houses, with fewer neighbors, in less clean and less safe streets (sure they were never really clean, but then they were more filled and thus safer, too). In most places, owing to insufficient demand and bigger supply-side

3 "Business in the Community" website: www.bitc.org. For a broader perspective on the interaction between entrepreneurship and local development, check the OECD LEED Program on www.oecd.org, which also includes a guide to "*successful partnerships*", et al.

4 The Antwerp-Liège-Charleroi "triangle" was comparable to North of England in the 19th and first half of 20th century. The region is also comparable to former "black" coal-and-steel areas, such as Ohio's Youngstown (sung by Bruce Springsteen, from which the quoted words are excerpted), or Pennsylvania's Pittsburgh (with which Charleroi is twinned). The latter made a more successful transformation due also to entrepreneurship than the declining and politically mismanaged Walloon metropolis. Pittsburgh consistently ranked among U.S. cleanest and most livable places these last years (see e.g. "*The World's Cleanest Cities*", in Forbes, April 16, 2007).

alternatives (department stores are leaving their mark here too), grocers, butchers, bakers, brewers, et al. are gone.

Externalities and responsibilities: doing nothing or doing some good

Externalities – i.e. benefits or external costs and thus the positive or negative impact on any unrelated or third party of an economic decision or activity – have always existed in economies and capitalism. The difference between now and then is that in Adam Smith's times externalities were not as important and expensive to enterprises, the whole economy, and the environment. In the "Black Countries" neighborhoods referred to above, the steel industry (and what is still left of it now) offers a good (?) example of negative externality; directly through its pollutants sent into the air; and indirectly through poorer quality of life, increased medical expenses, dirt and dust, decreased property value… In an influential paper published in 1960, Ronald Coase suggested that "*private parties that generate or are affected by externalities will negotiate voluntary agreements*" might apply to a world of "*perfect competition*" and "*clearly defined property rights.*"[5] As this is not the case, both for competition (which is rarely perfect), and property rights (who owns the air up and around the steel mill? Are some owners not bigger than others?), and as externality costs have sometimes become so big, the suggested "agreements" are illusory. In the case of steel – and if it was about this only – many companies simply did not care about externalities and, more broadly, about their social and environmental responsibility for decades. When the times changed, the balance of power often resulted in… unbalanced agreements.

To make things worse, a growing number of products are defined by selfishness or generate carelessness, with externalities

5 Ronald Coase: "*The Problem of Social Cost*" in the Journal of Law and Economics (October 1960).

that sometimes outweigh internalities. A car is often oversized compared to a driver's actual needs. For commuting trips, the driver is frequently alone (have you counted how many times the back seats are occupied?). Last but not least, car driving drives many people crazy, or, to put it another way, an increasing number of individuals are driving irresponsibly. The use of a mobile phone has become as much of a disturbance factor and impoliteness as a communication object, which was its primary purpose.[6] Sony's Walkman and Apple's iPod can quickly turn into kinds of autistic devices. And these are just a few examples.

This is where the principles of "sustainable development" came in – and are here to stay. Probably coined by the U.N. Brundtland Commission as development that "*meets the needs of the present without compromising the ability of future generations to meet their own needs*", the concept has since then been translated into various terms: sustainability, corporate social responsibility (CSR), responsible business, corporate citizenship, stakeholder reporting, "Triple bottom line", "Balanced scorecard", etc.[7] Acting more responsibly or sustainably in business does not necessarily mean distraction from selling products to customers to make profits required for future investments, and so on. Side effects are of course inevitable in almost every business (at a very small scale, the butcher and the baker must park and dispose of their waste, among other things). Responsible business goes beyond self-interest and is about taking care and managing externalities and a wide range of outside stakeholders in their broadest meaning.[8]

---

6 This may sound old-fashioned to some but I was taught not to interrupt a conversation with someone to call or pick up the phone.

7 United Nations "*Report of the World Commission on Environment and Development*" (1987), chaired by Gro Harlem Bruntland. See also the joint OECD/UNECE/Eurostat report on "*Measuring Sustainable Development*" (2008) on www.oecd.org. For updates, visit www.globalreporting.org.

8 e.com reporting analysts have identified 20 groups of stakeholders for an average listed company (see: www.reportwatch.net/home/staking/who-are-your-stakeholders/).

Ralph Waldo Emerson wrote: "*Doing well is the result of doing good. That's what capitalism is all about.*" Winston Churchill said: "*The price of greatness is responsibility.*" This may be the view echoed by the increasing numbers of responsible business people who act accordingly, or are striving to do so.

Do as I say… Acting and reporting responsibly

As Tania Ellis writes in a thought-provoking book, CSR may be treated as an "add-on" – and therefore as a rather conservative way of dealing with externalities – or as "strategic".[9] In this latter option, where "*CSR activities complement – or maybe even become – the core of business, more value is added to both society and the company: externalities are internalized*" and the benefits for the company may range from a better image to differentiation from competitors, from attraction and retention of new employees to the development of new products. Socially and environmentally responsible companies broaden their bottom line.

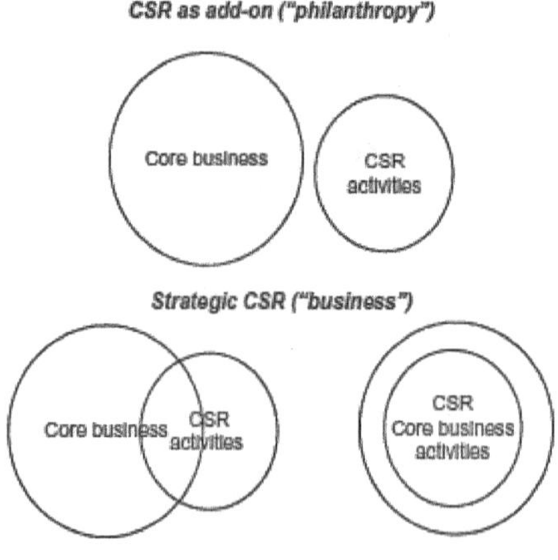

Source: Tania Ellis: "The New Pioneers"

9 "*The New Pioneers – Sustainable business success through social innovation and social entrepreneurship*" (Wiley, 2010): the book abounds with examples and ideas.

Many trees have been cut (and are hopefully being replaced) to write useful books on the subject matter and a number of links keep on bringing important contributions towards best practice.[10] Tania Ellis's book gives very good insights into these. In 2012, 6,000 companies were disclosing sustainability, environmental, social and governance data, compared with about 700-800 in 2005 and about 300 in 1996.[11] Let us point out a few notable cases and examples, based on efforts, results, achievements, as reported by various large companies from different countries and industries:

- In its 1998 "*Shell Report*", the UK-Netherlands-headquartered oil group, which used to be regarded as a pioneer in responsibility reporting practices (and not only because it once put its rivals to shame on those issues) was asking the question: "*Profits and Principles – does there have to be a choice?*"
- Danish health care group Novo Nordisk has offered trendsetting reporting for some years now, for its integrated economic stakeholder model, non-financial targets made as key as financial ones, and its specific accounting policies for sustainability measures. A number of companies have followed suit on these very precise aspects (see e.g. the Finnish retailer Kesko), but not yet as many as expected.
- In the same industry, Novartis reports annually as much on its responsibility as on its business.

10 www.csrwire.com/books updates regularly books published about CSR. On reporting aspects, read "*Reporting Nonfinancials*", by Kaevan Gazdar (Wiley, 2007). Go to www.sustainability.com, www.corporateregister.com, www.ethicalcorp.com et al. to find reports or updates on best practices. What about so-called sustainability indexes? Well, a bit like for rating agencies, these should be used with all due caution (what's the real meaning of Dow Jones Sustainability Index, for example? And who is the owner of Dow Jones?).

11 Figures from Patrick Eastwood, managing partner at Further (London) (Financial Times, October 4, 2010); and Curtis Ravenel, sustainability director at Bloomberg (Financial Times FTfm supplement, March 12, 2012).

- Among numerous quantitative measures and qualitative indicators, the Spanish retail group Inditex (which owns the famous brand Zara) reports extensively on suppliers' control.
- In a recent annual report, Accor (France) showed how to "*understand and manage water, energy and waste in an Accor hotel.*"
- Holmen, the Swedish pulp and paper group, made out a strong case in its rich responsibility report for increasing company's forests by 25 percent over the next thirty years. From the Scandinavian woods, other players are also delivering strongly on CSR.
- Although operating in the "dirty" fertilizer industry, one-third of the Canadian PotashCorp strategic goals are socially and environmentally driven.
- Apart from being involved in the U.N. World Food Program, TNT – the Dutch mail services group (since then acquired by UPS) – compared its carbon footprint measures for all transportation means. Also in the Netherlands, Philips, DSM, and AkzoNobel have made serious progress in integrating sustainability in their business.
- The U.S. coffee chain Starbucks has been disclosing progress made on purchasing practices for a number of years.
- A number of Japanese companies are leading the way on responsibility initiatives and measures. Kyocera, Ricoh, Sharp, Epson (who mapped how it changed routes to reduce emissions during product transportation), NHK Spring (which links its responsibility to the product lifecycle) stand on the list.

Amid the late-2000s financial crisis, former Nokia chairman Jorma Ollila commented: "*The crisis will lead to a rethink in the corporate world. It is not just about profitability, but it is also about values.*"[12] That said, a few years on, it is a bit surprising not to see more companies appointing a CRO (chief responsibility officer) or CSO (chief sustainability officer), which would demonstrate a high-level commitment to these issues. Worse, if a growing number of big corporations take the matter seriously, careless acts, lip service, shifty reports, misrepresentations, greenwashing, and big lies still abound.

Those examples, like many others, show that what is good for the neighborhood, the community, the society, stakeholders can be good for business too.

Up to no good – Corporate irresponsibility

"*What's good for the country is good for General Motors, and vice versa,*" said Charles E. Wilson, CEO of General Motors after the end of World War II.[13] Sixty years later, AIG's former (and ousted) Chairman Maurice "Hank" Greenberg wrote in a similar vein in the Financial Times: "*It is in America's interest to save AIG*" – not less! – to call for a huge rescue plan to be paid by the taxpayer to escape insolvency.[14] The tone was somewhere between "*Don't cry for me AIG*" and "*Don't let me down*". Mr. Greenberg's tears paid off straight off: the U.S. government agreed to provide an $85 billion "emergency loan" in September, "restructured" it to $150 billion less than two months later, and came one more time to the rescue in

12 "Champion of Nordic capitalism" (Financial Times, March 23, 2009).

13 According to some sources, Mr. Wilson was slightly misquoted and just said: "*What's good for General Motors is good for the country*". Does this make it better or worse? We leave it up to the reader, but bear in mind that he later became U.S. Secretary of Defense...

14 Financial Times, September 16, 2008. Three years later, in another moment of brashness, Mr. Greenberg announced he was suing the government of AIG "takeover" in 2008! (www.reuters.com, November 21, 2011).

March 2009 with an extra $30 billion loan (on the same day that another $62 billion quarterly loss was announced)![15] The story could go as "Rich Hank, Poor Joe" or a kind of remake of "Rich Man, Poor Man."[16] "T*hat's how we got here – a near-total breakdown of responsibility at every link in our financial system*," wrote Thomas L. Friedman.[17]

A few weeks after the first AIG (and by this time other) bailouts, the then GM chairman was almost echoing the same "good for you, good for us" story from one of his predecessors, seeking government support to avoid bankruptcy, with a tone that even bordered on blackmailing. What to make of the $20 billion bailout of Bank of America in 2008-2009 (and keep in mind the additional $118 billion worth of "*guarantees against bad assets*" too)? Presented as "*emergency funding*", it was supposed to (sic) "*absorb the losses incurred when it bought Merrill Lynch*."[18] Absorbing? Merrill's marauders seemed to have moved from bucking trends to passing the buck! Quoting a book written by George Akerlof in the early nineties (light years ago by market measures), David Leonhardt wrote that investors and bankers acted "*as if future losses were somebody else's problem*."[19] In a similar vein yet much less seriously (no, really?) in January 2009 the U.S. adult entertainment industry (a politically correct word for the porn business) requested a $5

15 "*AIG gets $150 billion government bailout; posts huge loss*", on www.reuters.com (November 10, 2008), "*U.S. Is Said to Offer $30 Billion More to Help A.I.G.*" (New York Times, March 2, 2009). At the end of 2011, AIG was topping the list of U.S. bailed-out companies owing money to the government, with $50 billion still due (Washington Post, January 26, 2012).

16 A novel and a television series written by Irwin Shaw (Delacorte Press, 1970).

17 New York Times (November 26, 2008).

18 Financial Times, New York Times, Reuters (January 16, 17, 2009). A former M&A banker on Wall Street asked: "*How could the Bank of America chief not have known that Countrywide and Merrill Lynch were virtual bankrupt?*" (Financial Times, January 20, 2009).

19 "*Bailouts invite looters*", by David Leonhardt in the The New York Times (March 11, 2009). The book he was referring to is "*Looting*", by George Akerlof (out of print, unfortunately).

billion in federal bailout money, adding that it was not suffering from the crisis (sic), "*but why take chances?*"[20] Learning the hard way? We are not aware that the industry leaders came up with vital statistics (for another form of stress test?), and if such a bailout ever took place.

A high degree of selfishness and irresponsibility is actually one of the main features of the latest crises. In November 2008, the founder of Davos economic forum figured out the cost of the global financial crisis at about $5,000 billion, adding that this astronomical figure should be (quote) "*replaced*" by... the governments! Was this about running like clockwork (made in Switzerland, natürlich) or a Swiss chorus for "*Take the money and run?*" Anyway, it was about paying mountainous amounts for selfishness and corporate irresponsibility. One crisis later, and a few forums on, responsibility remains on top of the World Economic Forum's agenda. Business as usual...[21]

Today's bankers seem to act like truck drivers carrying a load of paper and rolling in the fast lane. They have not checked the value of all notes and bills before hitting the road (we mean that many of them do not know significant parts of what is in their balance sheet), then they lose some en route. When they have to put the brake on, accidents are waiting to happen. Paul Krugman sums it up: "*Wall Street's culture of excess seems to have been barely dented by the crisis. "Say I'm a banker and I created $30 million. I should get a part of that," one banker told The New York Times. And if you're a banker and you destroyed $30 billion? Uncle Sam to the rescue!*"[22] This comment about a crisis made in America applies perfectly

20 From http://edition.cnn.com/2009/US/01/07.

21 Late in 2008, and probably to look whiter than white, Professor Schwab decided to cancel invitations to the January 2009 event to famous bankers and sponsors at the last minute. Oh, three years later, the World Economic Forum 2012 was kind enough to invite Lord Turner, head of the UK Financial Services Authority, who lashed out at bankers' bonuses (interview with Sky News, January 27, 2012).

22 "*Bailouts for Bunglers*", by Paul Krugman in The New York Times (February 1, 2009).

to the Eurozone meltdown which, contrary to what is often presented by conservative politicians and reported in mainstream media, is not only a debt crisis due to governments' profligacy (and there is some, in Greece and elsewhere), but also another example of bankers' careless irresponsibility. After all, governments can borrow because they find lenders (and a German or other bank is never far, in Greece or elsewhere). Just before Christmas 2011, 523 banks borrowed a total of €489 billion – equivalent to 5 percent of Eurozone GDP, quite an amount, that is – from the European Central Bank. Though the ECB's chief Mario Draghi said a few weeks later in Davos (here we are again) that the action had "*avoided a major, major credit crunch*," the news went almost unnoticed. A second round took place two months later, with 800 banks (of which 460 were from Germany, including the largest, Deutsche Bank) taking advantage of another €489 billion cheap-year loan program, of which two-thirds were from three countries.[23] If that is not a bailout, it is at least QE (for "Quantitative Easing", another of these lovely euphemisms invented since 2008). Eurozone states' rescue measures are mainly about rescuing the financial sector, which, once again, has moved far away from the prudent man rule idea that prudence dictates.

Another Keynes, Stiglitz, or someone else, would be needed to compare the hundreds of billions (upper case) of dollars, euros and other currencies thrown around in the multiple and successive bailout packages with the hundreds of millions (lower case) still spent by companies on social responsibility issues. We have not read about that, but we are almost sure

23 A very good analysis by Ralph Atkins in the Financial Times: "*A deft way to buy time*" (February 8, 2012). See also: "*Bank's cheap loans support bond rally for Italy and Spain*"; "Eurozone's smaller lenders follow the road to Frankfurt"; "*Deutsche Bank tapped ECB for up to €10bn*" (Financial Times, February 29, March 1, March 9, 2012).

that CSR would be a big loser to the various forms of TAR.[24] Some will object that doing nothing to rescue (mainly) financial institutions - both in the American mortgage crisis and in the Eurozone meltdown - would have cost more in money and in jobs, and therefore have been... irresponsible. They have a point. Still, the price is high. Probably too high. Financially, economically, socially, and, not least, morally.[25] Because it rewards selfishness and will not put a brake on widespread self-serving behaviors. To quote London School of Economics Professor Willem Buiter, we have moved "*from financialisation of the economy to the socialisation of finance.*"[26] Now a chief economist at Citigroup, Buiter also stated that if the public underwrites the costs of bailouts, logically, "*banks should be in public ownership.*" To paraphrase Keynes in another context, the repeated bailouts, rescue plans, capital injections, or whatever you call it, represent the most spectacular cost of the economic consequences of irresponsibility[27].

---

24 TAR stands for troubled assets relief, named after the "Troubled Assets Relief Program" (TARP) set up by the U.S. government and approved by Congress in the fall of 2008.

25 At the peak of the 2007-2010 financial crisis, IMF estimates of the cost of banks' bailouts as a percentage of GDP were varying from about 4 percent in Germany to 6.3 percent in the U.S. to almost 20 percent in Britain.

26 Willem Buiter: "*The end of American capitalism as we knew it*", in the Financial Times (September 17, 2008). Let us remember, among many figures, that potential losses of the U.S. banking sector were estimated early in 2009 at 12 percent (twelve percent!) of GDP. For the potential impact of the Eurozone crisis, watch the Eurozone bank stress test set up by Thomson Reuters at http://graphics.thomsonreuters.com.

27 "*The economic consequences of the peace*" was John Maynard Keynes's first real book, published after World War I (1919. Republished recently by Book Jungle).

SIN NO. 5:
TOO GREEDY

"It is preoccupation with possessions, more than anything else, that prevents us from living freely and nobly."
HENRY DAVID THOREAU

"To convert the business man into the profiteer is to strike a blow at capitalism, because it destroys the psychological equilibrium which permits the perpetuation of unequal rewards."
JOHN MAYNARD KEYNES

Mr. Greed goes to Wall Street[1]

"*Greed is good*," said Gordon Gekko (played by Michael Douglas) in Oliver Stone's movie "*Wall Street.*" The film's main characters were a stockbroker and a corporate raider, inspired by the likes of Icahn or Boesky – little room for blue-collar workers here. Released in 1987, it was supposed to describe the financial excesses of the 1980s. Aptly titled "*Money Never Sleeps*," a sequel was released in 2010 to provide an update to those who thought the (financial) world had (not) changed. The plot and the characters were a bit different, but the "fundamentals" had remained, with the same degree of immorality and just more "toxic debt" and "troubled assets". What is it about? Just another gold rush story. Golden boys (and girls) carrying a gold card getting onto the gravy train, turning into golden geese in good days, and then being given the golden handshake in hard (no, really?) times. "*Rivers of gold flow there from all over the earth, and death comes with it. There, as nowhere else, you feel a total absence of the spirit,*" wrote the Spanish poet Federico Garcia Lorca about Wall Street.

Milton Friedman often said: "*Is there some society that doesn't run on greed?*" Let us admit we could agree on that, but where is the limit? What is the point for, say, Bill or Melinda in making 100, 200, 300 times more money than, say, Joe (remember the plumber?) or Sarah (forget the campaigner!)? Who and what can justify that Lehman Brothers CEO Richard Fuld earned over $500 million over the fifteen years that preceded his bank's collapse?[2] Why were Tyco's rich CEO and CFO

1 For some reason this chapter contains a higher number of musical and movie references. "Mr. Greed" by John Fogerty (from "*Centerfield*", Warner Bros, 1984); "*Main Street*" by Bob Seger (from "Night Moves" album, Capitol, 1976); "*Money For Nothing*" by Dire Straits (from "*Brothers In Arms*", Vertigo, 1985); "*The Wall Street Shuffle*" by 10cc (from "*Sheet Music*", UK Records, 1974). Others appear in the text.

2 Read e.g. "*How Much Did Lehman CEO Dick Fuld Really Make?*" (BusinessWeek, April 29, 2010).

accused of the theft of $150 million (including unauthorized bonuses and $1 million for a birthday party) from the company in 2002? How is former ExxonMobil chairman Lee Raymond spending (?) his time with his gigantic $398 million retirement package? How much mercy should we have for former GE chief Jack Welch's wife when she complained that the monthly $35,000 compensation proposed by her husband for divorcing was nowhere near enough to maintain her "*extraordinary*" living standard? Why was an estimated ten percent of the first U.S. stimulus package after the financial crisis dedicated to the compensation of loss-making executives? What to think about RBS's chief saying that a £7.7 million compensation package is "*low for the industry*"? Peanuts indeed, compared to the $190 billion that U.S. financial institutions paid as bonuses in 2010, only two years after the subprime crisis. Is there any justification for Apple's new CEO to receive a pay package that could be worth $378 million over ten years? Lastly, just for fun, should we talk about Paris and other Hollywood Hiltonities who, yet having sometimes starred in "*Simple Life*" stories (no joke), often show more money than taste?[3]

Down on Main Street

Many will admit that the above excesses have just joined a (growing) list of big exceptions to the rule, and we should not draw conclusions about the whole system. In other words, there would be "normal" and "abnormal" greed. That is, is an acceptable degree of greed probably (for Smithians and Keynesians) or absolutely (for Friedmanites and Hayekians) necessary to make the system work – and fuel it?

---

3 "*Top 10 Crooked CEOs*" (www.time.com, June 9, 2009). "*Exxon pension: How much is too much?*" asked the New York Times (April 16, 2006). "*Welch Walks Away From Perks*" (Forbes, September 16, 2002). "*RBS chief says £7.7m pay package is 'low' for industry*" (Daily Telegraph, March 17, 2011). "*Too Much Cash in the Corner Office*" (www.businessweek.com, February 15, 2012). For those who missed it, Paris Hilton starred in "*Simple Life*", a Fox TV reality series.

Greed is deeply rooted in capitalism. In her passionate and rather terrifying book "*The Shock Doctrine*", Naomi Klein points to "*a nagging and important question about free-market ideologues. Are they "true believers"..., or do the ideas and theories frequently serve as an elaborate rationale on unfettered greed while still invoking an altruistic motive?*"[4] Greed takes different forms, from benign to malign. The fact that benign forms of greed have spread across the economy and the whole of society leads many to envy the most successful (a large media segment continues to thrive on the rich and (in)famous, after all), and therefore to accept malign forms of greed. Furthermore, the lines between selfishness and rapacity are not always clearest and often blurred.

Let us attempt a few possible explanations to the causes that make greed a deadly sin:

- The capitalist system is based on and nurtured by various types of economic, social and other inequalities. These result in differences in possession, which in turn nurture and create new forms of inequality.
- No matter that Mark Twain wrote: "*Any so-called material thing that you want is merely a symbol: you want it not for itself but because it will content your spirit for the moment,*" consumption capitalism is largely driven by a craving to have and own more – more than you had before and more than the neighbors have now. Keeping up with the Joneses is about envy but then rapidly translates into greed. "*Mr. Greed, why you got to own everything that you see,*" sang John Fogerty.
- The conservative ideology, especially in its Anglo-American version, progressively (?) endorsed by other segments of the Left (and not only in the "Third Way"),

4 Naomi Klein: "*The Shock Doctrine. The Rise of Disaster Capitalism.*" (Penguin Books, 2008).

promotes an ownership society. This applies especially to home ownership, as well as to other related assets, stationary (a second residence) or mobile (one car or more). Even after (is it really over?) the terrible subprime mortgage nightmare, 38 percent of one survey's respondents in Britain regard increased mortgage availability as the best measure for the health of the UK housing market, while 75 percent of respondents in the U.S. still believe "*owning a home is essential to the American Dream.*"[5] Incidentally, we have here a perfect example of deception, as you really become the owner when the last installment is settled, and not any time before.

- Banks, insurance companies, and other credit "innovations" from the shadow-banking sector have thrived on the insatiable appetite for goods, which is in most cases – except for the wealthy who can afford paying in cash – now linked to an addiction to credit. It started with branches set up on main street, then with building a "*credit card nation.*"[6] This trend has particularly affected North America and the British Isles, but other economies followed.[7]
- "*Unfettered finance*" is characterized, among other features, by lavish compensation packages mostly, if not

5 Cited in "*The House Issue*" in Modus RICS magazine (September 2011).

6 Words used by Rochester professor and financial expert Robert D. Manning: "*Credit Card Nation. The Consequences of America's Addiction to Credit*" (Basic Books, 2001). Read also: "A Piece of the Action. How the Middle Class Joined the Money Class", by New York Times columnist Joe Nocera (Touchstone, 1995); and "*The Two-Income Trap*", by Elizabeth Warren and Amelia Warren Tyagi (Basic Books, 2004). It looks like those books were not dipped into before the 2007-2009 dip...

7 Another worrying sign: "*Citigroup to issue China credit cards*" (Financial Times, February 7, 2012).

solely, fueled by... greed (stock options are the perfect illustration of this).[8]

- To make things worse, some of the so-called sophisticated financial products and techniques are in fact heavily based on rapacity, in trading rooms and elsewhere, directly or indirectly.

Making money with money

"*In this world there are two ways to get rich. N°1: Produce something valuable and sell it to others. N°2: Find people pursuing the first strategy, and steal from them,*" wrote Harvard professor N. Gregory Mankiw.[9] Making money with products and services and deriving profit from that is the raison d' être of capitalism. Today's capitalism looks more like a world of users (a vast majority), producers, financiers, and stealers (a small yet very influential minority). Robert W. Sarnoff, the former chairman of RCA, said in the 1970s that "*Finance is the art of passing money from hand to hand until it finally disappears.*" A premonitory definition of today's financially driven capitalism:

- Finance is increasingly – and in some cases totally – disconnected from production and has grown into pure speculation. Daily trading on foreign exchange markets has grown from around $15 billion in the 1970s to $15 trillion these last years... Short-term money markets are 40 to 60 times more important than goods and service trading.
- The lines are blurred between good and bad finance. Bill Watterson, author of the comic strip "Calvin & Hobbes", said: "*To make a business decision, you don't need much*

8 Martin Wolf: "*The new capitalism. How unfettered finance is fast reshaping the global economy*" (Financial Times, June 19, 2007).

9 Fortune, June 12, 2000. Note that Mankiw's views hardly make him belong to the progressive camp.

> *philosophy; all you need is greed, and maybe a little knowledge of how the game works.*"

The size of the financial sector has exploded across the economies and its role as (de)regulator is unprecedented. The ratio of global financial assets to annual world output (GDP) had soared from 109 percent in 1980 to 316 percent in 2005, making the global stock jump from about $10 billion to $140,000 billion over the same period. Stock markets – on which €50,000 billion were traded in 2010, which happened to materialize and reflect the real economy – now lag far behind other purely financial markets, such as derivatives including the (in)famous CDS (€545,000 billion in 2011), or hedge funds (estimated value today: €1,500 billion).[10]

Making money with money is the favorite occupation for an increasing number of market players – sometimes self-appointed or dubbed as "market makers." Some economic analysts and authors even regard greed not as an excess but as a fundamental flaw (name it a sin) on which the whole system is now based.[11] A commercial lender himself, Mark Sunshine asked if speculators were not armed by banks to hurt companies and people.[12] Gillian Tett described in thrilling words the "*Genesis of the debt disaster,*" which originated with honorable bankers and insurers in respectable institutions who started

---

10 In another of his insightful articles published in the Financial Times: "*The new capitalism. How unfettered finance is fast reshaping the global economy*" (June 19, 2007) Martin Wolf also referred to a study from McKinsey Global Institute. He came back on the same issue in a FT column (April 2, 2008), where he points to the six-fold increase in the share of financial sector profits in U.S. GDP between the low of 1982 and the high of 2007. Other sources include: World Federation of Exchanges, IMF, Bank for International Settlements.

11 If even a conservative banker like Evelyn de Rothschild wrote that "*Ethical standards must be restored in finance*" (Financial Times, May 9, 2008) there must be trouble somewhere.

12 Michael Sunshine, COO at First Capital, in the Financial Times ("*Insight*" column, November 28, 2008).

playing with CDOs and "BISTRO" deals (no relation between these and the main street ones), et al.[13]

A growing sophistication of financial, credit and insurance services generate interstices for abuse and embezzlement, sometimes packaged as "complex products" which turn into "toxic assets" when the bad days come. In 2008, the New York Times asked the question about Countrywide, U.S.'s largest mortgage lender: "*Will Wall Street backlash lead to bankers on trial?*"[14] Wrong bet, the answer was very kind to those. Surprised? "*Always be nice to bankers,*" advised Lord Hanson. A recent book describes the fund management industry as "*legal theft at the expense of investors and beneficiaries.*"[15] Two specialists in risk management stated that a robbery best describes the latest financial crisis, marked by "*overcompensated bankers who got fat bonuses hiding risks, overpaid quantitative risk managers selling potently bogus methods.*"[16] In the worst-case scenarios, it is just money from and for nothing. Stock options are a good (we mean bad) example of this: many top executives and employees are being rewarded on the basis of share price, no matter what income statement results are (sometimes they are big losses) and what shareholders receive as dividends. Stock options are economically useless, and they are just short-term fueled greed derivatives, period.

---

13 "*Genesis of the debt disaster*", published in the Financial Times (May 1, 2009) makes a gripping -and worrying- read. It is an edited extract from "*Fool's Gold*", a very good book written by Gillian Tett (Little, Brown, 2009). BISTRO stands for Broad Index Synthetic (or Secured) Trust Offering.

14 New York Times, December 11, 2008.

15 "*Corpocracy. How CEOs and the Business Roundtable Hijacked the World's Greatest Wealth Machine – and How to Get It Back*", by Robert A.G. Monks (Wiley, 2007).

16 N. N. Taleb and P. Triana: "*Bystanders to this financial crime were many*" (Financial Times, December 8, 2008).

Pyramids and charades: another Wall Street shuffle

On top of Main Street's greed, which is primarily material, we now have Wall Street's (shorthand for the long arm of financial markets) rapacity, which is financial. Many investor portfolios are structured in the form of a financial pyramid. The base of the pyramid is (supposedly) made up of nonvolatile, liquid assets. The next level includes securities that provide both income and long-term capital growth. At the third level, a smaller portion of the portfolio is allocated to more volatile investments with higher potential returns and greater risk. And at the top level, the smallest percentage of the overall portfolio is invested in ventures that have the highest potential return but also pose the greatest investment risk. This is supposed to generate a high potential of significant returns if some of the speculative investments succeed without risking more than investors can afford to lose.[17] The whole financial system is now built on such pyramid-looking schemes, or is itself a pyramid. Many of these pyramids are risk-based, volatility-driven and... heavily greed-fueled – the motivation is to get and own more money, for the deals... and the dealmakers. Those pyramids can turn into houses of cards, especially yet not only when they are built on fraudulent practices (like in Ponzi schemes where returns to investors are promised out of the money paid by subsequent investors rather than from actual profits).

With all... undue respect, a significant number of economic players can be regarded as part of the irresponsible greed of these last years and decades, at individual and corporate level. And the game, at times referred to as "liar's poker" or

17 Explanations based on the "*Dictionary of Financial Terms*" (Lightbulb Press, 2008).

"monkey business" is not over.[18] Have a look at the following list: Charles Ponzi (one of the first famous wheeler-dealers in history); Barings Bank (gone bankrupt because of one single trader's losses); Ivan Boesky; Salomon Brothers (acquired by Travelers, which was acquired by Citicorp, which finally resold it); AIG (see above); Michael Milken; Enron (Enronitis was as much about greed as about short-termism); Parmalat; Tyco; Bear Stearns; RBS; Fortis; Lehman Brothers (with special mention for the former boss and his wife); Merrill Lynch (please do not stop the blame at Henry Blodget);[19] UBS and Credit Suisse (accused of "naked greed" by a judge in Montana in 2009); Fannie Mae and Freddie Mac; Jérôme Kerviel (and Société Générale);[20] Allen Stanford; and more, of course. The list, which is certainly not exhaustive, would be incomplete without the inevitable Goldman Sachs. About the latter, Rolling Stone magazine called the firm: "*a great vampire squid wrapped around the face of humanity, relentlessly jamming its blood funnel into anything that smells like money.*"[21]

All the names in the above list relate to cases of cupidity. Are there exceptions, rules, or exceptions that prove the rule? We are just asking (well, not only). After all, what was the official business of a once respectable firm called Bernard L. Madoff Investment Securities LLC? Besides the fact that the words

---

18 Words from the Financial Times associate editor John Gapper: "*This greed was beyond irresponsible.*" (September 17, 2008); "*Liar's Poker*" (Coronet Books, 1999), written by a former Salomon Brothers bond broker in... 1989; "*Monkey Business. Swinging Through the Wall Street Jungle*", by John Rolfe and Peter Troob (Business Plus, 2001), swings less than Chuck Berry's song though (Chuck Berry not being the least greedy man we have heard of. But that is another story).

19 696 Merrill Lynch employees (traders et al.) received a $1million bonus or more in 2008, i.e. when the investment bank lost money all year long and was then rescued by Bank of America, who (not so) surprisingly still uses the name in its corporate brand... (Herald Tribune, February 12, 2009).

20 A good summary of Kerviel's "game" can be found in "Le roman vrai de la crise financière" by Olivier Pastré and Jean-Marc Sylvestre (Perrin, 2008).

21 "*The Great American Bubble Machine*" by Matt Taibbi, in Rolling Stone (April 5, 2010).

"security" and "limited liability" sound strange in retrospect, the "*talented*" Mr. Madoff could also count on the Austrian Bank Medici (that has Bank Austria as main shareholder), once presented as Madoff's "gatekeeper", and on the Spanish Banco Santander, who used the "impeccable" adjective for Madoff's "*market timing*."[22] Lest some have forgotten, Madoff used to be a Nasdaq non-executive chairman. The size of the Madoff fraud and resulting loss for investors was first estimated in the $57-65 billion range and was then reduced to smaller amounts (still up to $20 billion, though).. For obvious reasons, the real amount will probably never be known. The core business of all those institutions and individuals has shifted from serving the economy to making money, and from making money to... playing with it. "*Money doesn't talk, it swears*," wrote Bob Dylan.[23]

Bankers: the good, the bad and the ugly

It may appear shocking to see in the above list respectable financial institutions mixed up with fraudsters and crooks. Sorry, but the distinction between individual and corporate responsibility is far from clear in many cases. Are there not still a few (hopefully more than that) good and trustworthy bankers in the global marketplace and around the corner? Are those stories not just about rotten apples? Some state that separating

22 The fallout of Enron's collapse in 2001 was a $4,000 billion loss of market value, making it the worst bust since 1929. BusinessWeek singled out bankrupt Lehman Brothers' former CEO Richard Fuld among "*The Worst Managers of 2008*" with the following comment: "*He drove his people hard and ignored warning signs, rewarding risk and greed.*" Bernard Madoff was called "*De illusionist van Wall Street*" by Belgian daily De Morgen (December 20, 2008) next to his track record of institutions and foundations cheated by ex-Nasdaq chairman. See also the Herald Tribune (January 7, 2009), the Financial Times (January 22, 2009), "*The Talented Mr. Madoff*", in the New York Times (January 24, 2009), "*Defending Bernie Madoff*" (Herald Tribune, March 12, 2009); and the book "*The Wizard of Lies: Bernie Madoff and the Death of Trust*" by Diana B. Henriques (Henry Holt, 2011).

23 In "*It's Alright, Ma (I'm Only Bleeding)*" (from "*Bringing It All Back Home*", Columbia, 1965).

the sheep from the goats would make the financial sector return to normal. Perhaps, but who are the sheep and where are the goats? Is that what we have seen after the worst financial crisis in fifty years or more? Certainly not.[24] Many financiers seem to be familiar with the old saying: possession is nine-tenths of the law (the tenth may be a bailout, when necessary.) Still, from corporate and investment banking to real estate and mortgage, from insurance to credit assessment, from fund management and trading to rating agencies; many financial sector business practices, if not the system as a whole, have now come into question.[25] In January 2012, a former Bank of America Merrill Lynch broker was fined £350,000 for tipping off a hedge fund investor to a rights issue. Six weeks later, the head of credit trading at Credit Suisse was fined £210,000 by the UK FSA for disclosure about a forthcoming bond. He reportedly said to his contact, a UK fund manager: "*We could play this game. You're going to be my charades partner.*"[26] Gaming – or gambling – is what the financial business is all about. The optimists (would like to) think that greed and fraud happen on the margins. The pessimists consider them as fuel for large parts of it, or even as the heart of the system. A former Goldman Sachs executive director publicly resigned from the bank in March 2012, saying that: "*The firm has veered so far from the place I joined… that I can no longer in good conscience say that I identify with what its stands for… the interests of the client continue to be sidelined in the way the firm… thinks about making money.*"[27]

---

24 The embarrassment of Barack Obama and David Cameron regarding the return of bankers' bonuses means something.

25 For a hard example, check e.g. Ireland, where about 30 percent of growth in the last half-decade came from real estate and the building industry. For a funny tale, read: "*How is the Ku Klux Klan Like a Group of Real-Estate Agents?*" in "*Freakonomics*", by Steven D. Levitt and Stephen J. Dubner (Penguin Books, 2006).

26 "*Credit Suisse trader fined for wall-crossing charades*" (Financial Times, March 14, 2012).

27 "*Why I Am Leaving Goldman Sachs*" by Greg Smith, op-ed contributor to the New York Times (March 14, 2012).

The boundaries between "good" and "bad" banking are increasingly blurred. Even Alan Greenspan had his lucid moments about this: "*There's been too much gaming of the system... There's been a corrupting of... capitalism.*"[28] J.K. Galbraith once said: "*The man who is admired for the ingenuity of his larceny is almost always rediscovering some earlier form of fraud. The basic forms are all known, have all been practiced. The manners of capitalism improve. The morals may not.*" Was Madoff not considered a good guy in his heyday? The difference between good practice and malpractice is sometimes not most obvious. The "Good Guys" and the "Bad Guys"[29] sit and work next to each other, and are sometimes substituted for each other. Good guys sometimes turn bad at market speed. "*And rich guys working on Wall Street get greedy and cross lines they shouldn't cross,*" writes Joe Nocera. Are the bad guys the exceptions (the rotten apples), or isn't it that the rules have been bent and the rule book has changed? "*Where large sums of money are concerned, it is advisable to trust nobody.*" These words from Agatha Christie perfectly fit the situation.

"*The terrible, cold, cruel part is Wall Street... And the terrible thing is that the crowd that fills the street believes that the world will always be the same and that it is their duty to keep that huge machine running, day and night, forever.*" Garcia Lorca's words, written in 1929, still sound terribly true. These are hard times for honest men.[30] Before using (one of) your credit card(s) or cashing in your bonuses, reflect on the following thoughts. Aristotle wrote: "*All virtue is summed up in dealing justly.*" The Christian Bible considers greed as a form of

28 Reported by Ron Suskind in the New York Times (September 25, 2008), who refers to his account in his book: "*The Price of Loyalty: George W. Bush, the White House, and the Education of Paul O'Neill*" (Simon & Schuster, 2004).

29 "*Good Guys and Bad Guys*" is the title of a book written by Joe Nocera (Portfolio, 2008).

30 Words inspired from a John Mellencamp's song on "*The Lonesome Jubilee*" (Mercury, 1987).

idolatry. In the European Middle Ages, usurious interest rates were condemned by some church leaders. Buddhism regards cupidity as improperly connecting material wealth with happiness. Gandhi said: "*Earth provides enough to satisfy every man's need, but not every man's greed.*"

SIN NO. 6: TOO WILD

"Economic progress, in capitalist society, means turmoil."
JOSEPH A.SCHUMPETER

"A bald wig for Jack the Ripper who sits at the head of the chamber of commerce."
BOB DYLAN, "Tombstone Blues"

From the Wild West to the Far East

If the word "wild" itself can have more than one meaning, "wild capitalism" often refers to the earlier forms of capitalism, and for some its "natural state", growing through dog-eat-dog competition, without control and as few regulations as possible.[1] It has a positive content for its partisans and a negative one for its opponents. Having flourished from Manchester (among other places) to the Wild West, wild capitalism has move northward (where it has been tempered with social democracy), southward and to the Far East. Although some of the system's original brutalities, deviations, abuses, flaws, have been regulated or adjusted here and there, the system has a tendency to return to its natural (or wild?) inclinations. As a net result, the bad sides spoil or outweigh the good ones: opportunities vs. inequalities; jobs vs. unemployment; poverty alleviation vs. injustice (and new forms of poverty); booms vs. busts; creation vs. destruction; trade vs. shocks and wars.

It would be impossible to address all those issues in this chapter. We focus on three of them: inequalities; bursts, busts and shock (with a special focus the euro); and wars.

1 The Oxford Advanced Learner's Dictionary lists 8 possible meanings for "wild". Being linked to the neutral definition of "Economy" when you type "wild capitalism" on Wikipedia looks a bit strange.

Inequalities on the rise

Figure 1. Income inequality increased in most, but not all OECD countries
Gini coefficients of income inequality, mid-1980s and late 2000s

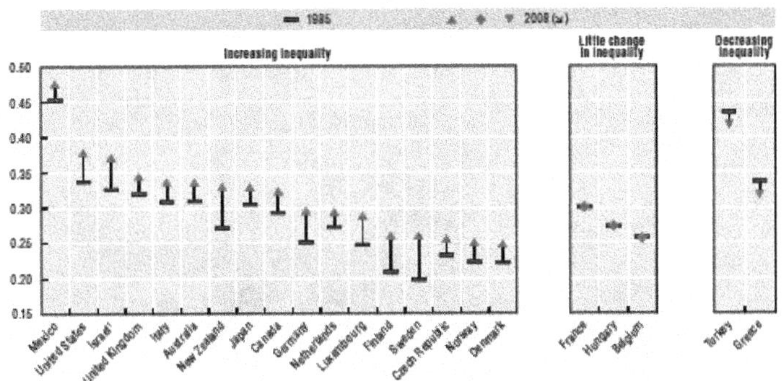

Source: OECD Database on Household Income Distribution and Poverty[2]

In a detailed review of inequality, the OECD reports that in its 34 member countries, the average income of the richest 10 percent is about nine times that of the poorest (see chart above). "*However, the ratio varies widely from one country to another,*" adds the report, which rates countries such as the U.S. (no surprise), but also Mexico, Chile, the UK, and Israel as increasingly unequal in the distribution of income.[3] Although not as big, disparities have tended to increase even in countries with more egalitarian cultures such as France, Germany, Austria, or The Netherlands.[4] Levels of income inequality in "emerging economies" (a word less and less appropriate to call newly developed nations) remain "*significantly higher*" than in developed ones, and, bar a few exceptions (e.g. Argentina, Brazil, or, to a lesser extent, Indonesia), have kept on increasing over the last decades. China, India, Russia, or South Africa

2 OECD: "*An Overview of Growing Income Inequalities in OECD Countries: Main Findings*" (December 2011).

3 "*Divided We Stand. Why Inequality Keeps Rising*" (OECD, Paris, December 2011) makes highly recommended reading.

4 See e.g. "*Why did earnings inequality increase in the Netherlands in the past two decades?*", by Paul de Beer (paper for the workshop on "*Inequality measurement*", University of Utrecht, January 2006).

have become less equal than they were (see chart below). Although sources of inequality remain different in emerging economies, new forms of inequality have appeared, and they are attributable to the adoption of capitalist systems, sometimes in their wildest style.[5]

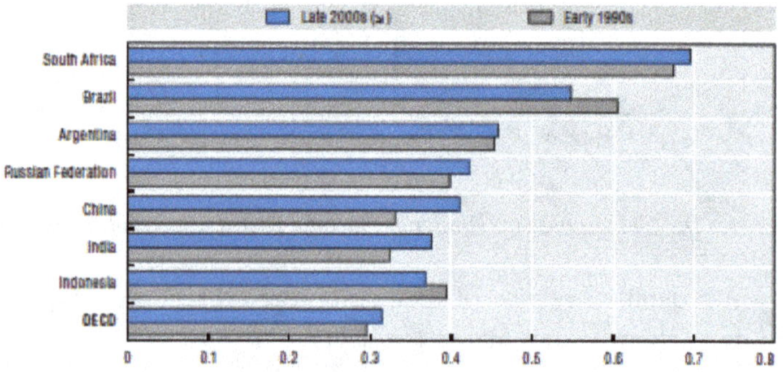

Source: OECD-EU Database on Emerging Economies, World Bank[6]

We have to live with that: inequality is inherent in a free-market society. The capitalist system is based on and nurtured by various types of economic, social and other inequalities. Consider them a useful growth ingredient, a necessary evil, a cost, inequalities do and will always exist.[7] Disparities in the way income, assets (mind also the liabilities!), purchasing power et al. are distributed represent a price to pay for making

5 The OECD report cites a large informal sector, widespread divides (e.g. between rural and urban areas), gaps in access to education, barriers to employment (e.g. for women) as major traditional sources of inequality in emerging countries.

6 OECD: "*Special Focus: Inequality in Emerging Economies*" (OECD, December 2011).

7 The late Alfred Sauvy, a French anthropologist and demographer, often said: "*C'est le riche qui crée l'emploi*" (*"Rich people create the jobs"*).

the system work,[8] and the price can be high. The U.S. has the most unequal income and wage distributions among all high-income economies. Income inequality in the U.S. is as big in the early 21st century as it was in the "Gilded Age", i.e. the end of the 19th century, when the country was still an "emerging" nation. After a period of stability in the 10 percent bracket between 1950 and 1980, the annual income share of the top 1 percent in the U.S. peaked at the same level (24 to 35 percent, depending on the sources) in 2007 as in... 1928. Note that this share went up again after the mortgage crisis. Reliable sources in the U.S. show that the income gap between chief executive pay and the average worker salary has grown from 24 times in 1965 to 300 times in 2010.[9] Equality is going backward, making comparisons with emerging economies both appropriate and terrible: today, one out of every two Americans lives in poverty or with the lowest income, while, at the same time, billionaires derive most of their income from capital gains. In Britain, the top 1 percent of earners have doubled their share of national income over the last 25 years. FTSE 100 chief executives were earning 133 times more than the average wage at the peak of the latest financial crisis, against 20 times in the early 80s.[10] Paul Krugman once compared J.D. Rockefeller making 7,000 times the average per capita income in 1894 with James Simon, a hedge fund manager, who took home $1.7 billion, i.e. 38,000 times (!) an average worker's pay a hundred years later. These are extreme figures, of course (maybe in sight for

8 The ratio of total household debt to aggregate personal income in the U.S. has risen from a 0.6 average in the 1980s to a 1.0 and higher average in the 2000s (source: http://repec.org. RePec stands for Research Papers in Economics, a collaborative effort of volunteers in 64 countries).

9 Source: Economic Policy Institute. The multiple may vary due to various components taken into account.

10 The Guardian journalist Oliver James incisively pointed out that "*under Brown's chancellorship the richest 0.3% nobbled over half of liquid assets*", increasing their share by 79 percent during the last five years (January 3, 2008). (Figures for the UK were also excerpted from that article.) See also: "*Social mobility. It's still not fair*", in The Economist (January 17, 2009).

future China and India billionaires, heaven forbid!), but they reflect a broader - and harder - reality. There is "*Too Much Cash in the Corner Office*," wrote BusinessWeek early in 2012.[11] Despite that, Mitt Romney's campaign team named Barack Obama's plan for a minimum tax on millionaires a "*war on capital*."[12] Knowing that 22,000 U.S. millionaire households are paying less than 15 percent in taxes (i.e. a slightly higher rate than an executive assistant), it is probably worth waging a war! The management guru Peter Drucker, hardly the founder of "Occupy Wall Street", was appalled at those ballooning figures. He had already openly criticized these trends in the eighties, naming them "*morally and socially unforgivable*".[13]

That was well before the use and abuse of other forms of compensation systems, such as bonuses and stock options. Though the principle of bonuses is not questionable in a market economy - rewarding executives, managers, and employees for their performance makes much sense - the extravagant amounts paid have turned completely unhealthy - and insane. Is it normal to exercise stock options rights when share price is up while profits are down -or even worse, when there are losses?[14] No. Is it logical to offer a golden parachute to executives who are rewarded for having done a wrong job and/or posted a company loss? No. Is it fair to make shareholders pay for executive failure fees, and pension plans, while taxpayers have to shoulder most of the burden of unemployment and retirement benefits, if any? No. Former General Electric CEO Jack Welch was less embarrassed (all meanings) when he

11 "*Too Much Cash in the Corner Office*" on www.businessweek.com (February 15, 2012).

12 "*Romney fights back on Buffett rule*" (Financial Times, April 13, 2012).

13 Peter F. Drucker: "*The Temptation to Do Good*" (HarperCollins, 1984).

14 In less than two weeks in February 2012 RBS announced that, yet reluctantly, the chief executive would forgo his bonus, the annual losses had widened, and that bonus cuts would be "*offset by big salary increases*" (Financial Times, Guardian). Call it bank transfers.

stated that overcompensation allegations were "*outrageous*" (quote) and that executive remuneration (including retirement plans, no doubt) should be dictated only by free markets.[15] More fundamentally, where are the "risks" associated with "free" markets if executives cash in a bonus when the company makes a loss? Is it just not no-risk capitalism?[16] Now retired, Mr. Welch has all the time to meditate on Keynes's words: "*The business man is only tolerable so long as his gains can be held to bear some relation to what, roughly and in some sense, his activities have contributed to society.*"[17]

Income inequality translates into an inequality of outcome, which has "a strong bearing on equality of opportunity" – a value on which political and economic liberalism normally fuse together.[18] Children brought up in deprivation face many more difficulties to get a decent start in life and find a job than the others. The net results go from unemployment to social exclusion and poverty. While many people in fast-growing "emerging" economies have been moving up the social ladder these last decades; the opposite trend is at work in developed countries. In the former case, more wealth is being created, at least in the short term, and is slowly trickling down from the rich to the poorer. In the latter, the supposed trickle-down effect, either as a natural consequence of increased wealth or through more artificial tax breaks (Reaganomics-style policies), is not working, or has reached its limits.[19] Raghuram

15 Welch's words on "*Hardball with Chris Matthews*" (transcript on www.msnbc.msn.com (July 13, 2006).

16 As Naomi Klein wrote in The Guardian (October 31, 2008).

17 Cited by Roger E. Backhouse and Bradley W. Bateman in "*Capitalist Revolutionary: John Maynard Keynes*" (Harvard University Press, 2011).

18 As Martin Wolf put it in "*Seven ways to fix the system's flaws*" (Financial Times, January 23, 2012).

19 See e.g. J.K. Galbraith's remarks in "*Recession Economics*" (New York Review of Books, 1982), or Robert Reich: "*Trickle-Up Economics*" (2004) on www.robertreich.org.

Rajan, a former IMF chief economist, has partly attributed the credit explosion in Anglo-Saxon economies to real wage stagnation, which encourages people to borrow. There can be surprising side effects. Robert Frank points for instance to some middle-class families' consumer behavior:

- With or without tax breaks, some people spend so much money on buying larger houses or a bigger cars (and other household assets) that it is to the detriment of education or other expenses.[20] A vicious circle is then triggered;
- Less income results in less purchasing and investing power (this is worsened by debt, too);
- This leads in even less resources for education (e.g. with children in lower-level schools);
- As a consequence, it diminishes job qualification and its improvement;
- This results in substitution of technology for labor force at a microeconomic level and deindustrialization at macroeconomic level;
- That generates more unemployment;
- It increases the income gap and inequalities.

That downward spiral is not only a trademark of Anglo-Saxon countries. It has spread to other places, not least emerging markets. And the losers are: the poor, the working class, as well as the increasingly impoverished middle class. Once epitomizing the success of capitalism, and not just on

20 Read, among others, "*Falling Behind: How Rising Inequality Harms the Middle Class*", by Cornell Professor Robert H. Frank (University of California Press, 2007) (you may also visit Economic Scene on www.robert-h-frank.com); or "*The Race between Education and Technology*", by Harvard Professors Claudia Goldin and Larry Katz, (Belknap Press, 2008).

TV, the middle class – or at least some of it – is now moving down the social ladder.[21]

When it comes to inequality, and contrary to what its exponents still state, globalization is not always a win-win game. Rising working and middle classes here are "paid" by dwindling ones there. Walking down the back alleys of, say, Bandung or Brazil's favelas will show you the privations of old poverty. But driving down some streets of, say, Brussels or Madrid will make you see the hardships of new poverty.[22] Equality is definitely not capitalism's business. As Robert Reich puts it: "*Capitalism's role is to enlarge the economic pie. How the slices are divided... is up to the society to decide.*"[23]

Bursts, busts, and shocks

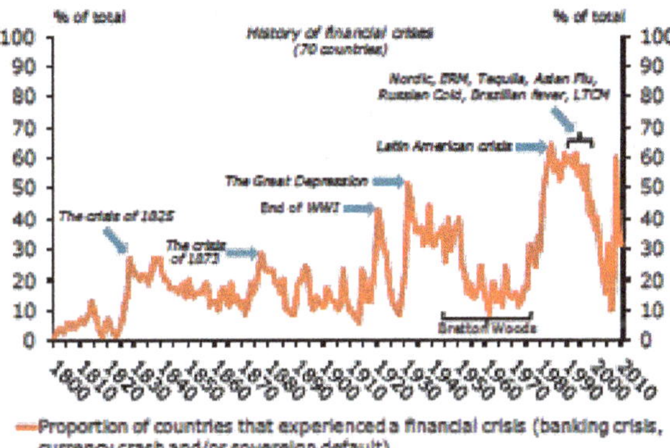

Source: Rabobank Economic Research Department (2011)

21 Read the above-mentioned "*Divided We Stand. Why Inequality Keeps Rising*" (OECD, Paris, December 2011). The impoverishment of the western middle classes is naturally explicable by the growing purchasing (and saving) power of the eastern-based ones (Southeast Asia, China, India, and, to a lesser extent, Eastern Europe). However, other causes may be found "inside" the system as well (see: greed, selfishness, buying and saving behavior, etc.)

22 To be fair, poverty in developed countries is not entirely capitalism's fault. Poor urban planning, misused taxation policies, uncontrolled immigration flows, political errors are much (and sometimes much more) to blame.

23 Robert Reich, a former U.S. Secretary of Labor under Bill Clinton: "*Supercapitalism: The Transformation of Business, Democracy, and Everyday Life*" (Vintage, 2008).

Crises are nothing new. Shahin Kamadolin, an economist at Rabobank, points out: "*Not a single year has gone in the past two centuries where there was not a financial crisis somewhere in the world.*"[24] "*The beginning of wisdom is to recognise that booms and busts have been a feature of capitalism from the start,*" says Financial Times columnist Samuel Brittan.[25] I could not agree more. Today's mainly financial capitalism is as much about burst bubbles as about bust booms. Those are defined either as short economic cycles (and related stock booms), or as artificial surges in equity or asset prices (increasingly and irrationally disconnected from fundamentals). The increased role of financial markets, short-term-driven investment strategies, speculation, and interconnected economies tend to inflate bubbles (or booms) more quickly than in the past. Is the whole economy itself not a kind of bubble after all, with securities, bonds and bank assets now representing between 400 and 500 percent of global GDP? Bubbles always end up bursting. The 1997 Asian financial crisis was caused by excessive capital inflows mainly used as "hot money" to finance (mainly) property bubbles in Thailand, Malaysia and other countries, then followed by a quick and massive outflow that resulted in a market crash. The famous 1995-2000 dot-com bubble cost a lot of money to investors but also hundreds of company bankruptcies and thousands of jobs in the IT sector and beyond. Some authors view the 2000s subprime crisis as a succession of bubbles, another "Minsky moment", which is

24 "*Asset bubbles, financial crises and the role of human behaviour*" by Shahin Kamalodin, Rabobank Economic Research Department (January 2011). This excellent overview is based among others on thorough research conducted by Carmen M. Reinhart and Kenneth S. Rogoff. Read e.g. "*This Time is Different: A Panoramic View of Eight Centuries of Financial Crises*" (NBER Working Paper 13882, March 2008).

25 Samuel Brittan: "*The financial crises of capitalism*" (May 9, 2008).

probably the right analysis.[26] The 2010s Eurozone crisis bears a striking resemblance to some of the above, not least because of the property bubbles in Spain and Ireland. Lastly, bear in mind the increasing role of algorithmic and high-frequency trading, which can cause flash crashes in a few seconds. As Paul Wilmott puts it: "*Financial markets are being made even more dangerous by the unthinking power of machines.*"[27] It is no risky bet to say that (at least) one other bubble is growing somewhere.

If booming cycles may go higher or be longer than in the past, busts seem to repeat more often. The contractions or recessions that follow are bigger, hit harder (hence the need for safety nets, which brings us back to the inequality issues – see above), and spread at a larger scale (due to globalization).[28] This seems especially true when a financial crisis causes and then amplifies the downturn, as IMF's World Economic Outlook showed on the subprime-based crisis. Commenting on this IMF report, Tony Jackson added: "*[recessions] tend to be worse again if the crisis is in banking, rather than in securities markets... And the countries hardest hit are those with... arm's length financial systems.*"[29]

In April 2008, the IMF predicted that the credit crisis – the biggest since the 1930s – could cost nearly $1 trillion. In June

26 Hyman Minsky was a Chicago-born economist who created a model for credit-driven asset bubbles. See e.g. "*Minsky's moment*" in The Economist (April 2, 2009). Read also the very good analysis of Peter C.B. Phillips and Jun Yu (Singapore Management University): "*Dating the Timeline of Financial Bubbles During the Subprime Crisis*" (September 13, 2010). Paper available at http://papers.ssrn.com.

27 Quoted in the New York Times (July 30, 2009). An expert in quantitative finance, Paul Wilmott is one of the authors of the Financial Modelers' Manifesto.

28 According to the U.S. NBER (National Bureau of Economic Research), cycles are as numerous but longer and more asymmetrical than in the past. Go to www.nber.org/cycles/recessions.html. Other theories say the opposite.

29 Outlook available on www.imf.org/external/pubs/ft/weo. "*IMF thesis gives no reason to think the worst is over*", by Tony Jackson, in the Financial Times (November 3, 2008). Read also the penetrating "*The Five Phases of a Bubble*", by John Bellamy Foster, in "*The Financialization of Capital and the Crisis*" on www.monthlyreview.org, April 2008).

2008: "*12 months after a Wall Street era of superlatives... nearly half of the profits that major banks reaped during that age of riches have vanished... Worldwide, the reckoning totals $380 billion.*" In November 2008: "Financial groups' losses approach $1,000 billion." In August 2009, the IMF put the total cost of crisis at $11 trillion. In May 2010, the U.S. Treasury Department estimated that household net wealth fell by approximately $17 trillion in the last three years. And those astronomical figures are just the money cost. What's to be said about the cost to main street? More U.S. workers, i.e. 2.6 million, lost their jobs in 2008 than in any year since World War II. Unemployment in the UK hit 3 million in 2009. Japan faced its worst recession since the post-war days. More than 53 million people worldwide fell below the extreme poverty level in 2009.[30] Numbers indicate the misery... Five years later, nobody would dare say that the effects of that crisis have been wiped out. "*Curious, isn't it, that depression is the word for both economic collapse and nervous breakdown.*"[31]

Bertrand Russell wrote: "*Advocates of capitalism are very apt to appeal to the sacred principles of liberty, which are embodied in one maxim: the fortunate must not be restrained in the exercise of tyranny over the unfortunate.*"[32] A little help from friends in politics or the military is sometimes needed to adopt or impose "shock policies" that the "unfortunate" would not accept or even have refused democratically.[33] In her well-documented book, described by John Le Carré as "*wonderfully*

30 Herald Tribune, April 8, June 16, 2008; Financial Times, October 31, November 13, 2008, January 31, 2009; The Guardian, January 15, 2009; The Economist (March 14, 2009); Daily Telegraph (August 8, 2009); et al.

31 James P. Carroll: "*Surviving the dark winter solstice*" (The Boston Globe, December 8, 2008).

32 Bertrand Russell: "*Roads to Freedom*" (Spokesman Books, new edition, 2006).

33 The word "shock policies" was used by Milton Friedman himself to describe the Chilean "experience" after Augusto Pinochet's military coup. J.K. Galbraith once said about it and other Chicago Boys' policies: "*Milton Friedman's misfortune is that his policies have been tried*".

controversial and scary as hell", Naomi Klein reported extensively about those "*shock therapies*" whose most (in)famous examples have included Chile, Bolivia, Argentina, Uruguay; but also Yeltsin's Russia, and post-communist Poland, to name but a few. Whether in the hard Chicago Boys' version or in the more polished (no pun intended) Harvard style, those policies and their impact display capitalism in its wildest form.[34] Developed Western economies have had their share of shock-based capitalism, presented then as "without alternative" ("TINA" was the slogan): those were the Reagan and Thatcher policies. In all those cases, and somewhat ironically (Hayek was Thatcher's favorite reading), Hayek's definition of "*the road to serfdom*" might have a very different meaning from the one expressed by the Austrian-born economist: for those who suffer from shock policies it would mean serfdom to capitalist deregulation, more than the much despised socialist alternatives.[35]

The euro: a very hard currency

A cautionary statement is needed here. The euro was not an invention of capitalism, which should thus not be blamed in the first instance for another of its sins. That said, in an unlikely coalition with political bureaucrats and financial technocrats, capitalist forces have taken over the European currency. The

34 South America's shock therapies were most inspired by the Chicago school, while Eastern Europe extensive privatization and deregulation policies were carried out under the influence of Harvard economists such as Jeffrey Sachs. Naomi Klein's "*The Shock Doctrine*" (Penguin Books, 2007) certainly stands out as one of the most researched books on economic shock therapies. Disqualifying Naomi Klein as a "Marxist" (why should this be an insult, after all?), as Cato Institute's Johan Norberg (author of "*In Defense of Global Capitalism*", Cato Institute, 2003) does in "*The Klein Doctrine: The Rise of Disaster Polemics*" (May 2008, on www.cato.org) makes up a very mean counter-attack.

35 Friedrich August Hayek: "*The Road to Serfdom*" (Routledge, 2001 edition). Note that, like other observers, including in the "Third Way", I do not consider all the aspects of Reagan and Thatcher policies as evil. Some parts of the economic system needed to be reformed at that time, but not that way.

Eurozone crisis that started in 2010 is therefore a hybrid result of the fallacies of European bureaucracy and the sins of financial capitalism.

Much ink has been spilled over the euro and Eurozone troubles. To cut it short, and after the EMS, ECU and EMU phases – which, as many in Brussels seem to have forgotten did not prove very successful – the push for a single currency mostly (yet not only) came from French politicians and technocrats. These were both inspired by a desire for further economic union and by a fear of German reunification. Introduced in 1999 in a non-material form, it was launched as a real currency in 2002. That was about building up a monetary union through a currency but without the other components of a real union (i.e. budget, fiscal and economic policies). "*A money too far,*" as Paul Krugman wrote in the New York Times. Eighteen months later, he added: "*the European elite, in its arrogance, locked the continent into a monetary system that recreated the rigidities of the gold standard, and – like the gold standard in the 1930s – has turned into a deadly trap.*"[36] Transmitted until now via member states – mainly the Franco-German couple – Eurocracy's hubris is now working on its own. Between the two rounds of the 2012 French presidential campaign, the Euro Group's president lectured the socialist tender and said it would be "*a dream*" to deeply modify the treaty proposed a few months before.[37] Such interferences were hardly imaginable ten or twenty years ago. The French economists André Orléan and Michel Aglietta once co-wrote a book titled "*La*

36 "*A Money Too Far*" (New York Times, May 6, 2010); "*The Hole in Europe's Bucket*" (New York Times, October 23, 2011). For the sake of clarity, I used to view the euro as a rather good idea, provided it would go with a deeper union. I have now changed my mind, and no longer believe in a "union" as national and regional realities in Europe will remain different – and that's a good thing – probably forever.

37 Not long after having won the election, the newly elected socialist president backed down from his campaign promises and asked the Parliament to vote for the treaty.

Violence de la monnaie".[38] Though this could be correctly translated as "*Violence of Money*," the Eurozone version of the book title would certainly go today as "*The violence of a currency*" or a shock therapy "à l'Européenne" (the European way).

If Greece – but we might as well take the other "PIIGS", i.e. Ireland, Portugal, Spain and Italy as other examples – is not a case study for a shock capitalist therapy in disguise, what is it then? Admittedly, Greek politics and economics stand as bad examples of profligacy and number-fudging; "Rhenish capitalism"[39] is not comparable to monetarist economics; the government has been democratically elected (um, not sure); the political objectives are different (but what are they, really?); etc. Still... Early in 2012, Greece's GDP was down by 13 percent compared to 2008. By comparison, Britain's GDP never fell more than 10 percent during the Great Depression in the 1930s. More than a half of the decrease may be attributed to the Eurozone crisis. In 2013, it will be back to the GDP level before the country joined the euro, meaning that all supposed growth benefits of the adoption of the currency have been written off in a decade. Adjusting the current-account deficit by spending less would require an additional 25 percent fall in GDP. Adjusting by raising exports would mean a 50 percent increase of these. With a manufacturing export sector making up 7 percent of economic output and without devaluation (made impossible within the euro), the task is herculean. The EU's cutback dogmatism is far from enabling even a small part of this hypothetical recovery track. In Great Recession style, the average worker's pay decreased by 25 percent in the year 2011. 100,000 small businesses have gone bust these last two years,

38 "*La Violence de la monnaie*" (PUF, 1984). By the same authors, read also "*La Monnaie souveraine*" (Odile Jacob, 1998). Orléan and Aglietta stand out as two brilliant representatives of the French school of economic regulation.

39 A term coined by the French economist Michel Albert in "*Capitalisme contre capitalisme*" (Le Seuil, 1991). Some authors talk about a coming war between different capitalist models: see e.g. "*La guerre des capitalismes aura lieu*", edited by Jean-Hervé Lorenzi and the French Cercle des économistes (Perrin, 2008).

while the youth unemployment rate jumped from 25 percent to almost 50 percent. As a condition to the second bailout package, international creditors and the "Troika" (a name reminiscent of Soviet style) demanded a 22 percent cut in the minimum wage. In many areas, living conditions have become unbearable. "*And the 'rescue' money often goes to bond investors rather than widows and orphans,*" wrote BBC News economics editor Stephanie Flanders less than three weeks before knowing about another longer-term refinancing operation (LTRO) provided by the ECB to 800 European banks for an amount four times bigger than the second Greek bailout. To add insult to injury "*the eurozone wants to impose its choice of government on Greece – the eurozone's first colony,*" added FT commentator Wolfgang Münchau. The Greek colonels are long gone, but the results and realities are in the generals' policy style.[40] This raises one of the big questions of our times: will the EU elites achieve through peace but at all cost the united Europe that Charlemagne, Charles V, Napoléon, and Hitler before them were not able to achieve by war? That would come at a high social price, and could even backfire. "*The risk is that contempt for our discredited economic model will fuse in various parts of the world with contempt for our political model, democracy,*" wrote Anatol Lieven in the midst of the mortgage-based crisis. These words fit even more Europe's crisis "management" and its possible populist and nationalist backlash.[41]

---

40 Figures from the Financial Times, Reuters. Read: "*Europe failed to learn from emerging defaults*" by John Dizard (FTfm supplement, July 4, 2011); "*Ireland can show Greece a way out of the crisis*" by Ricardo Hausmann, a Harvard professor (Financial Times, February 9, 2012); "*Greece will have to default if it wants democracy*" by Wolfgang Münchau (Financial Times, February 20, 2012); "*Greece: Who is being 'bailed out'?*" by Stephanie Flanders (on www.bbc.co.uk/news, February 10, 2012); and another scathing article by Peter Osborne in the Daily Telegraph ("*The callous cruelty of the EU is destroying Greece, a once-proud country*", February 15, 2012).

41 "*Europe has to guard democracy amid crisis*" (Financial Times, December 11, 2008).

War, what is it good for?[42]

In his sagacious paper on the "Economic Causes of War," Ludwig von Mises wrote words that some of his ideological disciples should read again before selling us – and waging – the next wars: "*Viewed as an economic means for the attainment of certain economic benefits, the policy of aggression and conquest is self-defeating. Even if technically successful in the short run, it would never attain in the long run the ends at which aggressors are aiming.*"[43] That was written in October 1944 when World War II was far from over. An underlying von Mises assumption was that free markets and capitalism could deliver better than wars, but could also help in avoiding wars or preventing them. "*The individual citizens do not derive any profit from the conquest of a territory,*" contended von Mises. "*Commerce with all nations, alliance with none, should be our motto,*" said Thomas Jefferson.[44] Like Montesquieu, who wrote "*Où il y a du commerce, il y a des moeurs douces,*" our first inclination would be to believe that free markets and trade are a part of civilization and therefore (should) play as "*weapons of peace.*"[45] After all, hasn't post-war democratic Germany achieved economic dominance over Europe through peaceful means and succeeded where the Nazi regime – which was, lest we forget, as much about state-protected capitalism as national socialism – had failed by means of aggression? Is Volkswagen,

---

42 Words inspired from "*War, huh, yeah. What is it good for? Absolutely nothing,*" a song written by Strong and Whitfield, and sung by Edwin Starr (Gordy, 1970).

43 Available on the website of the conservative-libertarian von Mises Institute: http://mises.org/story/. Ludwig von Mises also wrote an essay about "*The Anti-Capitalistic Mentality*" (Van Nostrand, 1956). For "self-defeating" estimates in modern times wars: "*The Three Trillion Dollar War*", by Joseph Stiglitz (W.W. Norton, 2008).

44 U.S. (neo)conservatives, the Christian Right, and other Tea Party goers seem to have forgotten the words from one of the nation's Founding Fathers.

45 To use the words of Samuel Pisar referring to trade with the Communist bloc as a better weapon than using the military during the Cold War.

among other Konzern, not a long-term winner of World War II? Yet at a very high cost (remember Vietnam, "Star Wars", etc.), and to the benefit of some, was the "Cold War" not preferable to engaging the enemies in real battles?

Capitalism does not need wars to prosper, but it may occasionally live with war. More than once in recent history, "free" markets have also thrived on war. This is not to say that capitalism is the source of all wars. Nationalism, ethnocentrism, religion, kings (and queens), generals (or colonels) have done more than their share. But this does not make it an open-and-shut case. Jonathan Nitzan and Shimshon Bichler make out a strong case in analyzing the relationship between "*Capitalism and War*" in what they define as the weapon-petrodollar coalition, e.g. when they link oil-industry profit performance to conflicts. In this case, like in other situations, "*war serves to boost the economy.*" For those who might think we are conceding too many points to the Left (not exactly von Mises's angle, though), may we refer to John T. Flynn, described by Justin Raimundo as a "*master polemicist of the Old Right*", who wrote that America had "*surrendered to militarism as an economic device*"[46].

Referred to by President Eisenhower (a former general...) in his farewell address as the military-industrial complex (or MIC), by Bob Dylan as "*Masters of War*", as the "*weapondollar-petrodollar coalition,*" or as a "*New American Militarism,*" the growing connections (or collusion) between the economy and the military in the U.S. more than anywhere else have been

46 Jonathan Nitzan, a Canadian professor, and Shimshon Bichler, an Israeli professor in a well-grounded and very convincing paper "*Capitalism and War*" (November 2006), published on www.globalresearch.ca. Justin Raimundo: "*Inauguration Day, 2009: A day of Mourning*" (January 19, 2009), among his many incisive analyses on www.antiwar.com.

a worrying development ever since.[47] In his 2012 presidential campaign, Mitt Romney declared: "*I will insist on a military so powerful no one would ever think of challenging it.*"[48] Besides the fact that it overlooks the Vietnam and Afghanistan "challenges" and the failure in Iraq, among others, such a statement could be written by a 20th century dictator rather than by a modern democratic leader, and still reflects how many U.S. politicians are hijacked by MIC's interests. An overview of major MIC-driven economies in the last hundred years would of course show Germany's second (or Deutsches) and Third Reich, Japan Empire, the USSR, i.e. not exactly models of free-market democracies. One of today's major strategic questions is to know if China and India are moving towards these models. Perhaps the U.S.A. and Israel should be added to the list. Strange bedfellows? To be sure, the two latter countries are also market systems and democracies that produce many more valuable goods than just barrels and cannons. Point taken, but case sustained nevertheless. With over $600 billion a year, the U.S. keeps on spending almost half of worldwide defense budgets – and the figures do not include other permanent appropriations or "entitlements" which would, according to some sources, make the "real" or "total" defense-related expenses reach about 20 percent of national budgets.[49] Some calculations for Israel reach the same percentage brackets (note that Saudi Arabia is

---

47 Dwight D. Eisenhower, who, lest some have forgotten, was a true wartime commander-in-chief and not a bogus peacetime one. "*Masters of War*", by Bob Dylan (on "*The Freewheelin' Bob Dylan*", which also included "*Talkin' World War III Blues*", Columbia, 1963). "Coalition" term used by Jonathan Nitzan and Shimshon Bichler (see the reference below). "*The New American Militarism*" is a provocative book written by Andrew J. Bacevich, professor at Boston University, West Point graduate and a Vietnam veteran (Oxford University Press, 2005).

48 Speech made in Florida, cited by Edward Luce in "*The reality of American decline*" (Financial Times, February 6, 2012).

49 Figures from Budget of the United States Government Fiscal Year 2010 and "*World Wide Military Expenditures*" (on www.globalsecurity.org). See also "*What Do the Pentagon's Numbers Really Mean?*", by Winstow Wheeler, on www.cdi.org (February 4, 2008).

still spending more on defense as a percentage of GDP than the U.S., with a little help from the MIC, of course). More than twenty years after the end of the Cold War, the U.S. military budget is still higher than the next twenty largest spenders combined. Those figures would be significantly higher than Russia and China's current defense budgets... Even in decline, the U.S. remain the most capitalistic, imperialistic and militaristic power ever seen in history. Before, and based on similar capitalist ingredients, the British Empire achieved a lot, yet not in the same style. The Roman Empire and Spanish colonization were impressive in scale and dominance, but did not typify the capitalist model that would rise centuries later. The U.S.'s MIC seems to work as "*an informal and changing coalition of groups with vested... interests in the continuous development of high levels of weaponry, in preservation of colonial markets and in military-strategic conceptions of internal affairs.*"[50] The Chinese menace and the "Iranian threat" (to whom?) are the latest MIC tricks.[51]

A number of examples come to mind to illustrate the power of the MIC; Lockheed Martin is a case in point. The company, whose motto once was "*We never forget who we're working for*" (a registered trademark, naturally), received $25 billion per year of taxpayer money in 2005 alone (compare this for example. with $35 billion total company revenues during the Iraq war years). During 2004-2008, gross profit and operating profit increased by 56 percent and 118 percent, respectively. A congressman noted that the amount of public contracts was exceeding the GDP of 103 countries including poor Costa

50 Carroll W. Pursell: "*The Military-Industrial Complex*" (Harper & Row, 1972).

51 Don't get me wrong. Iran's Islamic republic is not my favorite political model. Likewise, I certainly do not underestimate radical Islamism as a threat to democracy, liberties, and secular States (what's left of the "Arab Spring"? Not secularism, for sure). But mixing this up with interferences in country politics and the right to build nuclear power facilities (what about Pakistan?) is a bit of an amalgam. As to China, the threat looks as exaggerated as Russia was in the good old days of James Bond.

Rica or (still) rich Iceland, and that it was also larger than the combined budgets of three U.S. ministries (plus the legislative branch of government). According to William Hartung, even Eisenhower would have not imagined a company wielding so much power in the MIC. As Naomi Klein writes, it does not only make the company qualify as an "emerging market" (a very mature one in this case) but "*the scale of the revenues at stake is certainly enough to fuel an economic boom.*"[52] Diverting resources to a military purpose can also lead to bad consequences for the other businesses. Consider Raytheon, often regarded as the inventor of the microwave oven, which has succeeded in producing missiles and security systems for military use far more than it did in making and selling ovens to private customers. In 14 years, it sold 10,000 ovens, while it took four or five orders to Toshiba to sell the same quantity and then become a market leader.[53] Some studies have also showed that doing military business seriously hampers productivity. When the war is over (or, in other words, the "mission accomplished") comes the reconstruction, sometimes for the better - e.g. a mutually beneficial Marshall Plan - sometimes for the worse, e.g. Iraq's rebuilding (estimated as three times more expensive than the one after the Asian tsunami) and legal (?) plundering.[54]

Two sides of the same coin? Capitalism can be as much about destructive creation as about creative destruction.[55]

---

52 About Lockheed Martin, read "*Prophets of War: Lockheed Martin and the Making of the Military-Industrial Complex*" by William D. Hartung (Nation Books, 2010). Naomi Klein reported at length on Lockheed Martin in "*The Shock Doctrine. The Rise of Disaster Capitalism*" (Penguin Books, 2008). Other data come from company annual reports and from BusinessWeek.

53 The Raytheon example is cited by Robert Heller in "*The Decision-Makers*", Hodder & Stoughton, 1989).

54 Naomi Klein commented thoroughly about the privatization of war and reconstruction matters, in Iraq and elsewhere. See also: "*In Rebuilding Iraq's Oil Industry, U.S. Subcontractors Hold Sway*" (New York Times, June 16, 2011).

55 The economic definition of creative destruction comes from Joseph A. Schumpeter in "*Capitalism, Socialism and Democracy*" (first published in 1942, republished by Harper, 1962, et al.).

SIN NO. 7: TOO MUCH

"To allow the market mechanism to be sole director of the fate of human beings and their natural environment, indeed, even of the amount and use of purchasing power, would result in the demolition of society."

KARL POLANYI

"Not everything can be regulated by the market: we must resist the merchandization of our entire life, both individually and collectively."

ANDRÉ COMTE-SPONVILLE

TINA and the market religion

1989 was marked by the fall of the Berlin Wall. Almost twenty-five years later, the Great Wall of China is still there yet, in the meantime, Deng Xiaoping was credited with saying "*To get rich is glorious.*"[1] In 1989, Francis Fukuyama also wrote his essay "The End of History" in which he noted: "*What we may be witnessing...is the universalization of Western liberal democracy as the final form of human government.*"[2] This statement implied that the market economy would prevail as an "*end point.*" Besides its Marx-style determinism and more than a trace of Western ethnocentrism, a number of facts have proved him wrong, but one thing is sure, market capitalism, in various forms, rules the world economy and society to an extent never seen before. With so many people now "*free to choose*" would Milton Friedman have the last laugh?[3]

From the good (?) old "laissez-faire" (tempered over the years with more democracy, distribution, public policies, etc.) defined as an economic system, capitalism has turned into an all-embracing ideology, sometimes bordering on religion, whose virtues are preached by free-market fundamentalists.

---

1 As the Los Angeles Times wrote it, there is no proof the Chinese leader actually said that, and if he said so, the full quote also says that socialism should not mean poverty ("*Great Idea but Don't Quote Him*", Los Angeles Times, September 29, 2004). By the way, don't misinterpret me, I do not wish the Great Wall of China would fall.

2 "*The End of History and the Last Man*", by Francis Fukuyama (The National Interest, 1989; expanded book in Free Press, 1992).

3 "*Free to Choose*" is the title of a book co-written by Milton and Rose D. Friedman (Harvest Books, 1990). A former finance minister of Poland once declared: "*I live in a Poland that is now free, and I consider Milton Friedman to be one of the main architects of my country's liberty.*" (cited by Naomi Klein in "The Shock Doctrine"). Really? Fortunately, Friedman did less "for" Poland than against Chile, and, at least, a free democracy came there as a prerequisite, and the Polish people took care of this job, without support or almost from abroad. That makes some Poles or Central Europeans' ecstatic pro-Americanism surprising -or doesn't (mind the Russians)?

A sort of "*common core of wisdom embraced by all serious economists*," in the words of John Williamson, who is considered the inventor of the term "Washington Consensus". "*Every regulation hurts people's freedom. The more regulation we get, the worse we do,*" said Hoover Institution economist David R. Henderson. Another "Chicago Boy" (and Nobel Prize winner), George Stigler, stated that "*When the facts contradict theory, they are wrong and theory is right*"?[4] Note that those words come from more subtle minds than the likes of Romney, Gingrich et al. Note also that this is not breaking news. In 1846, in the heyday of "Rule Britannia", the British liberal businessman Richard Cobden already declared that free trade was "*a sacred principle.*"[5]

If that is not ideology, what is it then? "*Voodoo economics*", "*La ideologia del mercado*", a panacea, "*Supercapitalism*", "*The Religion of the Market*", market hegemony, "*La pensée unique*" (French for "*The single thought*") have been among the words used by outspoken critics of the market religion in recent years. Maggie Thatcher's famous (last?) words "TINA" – for "There is no alternative"– epitomized the triumph of all-to-market policies which seemed to become the way of the

4 Read, among others, the note about Stigler in Robert J. Barro's "*Getting It Right: Markets and Choices in a Free Society*" (MIT Press, 1997).

5 Cited by John Ralston Saul in his book "*The Collapse of Globalism and the Reinvention of the World*" (Penguin Books, 2005).

world.[6] Adopted from the right to the left, from the west to the east and from north to south, liberalization, privatization, deregulation – which, behind their apparent synonymy, remain three different concepts – have been implemented, now and then with subtlety, here and there with brutality.[7] As Dani Rodrik, a Turkish professor at Harvard University, put it: "Stabilize, privatize and liberalize" became the mantra..."[8] Concluding that the results of those all-to-market policies are mixed would be a kind judgment. The worst consequence is to have brought too much capitalism – and money – in almost every aspect of everyday life.

---

6 Though naturally invented in France, the "laissez-faire" concept, and its implementation even more, has spread first through Britain after its use by John Stuart Mill and others. Curiously, "*Voodoo economics*" seems to have been used first by George H.W. Bush about his fellow Ronald Reagan's politics. Since then, stronger critics have used it otherwise, e.g. Paul Krugman in "*Wall Street Voodoo*" (New York Times, January 19, 2009). David R. Henderson's quote from "*The Free Market: A False Idol After All*" (New York Times, December 30, 2007). Robert Reich: "*Supercapitalism: The Transformation of Business, Democracy, and Everyday Life*" (Vintage, 2008). "*The Religion of the Market*", by David R. Loy, a former professor of philosophy at Bunkyo University (Japan), in the Journal of the American Academy of Religion (Summer 1997). Market fundamentalism, probably best embodied by its preacher Milton Friedman (among others in "*Capitalism and Freedom*", University of Chicago Press, 2002), has been criticized by many, including J.K. Galbraith, and, more recently Joseph E. Stiglitz ("*Globalization and Its Discontents*", W.W. Norton, April 2003), the Longview Institute (www.longviewinstitute.org), Naomi Klein, et al. "*La pensée unique*" seems to have been coined by Ignacio Ramonet in Le Monde Diplomatique, before spreading to the media as a criticism of the all-to-market conformist ideology. "Washington Consensus" was first used by John Williamson in 1989 to set up a list of economic policies based on liberalization (in "*The Political Economy of Policy Reform*", on www.petersoninstitute.org.); about this, read also "*Fads and Fashion in Economic Reform*" on www.imf.org).

7 On the brutal methods, Naomi Klein's "*The Shock Doctrine*" (Penguin Books, 2008) gives an often frightening account.

8 Dani Rodrik: "*Goodbye Washington Consensus, Hello Washington Confusion?*" (Harvard University, 2006).

Angela and the deficit dogma

Those who thought that "TINA" was out of business and the late 2000s financial crisis had knocked capitalism as we know it now off its pedestal should think twice. Apart from a predictable return to fashion in North America (was it ever out?), and traveling preachers everywhere, it came back with a vengeance in the long-lasting Eurozone crisis, courtesy of the EU elites and several governments. Although, as written earlier, the euro was not an invention of capitalism, market forces have taken over. Many of the ingredients of the previous crisis are still there – the banking sector and its practices, bonds and growing debt amounts and percentages (at public and private level), the role of rating agencies, and awkward government policies on top. Most of capitalism's deadly sins and a number of venial ones have come into play to make the situation worse, even more as governments are increasingly subservient to financial markets (which are not as anonymous as they look, lest we forget).

The EU had already followed suit on the Washington (we might as well write Wall Street) Consensus in recent decades, adopting all-to-market options in a mode varying from minor to major, depending on the countries and governments' political options. The Eurozone crisis provides an opportunity to carry on those policies. Besides simply repeating the criteria used in the Maastricht treaty (signed in December 1991…) – i.e. budget deficit below 3 percent (or 0.5 percent structural) and public debt below 60 percent of GDP – the latest (but certainly not last) EU treaty commitment purely and simply outlaws expansionary or Keynesian policies.[9] Saying, like Angela Merkel, that budget limits will be "*eternally valid*" has much to do with religion – and conservatism as usual – but very little with economics, and even less with politics, where

9 To use the words of Kirsty Hughes in "*Another summit, another bleak day for European democracy*" on www.opendemocracy.net (January 31, 2012).

nothing is eternal. Martin Wolf says: "*Putting an unmeasurable concept into the law seems mad.*"[10] Never mind. Once again, it is about bowing down to unstable financial markets that, somewhat paradoxically, prefer a stable environment and lower or zero deficits to prosper. Keynes would have rolled over in his grave if he could have seen 25 EU member states approving the so-called "fiscal compact" demanded by Germany early in March 2012.[11] A glance at past states' performance on those two criteria shows how eternity can be... temporary. As, apparently, EU members have not learned from the past, they will probably find out in time.

Though it is easy to acknowledge that a budget surplus is preferable to a deficit, deficit is not bad per se, it is the use of it that matters. Determining at what level a deficit is "good" or "bad" is about macroeconomic fine-tuning, not a dogma. Samuel Brittan (not exactly a leftist) wrote: "*For this we need not so much a political as an intellectual revolution, namely the overthrow of the balanced budget fetish.*"[12] The same line of reasoning may apply to public debt. Gross government debt for the whole EU was 80 percent of GDP in 2010, compared to 94 percent in the U.S., and way above 200 percent in Japan. Note also that Spain's public debt is lower in percentage terms than the UK or Germany's, often overlooked in the usually negative comments about the Spanish situation.

Numbers do not give the full picture. Who holds government debt matters as much as, if not more than the amount itself. As the chart below shows, Japan has a much larger debt than Greece, but most of it is in the hands of the Japanese citi-

10 Martin Wolf: "*The pain in Spain will test the euro*" (Financial Times, March 7, 2012). Martin Wolf also asks: "*Would elected governments accept the guesstimates of unaccountable technocrats?*"

11 "*Highlights: Leaders' comments from European Union summit*" on www.reuters.com (March 2, 2012). Do leaders have shorter memories than their people? It is worth remembering that among the first countries that broke the Maastricht rules were Germany and France.

12 Samuel Brittan: "*Mistaken Marxist moments*" (Financial Times, August 25, 2011).

zens. One of the reasons for the Eurozone crisis is that Greece, Ireland and Portugal's public debt is largely held by foreign bondholders.[13] Had these countries kept their currencies, they could have significantly reduced the debt burden through inflation and devaluation. Numbers do not tell the complete story. "*We should indeed avoid burdening the future with unproductive debt. Yet productive debt is not a burden, but a blessing*," rightly writes Martin Wolf.[14] Debt can be used for useful purposes, e.g. health care, education, capital expenditure, infrastructure, social services...

Government debt in selected countries as a percentage of GDP

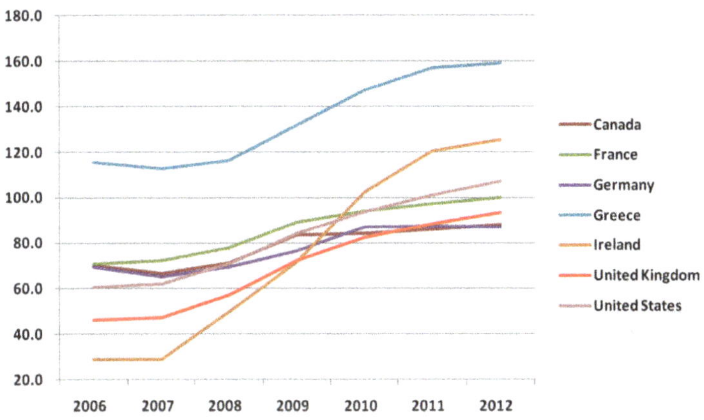

Source: OECD World Economic Outlook 2011

Never mind, the motto has become: "*Reduce deficits. Decrease debt levels.*" At all costs. ECB President Mario Draghi (a former

13 See: "*Public Debt as Percent of GDP 2006-2013*" in Global Finance (www.gfmag.com); "*Debt, deficits and the markets*" (www.economist.com/blogs, September 21, 2011); "*Europe has lower deficits than America*" (The Economist, February 20, 2012). As The Economist explained it, Japan's figures would bring down debt to "*a more manageable*" 130 percent thanks to big offsetting financial assets. That is still a large amount, but it is mostly held by the Japanese.

14 Martin Wolf: "*Assets matter just as much as cutting debt*" (Financial Times, November 26, 2010).

Goldman Sachs director) put it bluntly: "*The European social model has already gone.*"[15] Stabilization, liberalization, privatization are back on the table – were they ever really out? Some measures threaten key components of the social fabric. Had Iceland been a member of the EU it would never have been able – and authorized – to take the rescue measures that have helped to slowly rescue the country from its great financial disaster. Who has not read one those depressing stories about Greece, Ireland, Spain, or Portugal? Unemployment is rising, social security spending is reduced, health care benefits are diminished (or even privatized), public assets are sold (off) – often to the detriment of resource control and independence – the nation's youth is fleeing (and, quite significantly, mostly not to EU countries where they do not think there is a future).[16] Last but not least, democracy itself is under pressure.

When more market means less democracy

Many Europhiles – some of them sincere and respectable (the author used to stand among them...) – and not only a bunch of Eurocrats who want to save face, will be spluttering with indignation here, but, despite cosmetics and "democratic" makeup, the European project is no longer a democratic one. It is about saving the Eurozone, the euro, and at least according to some, the whole EU at all cost. As Paul Mason wrote in The Guardian, the political and economic elites of Europe "*have convinced themselves the single currency and the European Union are the same project, and that the collapse of either would be the end of the world. Therefore it cannot end. This fallacy is now about to*

15 "*Q&A: ECB President Mario Draghi*" on Wall Street Journal Blogs (http://blogs.wsj.com/eurocrisis, February 23, 2012). Read also: "*Quand les peuples européens se contentent de l'austérité*" by Laurent Pinsolle, in the French magazine Marianne (www.marianne2.fr, March 1, 2012).

16 "*Portugal's jobless graduates flee to Africa and Brazil*" (www.bbc.co.uk/news/world, September 1, 2011); "*Soaring youth unemployment stokes fear of long-term harm*" (Financial Times, July 3, 2012).

be tested."[17] Where are the noble European ideals? The means of maintaining the European Union project are increasingly undemocratic. As Gandhi said: "*And there is just the same inviolable connection between the means and the end as there is between the seed and the tree.*"[18]

Drastic measures to make the economies of the Eurozone's "bad guys" work (again) is serious enough, imposing them without democratic control is more serious, and wanting to change the ways people live in societies is very serious indeed. That is exactly what is happening in Europe right now. This is not to say that Greeks – and others – are angels and Germans – and others – are devils and vice versa, but that a Greek should not necessarily behave like a German. After all, are German (and other) tourists not going to Greece or Spain to enjoy a different way of life?[19] Naturally, we admit that public spending has to be controlled, loans must finance material things and not political whims, and the use of bailout funds has to be monitored. But it is also about living and letting live! FT commentator Wolfgang Münchau rightly said: "*We are at the point where success is no longer compatible with democracy. The German finance minister wants to prevent a "wrong" democratic choice... The eurozone wants to impose its choice of government on Greece...*"[20] As a former Citigroup executive said: "*It is imperative that a government be able to present the reform program as one of 'national'*

17 Paul Mason: "*The European dream is in danger: prepare for another rude awakening*" (The Guardian, May 24, 2011).

18 Source: Gandhian Institute Bombay Sarvodaya Mandal and the Gandhi Research Foundation (website: www.mkgandhi.org).

19 In another example of utmost hypocrisy, the Dutch populist leader Geert Wilders, who was among the ones lecturing Greeks about deficits and compliance, walked away from the right-wing governing coalition because he refused austerity measures that would affect the population. Do as I say...

20 "*Greece will have to default if it wants democracy*" by Wolfgang Münchau (Financial Times, February 20, 2012).

origin to avoid the perception that it was imposed, rather than supported, by an outside source."[21]

Far beyond the shores of Crete, the EU governments do not even take those political precautions anymore. In France, the president justified unpopular measures simply by the need to follow the "best-in-class" German model, and, in another of his countless political turns, proposed to put deficit limit as a "Golden Rule" in the country's constitution. In Belgium, a socialist prime minister and its composite government bowed down to EU "recommendations" through budget corrections announced on an almost weekly basis in the first quarter of 2012. The list of EU (un)democratic tricks is long – and getting longer: backdoor procedures for treaty signing, the Irish double-round referendum, special appointments for Italian and Greek prime ministers, and so on. Latest institutional example: to take effect, the "fiscal compact" approved (?) by the 25 EU member states early in March 2012 had to be ratified by 12 Eurozone states. Is this democracy? Somewhat ironically, the Eurocrats have staged their own version of Maggie Thatcher's "TINA" ways and means: there would not be any alternative to the euro, the Eurozone, euro-austerity, or any euro-something. The Washington Consensus had spread across the globe. At least in Europe, it has now been substituted with the Brussels diktat, mixed with submissiveness to markets, as perfectly summed up in the words of EU Council president Van Rompuy: "*We must maintain the budgetary objectives and if we don't do that in a consistent way, then the financial markets will punish us.*"[22] Yes, it is about punishment!

21 Rhodes knows what he's talking about, as he was a lead negotiator for its bank in Nicaragua's debt restructuring in 1980 (cited by John Dizard in "*Europe failed to learn from emerging defaults*" (FTfm supplement, July 4, 2011).

22 "*EU summit: All but two leaders sign fiscal treaty*" www.bbc.co.uk/news; "*Highlights: Leaders' comments from European Union summit*" on www.reuters.com (March 2, 2012). In the same sadomasochistic mood, note the words used by EC commissioner Olli Rehn about the suspension of funding to Hungary: "*This decision is to be regarded as an incentive to correct a deviation, not as a punishment.*" (Financial Times, February 23, 2012).

It is not the first time in history that market forces, their high-level representatives in the economy (especially the financial sector), and their servants in politics operate or consider themselves above national law and/or turn these to their own advantage. Under the mix of EU bureaucratic power, German domination and financial markets' short-term pressure, that is what has been going on in Europe in recent years.

Private gains and public losses

For all its failings, flaws, and... sins, the market economy still provides optimal responses and effective solutions to many problems and, although with necessary adjustments and regulations, contributes to prosperity and well-being.[23] Micro- and macro-economically, capitalism has proved to be a formidable wealth creation machine.

However, the market does not have the answer to all problems. Had policymakers – and social forces – left it to market forces the benefits of income redistribution (see other sins) and social expenditure would simply not exist, or would have been wiped out, in many places. It would be wild capitalism at its best (according to the right) or its worst (as viewed from the left). As the following chart shows, there is still room for improvement.[24]

23 All-to-market fanatics seem to have forgotten, or prefer to ignore, that some forms of regulation were acknowledged, and even sometimes advised by the founding thinkers, including Adam Smith himself.

24 To make things clear, public expenditure, social security must also be under control (some transfers from the public to the third and fourth sector sometimes make policies more efficient than central government polices). From a liberal perspective, income redistribution should of course not penalize excessively responsibility and risk-taking.

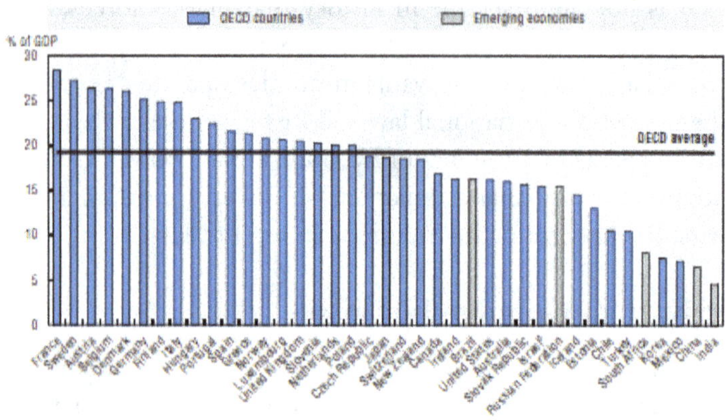

Source: OECD: "Special Focus: Inequality in Emerging Economies" (December 2011)

Over the last decades, many governments have embarked on all-to-market policies and implemented liberalization, privatization and deregulation guidelines. While some of those policies were, and still are, at least partly necessary and brought some benefits (for whom and how long is a legitimate question), many may be disputed in their implementation, and may even be questioned as such. Those policies have certainly injected a lot of private money into some sectors, but they have also instilled more monetary power (often disguised as "shareholder value"). On balance, their results are uneven, and the outcome sometimes looks more like destructive creation than "creative destruction". The zero-sum game described by Lester C. Thurow about American society in the 1970s may now be extended to larger parts of the world. Richard Murphy argues brilliantly that "*the private sector does not always work best...*"[25] Far from that. Should air, earth, water, subsoil, food, health, education, energy, electricity, waste, science, justice, art, sports... be wholly left to

25 Richard Murphy: "*The Courageous State: Rethinking Economics, Society and the Role of Government*" (Searching Finance, 2011): read e.g. "*Chapter 6 - Where only the state may venture.*"

market forces? The answer is a straight no. The costs – social, cultural, political, and even at times economic – equal or are higher than the (supposed) economic benefits. What is gained privately is not always in the public interest.[26]

Common goods or just commodities?

In November 2002, the U.N. declared access to water a human right, and stated that water was a common good, and not merely a commodity. For more than one billion people, water is a daily concern, and twice as many have no access to a safe toilet. Up to 50 percent of diseases are transmitted because of insufficient water quality or inefficient supply.[27] Even though current estimates show that only about 10 percent of water is in private (or privatized) hands worldwide, some are pushing for a larger role of the private sector and market solutions. France is an example: as opposed to a majority of countries, and as paradoxical it may sound in the country of Colbert and Général de Gaulle, 80 percent of French drinking water distribution is in the hands of a private sector oligopoly. In spite of evident privatization failures – witness some South American experiences or the Philippines, where the implementation purely and simply ran out of control – early in 2012, Madrid's local government was preparing to sell a stake in its water company Canal Isabel II. The main reason? Easing the region's spiraling debts to meet Eurozone convergence requirements.[28]

---

26 Lester C. Thurow, former dean of MIT Sloan School: "*The Zero-Sum Society – Distribution and the Possibilities for Economic Change*" (Basic Books, 1980). As a Guardian reader humorously put it about the planned privatization of motorways by the UK government: "*Coming next... air to be privatised because it will be more efficient if it's delivered by private equity firms.*" ("*David Cameron unveils plan to sell off the roads*", The Guardian, March 19, 2012). See also: "*Putting a price on the rivers and rain diminishes us all*" by George Monbiot (The Guardian, August 6, 2012).

27 Figures from the Global Water Challenge (www.globalwaterchallenge.org).

28 "*Madrid prepares water and metro sell-off*" (Financial Times, February 6, 2012). Note that Madrid's water company has several controlling interests in Latin America.

A founder of the Group of Lisbon and a noted expert on the matter, Riccardo Petrella is absolutely right when he states that access to water should be regarded as a human right. Logically, he advocates viable alternatives to the growing pressures from large companies towards "liberalization". If only a fraction of the money spent on bailing out irresponsible financial institutions could have been used for finding solutions to the water problem this could probably be solved within a few years.[29] This statement can also apply to the broader infrastructure issues. According to some sources, new public infrastructure needs worldwide will amount to $50 trillion in the next 25 years, consuming 3.5 percent of global GDP. As the OECD experts say, this goes beyond the capacity of governments and public sector financing.[30] PPPs (public-private partnerships) often constitute a more optimal answer than leaving it all to the private sector as this would rather go for more short-term-driven investments and is often only interested if there is a "leverage effect" arising from a public stake. After all, that is what happened in the early stages of capitalism: the public sector in various forms cared about infrastructure while private businesses did not want to spend money on that, yet benefited from the effects of public spending. That does not mean that private initiatives should not play a significant role and that efficient management methods should not apply, but the process should be – very – strongly regulated. And all profits should be reinvested and not (only) go into the pockets of private shareholders.

---

29 Riccardo Petrella: "*The Water Manifesto. Arguments for a World Water Contract*" (Zed Books, 2001). See also: "*Water is a human right*" on www.eudebate2009.eu.

30 Ernst & Young estimates and OECD words, cited in Modus RICS magazine (April 2012): "*Private sector investment is crucial to meeting the UK's infrastructure needs. But is it time for a new approach?*".

Energy: privatizing is not always electrifying

What (and who) is left from the privatization of energy and electricity companies and utilities in the UK? Powergen is now in the hands of the German E.On, Scottish Power has been acquired by the Spanish Iberdrola, British Energy was sold to the French EDF. In other words, the family silver has been sold off. The same acquisition stories abound in many other areas (e.g. Argentina, Belgium, and probably soon, Ireland). Some countries and areas have now ceded control of energy policy instruments and channels. Operators have become much bigger, headquarters – and investment decisions – are located farther away, and, yet to a lesser extent than in other sectors, short-term earnings weigh much more on strategies, e.g. through tariff policies which have more to do with the bottom line and shareholder value than with economic transparency or users' benefit.[31] This is not to say that those sectors should be entirely state-controlled, yet it is often ignored that some state-controlled companies have proved very effective in the energy sector too (see e.g. EDF in France, Hydro-Québec in Canada, or Vattenfall in Sweden). As an Ernst & Young study shows, ownership matters less than governance, and some publicly-held companies perform well on this issue too.[32] Between all-to-state and the deregulated U.S. model, there is a range of options. The U.N. estimates that 1.4 billion people have little or no access to electricity. Thinking that the private sector can – and wants to – solve that problem is not only an illusion, but a real threat. Mixed economies are probably the optimal solution, yet national and regional companies from the public sector should stay in the game, e.g. to guarantee a universal

31 I used to be a staunch advocate of full-fledged privatization and liberalization processes in most industries, not least in the energy sector – yet in my case with necessary caution and regulation. Realities kicked in. I must thank Pierre Wathelet and Philippe Bouix for having played the role of eye-openers.

32 "*Government as best in class shareholder*" (Ernst & Young, 2010).

service obligation and appropriate regulations which are less easy to impose on foreign groups headquartered elsewhere.

Health: who is taking care?

Facing the growing costs of health care, some hardliners keep pushing towards free-market remedies. If an entirely state-based system for providing health care has certainly not proved very efficient, relying mostly (or only) on market forces would be disastrous. As Karl Marx wrote: "*Capital is reckless of the health or length of life of the laborer, unless under compulsion from the society.*"[33] The U.S. example speaks for itself. In 2009, the U.S. government spent $3,800 per citizen on health care, compared to $3,242 in Germany, $3,100 in France, and $2,935 in Britain. As a percentage of GDP, U.S. public spending is comparable to Britain and slightly lower than France or Germany. Including private spending – half of total spending, required due to insufficient public means – the U.S. spends more than 17 percent of GDP on health care, compared to about 12 percent in European countries.[34] Are U.S. citizens healthier thanks to an increased role of the private sector? Nearly half of the global revenues of the pharmaceutical sector are generated in the U.S., for more than 300 million inhabitants. For all of them? Not really. Despite such high levels of health expenses, in 1993 there were 37 million Americans without health care insurance; less than 20 years later, the number has risen to 47 million, i.e. 10 million more. Moreover, a large proportion is underinsured. Recent studies show that insured people received the required health care cover 50 percent of the time. Even in Europe, where the mainly public health care sector delivers better than in America, times are changing.

33 Karl Marx: "*Das Kapital. Kritik der politischen Ökonomie*" (1867) (available in an abridged version (544 pages long!) at Oxford University Press, 1999).

34 Sources: OECD, The Economist (see e.g. "*Europe has lower deficits than America*", February 20, 2012).

Hospital stays are made shorter for budget reasons; public hospitals are increasingly leaning towards hotel-style billing policies; private retirement homes are on the rise, many being managed like real-estate facilities (at the related price, for those who can afford it, and with lax rules regarding health services); home-care services are not sufficiently developed.[35] There is growing discontent at a two-tier health care system. Those rich people's concerns should not distract our minds from the poor sanitary conditions still prevailing in Africa and other emerging countries.

Too much food?

There is too much food available (yet not equally distributed). Surplus results in mounting social costs. The time has come to face the music. There is too much food on the table (at least for some). Is growing obesity caused by capitalism? Let us not mince or eat our words. The answer is a straight yes. If The Economist uses the Big Mac as an index, that certainly means something! There is a new form of malnutrition, which is the product of the consumer society and the heavy use of four highly capitalist specialties: the automobile (plural), the screens (plural too), the (fast) food, and the soft drinks. The proof of the pudding is now in… China, where the number of obese people has risen from 18 million in 2005 to more than 100 million in 2010. Chinese officials blame the people's rush to emulate Western culture and the plethora of fast-food outlets. They are right, the curse is a direct import from American-style consumption, and they should act soonest. India's big cities now suffer from obesity too. In 2010, 74 percent of U.S. and 61 percent of British and Australian adults were overweight. In Mexico, where obesity was almost unknown in 1980,

35 To be fair, part of the blame may surely be put on non-capitalist factors, such as users' overuse and abuse (sometimes encouraged by irresponsible healthcare actors' behavior; as well as a lack of professional management. That said, merchandization is also at work.

30 percent of adults are now obese. The costs are high. By 2018, the U.S. will spend an astonishing $344 billion a year to treat obesity-related problems (the figure is coming close to military expenses…). A likely outcome is that all American adults would be overweight by 2050. The total cost of diabetes, one of the related consequences of excess weight, is already high: many more people die from diabetes each year than from HIV/AIDS; in the U.S. diabetes-related expenses already exceed $200 billion. "*Diabetes threatens to 'bankrupt' NHS within a generation*," wrote The Guardian about the situation in Britain. The only good news is for the health care industry.[36]

On the rails, in the air, in the box: all to markets

Is the deregulated airline industry delivering more competitively? For customers, flying with one company has never looked as similar as flying with another. For stakeholders, high costs and losses have moved from the taxpayer to shareholders, with governments coming to the rescue when necessary (this happens frequently). The truth is that over a long period, airlines have been for many years a loss-making sector, no matter who the owner is. Are privatized airports better run than publicly controlled ones (compare e.g. Heathrow in London with Singapore's Changi) and do short-term profit objectives better serve safety? More strategically, is it healthy to leave airport and air traffic control in the hands of foreign interests?

36 A labeled American export, the sickness -we refer to sociocultural obesity, not to hereditary or psychological one- has now invaded the whole planet. Read: "*Obesity belt is exposed by fat map*", in the Financial Times (August 27, 2008); "*L'obésité, nouveau fléau des pays émergents*", and "*Le lien entre surpoids et surmortalité est établi*", in Le Monde (January 17, March 19, 2009); "*Put the Obesity Epidemic at the Top of the Agenda*", by Kenneth Thorpe (Huffington Post, November 17, 2009); "*China's spoilt generation takes obesity to new level*", in the Sydney Morning Herald (June 25, 2011); "*The nutrition puzzle*" (The Economist, February 18, 2012); "*Diabetes threatens to 'bankrupt' NHS within a generation*" (The Guardian, April 25, 2012). Some data for diabetes come from Novo Nordisk recent annual reports and website.

Are the liberalization and privatization of services such as railways good things? Well, just ask the users! A Financial Times editorial asked: "*The real question is not so much 'why sell the Royal Mail but 'who will buy it'?*"[37] Sorry, but the first question is the one that matters most here. Do liberalized postal services work as effectively as they should – and as they did in the past, e.g. in fulfilling both a postal and a social mission in remote areas (towards elderly people, for example)? With all users (renamed clients to be in market fashion) lining up to be served, "liberalized" post offices in some countries now look more like Russian stores in the communist era. Ironic, isn't it? Why not make postal missions evolve instead?[38] And in a number of sectors and cases, have state-controlled monopolies not been just replaced by private-owned oligopolies?

Made in sport

Even the most enthusiastic aficionados have to admit it: there is too much money in sports today. These are fouled up by big bucks. The most popular sport in the world, football, is a case in point. In most countries, shirts advertise sponsors and do not even show the club's name; stadiums are named after airlines, beverages, lotteries, etc.; players are traded as slaves bought and sold at any time in the season, or act as mercenaries who do not even care about the origin and location of the team they are playing with. How many still believe FIFA's claims that corruption allegations are "*ridiculous*"?[39] With endorsement income much higher than tournament earnings, are golfers just rich sandwich-board men – or commercial paper tigers? Supposedly reserved for amateurs, the Olympics now include

37 "*Selling Royal Mail*" (Financial Times editorial, March 29, 2012).

38 A balanced view would recognize that responsibility also lies with a public sector that neither anticipated nor adapted its service offering, e.g. to compete with and then to embark on online activities.

39 "*Fifa's corruption probes described as ridiculous*" (www.bbc.co.uk/sport: April 2, 2012).

athletes paid all year long for their (de)feats. Would it be sadistic to ask about the real drive behind Formula One? Certainly not racing. More trivially, the United Arab Emirates launched a cycle race in which the winner made €772,000, i.e. a hundred times more than for similar races run in areas where cycling is at least part of the local culture, which is hardly the case in the desert. Is that about sport? Not at all, it is just about money.

Unfortunately, the music business – an awful term for talking about arts – is the same story. With their one-minute culture, would any studio bean counter take the trouble to listen to – and record – Mozart, Gershwin or Duke Ellington today? Many of the pop stars' tours are less about rolling stones than just rolling in the money. What happened to bands such as U2 and the Rolling Stones? Described as *"a way of life"* – and not just a band – on the sleeve notes of their first record, the latter were named *"the Rolling Stones Inc."* by Fortune magazine in 2002, and dubbed *"a multimillion dollar global brand"* by the Financial Times in 2012. A way of life indeed. At Cannes MIDEM 2008, U2's manager Paul McGuinness said that (sic) *"it would be pathetic to do good music and not good business."* Many have turned moneymaker shakers, more celebrated about what they are worth in tour revenues and assets than what their music and lyrics (still?) mean.[40] The old blues is long gone.

40 *"Shake your moneymaker"* was a song written by the late bluesman Elmore James, *"Rolling Stone"* is from Muddy Waters. Sleeve notes of the first Rolling Stones record were written by their producer Andrew Loog Oldham. That was a long time ago. In 2002, Fortune magazine wrote a lead story about *"Inside the Rolling Stones Inc."* (September 30, 2002). In 2007, the Stones played at a party for Deutsche Bank employees. In 2012, their anniversary was also celebrated in a financial newspaper (*"Rolling Stones at 50"*, Financial Times, July 13, 2012). Among U2 megalomaniac dreams was a 120-meter tower in Dublin that should be used as a recording studio. Bono is also a major investor in Facebook.

Beware a market society

All-to-market-based deregulation looks a bit like removing all (or most of) the signs and the traffic lights from the roads, and therefore leaving drivers' conduct up to them. This goes even further than the law of the jungle in the economy. As Chris Patten, the last Governor of Hong Kong and a sharp-minded British Conservative, reminds us: "*Capitalism should operate within the law, not the law within capitalism.*"[41] Franklin D. Roosevelt once said: "*The liberty of a democracy is not safe if the people tolerate the growth of private power to a point where it comes stronger than their democratic state itself.*" It is not just business that is transformed, but also political systems. Should we chalk it up to a kind of "capitalist utopia"?[42] Or purely and simply to a political resignation and submission to the market religion that has led to "cowardly states," as described by Richard Murphy? In a review of Robert Reich's book "*Supercapitalism*," Vanessa Bush wrote: "*the economy has grown so efficient and effective that the human equation is lost and... democracy has become less and less responsive to common values.*"[43]

The intrusive presence of markets also changes the social fabric, culture, and everyday life. In the late 1950s, Karl Polanyi noted: "*Instead of economy being embedded in social relations, social relations are embedded in the economic system.*"[44] David Loy says that "*as market values lead to a decline in the quality of our social relationships, society becomes more like the aggregate*

---

41 Chris Patten: "*Not Quite the Diplomat. Home Truths about World Affairs*" (Penguin Books, 2006).

42 To use the words of Pierre Rosanvallon in his clever "*Le capitalisme utopique. Critique de l'idéologie économique*" (Editions du Seuil, 1979).

43 See Richard Murphy: "*The Courageous State: Rethinking Economics, Society and the Role of Government*" (Searching Finance, 2011). Vanessa Bush's review of "*Supercapitalism: The Transformation of Business, Democracy, and Everyday Life*" (Vintage, 2008) for Booklist, the American Library Association's magazine.

44 Vienna-born Hungarian Karl Polanyi wrote "*The Great Transformation*" (Beacon Press, 1957).

of individuals that economic theory pictures it as being."[45] Social networks and media, and Facebook in particular, are a reflection of that shift. André Orléan, a French economist, states that the whole life of individuals is now "*financialized*," while another French political scientist and economist, Jacques Généreux, goes further and talks about a "*dissociety*" characterized, among others, by a "*privatization of minds*" (and mindsets).[46]

Contrary to what fundamentalists and dedicated followers of the market fashion[47] tell us, capitalism does not deliver for all purposes, and is not good for everything. Too much capitalism has become a deadly sin – and not a minor one. French philosopher André Comte-Sponville notes: "*It would be a mistake to believe that wealth is sufficient to make up a civilization, or even a humanely acceptable society. That is why law and politics are also required. And as politics and law are not sufficient either, we need morals, love and spirituality. Let us not ask economics to fulfill all those needs!*"[48]

On the whole, a market-based economy is beneficial, but a wholly market-driven society is damaging. There is life outside of capitalism.

---

45 David R. Loy: "*The Religion of the Market*" in the Journal of the American Academy of Religion (Summer 1997).

46 André Orléan, a leading French economist, president of AFEP (Association française d'économie politique): "*La finance est devenue une pensée de la vie*" (www.marianne2.fr, March 20, 2010); Jacques Généreux: "*La Dissociété*" (Editions du Seuil, Points, 2006, 2008).

47 The words refer of course to The Kinks' "*Dedicated Follower of Fashion*" (Pye, 1966). One of the many songs written by Ray Davies, which gives sharper insights into conservatism, Britain and the modern world than a book does.

48 From André Comte-Sponville: "*Le capitalisme est-il moral?*" (Albin Michel, 2004), a compelling read.

PART 2
SEVEN OTHER NOT SO VENIAL SINS

"The inherent vice of capitalism is the unequal sharing of blessings..."
WINSTON CHURCHILL

"Sins cannot be undone, only forgiven."
IGOR STRAVINSKY, Russian music composer

SIN NO. 8: PROGRESS AND GROWTH: THE GOOD AND THE BAD

"What we call 'progress' is the exchange of one nuisance for another nuisance."

HAVELOCK ELLIS

"If you can't count it, it doesn't count"

"*Do you want my one-word secret of happiness? It's growth – mental, financial, you name it*," said the grown-up Harold S. Geneen, CEO of the once famous ITT. Making growth synonymous with happiness? Rich man, poor man! Some might say that such a statement is typical of golden age, American-style capitalism, and directly inspired from or reflected in the writings of W. W. Rostow or the Hudson Institute, et al.[1] Actually, the cult of growth has spread across economists, business leaders, trade unions, and the whole political spectrum. Governments anticipate growth figures like patients waiting for hospital scan results.[2] Almost every day, newspapers and other media report that higher economic growth is a boon and slower or negative growth a bane.

What are the measures? And what is measured? An old saying, probably coined by a bookkeeper (or was it a macroeconomist?) goes: "*If you can't count it, it doesn't count*." Although GDP still has its virtues, not least by making it "*clear about what it includes and excludes... and is comparable across countries*," it has shown its limitations too.[3] GDP growth is usually calculated in real terms, i.e. adjusted for inflation. Is inflation effectively measured? Not 100 percent sure. The subprime mortgage crisis was preceded by an unprecedented ten-year surge in asset prices (property prices doubled in most developed economies). How was this recorded when inflation

1 Walt Whitman Rostow was the author of the famous "*The Stages of Economic Growth*" (Cambridge University Press, 1962), often used as a manual in schools from the U.S. to Vietnam and other places. Leaving aside its "*my way or the highway*" tone, it still makes a worthwhile read on the process of growth. The Hudson Institute is a conservative think tank founded by futurologist Herman Kahn and RAND colleagues.

2 To use the words of Andrew Simms, policy director of the New Economics Foundation, in the Guardian: "*Growth is good, isn't it?*" (January 25, 2010).

3 Quoted from "*A measure remodeled*", an interesting article about growth indicators by John Thornhill in the Financial Times (January 28, 2009). For an alternative, use the Happy Planet Index (www.happyplanetindex.org).

was calculated? Every consumer in the Eurozone experienced large-scale price roundups in the wake of the euro inception. Where was this accounted?

Another limitation is that growth and related measures are purely quantitative and virtually overlook qualitative aspects. To take four well-known examples:

- Productivity measurement "*poses no fewer problems than its definition*" (G. A. Oyeranti).[4] Without going into details, productivity is nothing more than an arithmetical ratio between an output, or amount produced, and an input, or amount of resources used. Whatever the sophistication of models used to refine the definition and metrics, increasing productivity means doing more, but not necessarily doing better.
- Oil extracted from the earth, sold and consumed is considered an addition to wealth, and not as a depletion of resources.
- The more cars on the roads the better for GDP, and traffic congestion is accounted only through the millions of liters of gas burnt (thus recorded as a positive economic indicator).
- Health care is measured by inputs rather than by outputs, i.e. the sale of medical services and drugs increases "wealth" while the number of healthy people (the ones having to use the medical services less often) does not! Highlighting for a U.S. Senate commission the absurdities of excessively mechanical measures, Jonathan Rowe, a Californian author, quipped: "*Next we will hear about the "disease-led recovery". To stimulate*

4 Gboyega A. Oyeranti, professor at the University of Ibadan (Nigeria): "*Concept and Measurement of Productivity*" (Department of Economics).

> *the economy we will have to encourage people to be sick so that the economy can be well.*"[5]

Accounting, valuation and reporting indicators at microeconomic and business level are also far from perfect, hence the efforts towards "Triple bottom line" and "Balanced scorecards". In a book that addresses the "glaring deficiencies of financial reporting," and explains what to do to overcome them, Kaevan Gazdar reminds us that "*Both goodwill and blue sky are intangible assets*" and therefore impossible to figure and value.[6] The growth model of the last decade(s) is now in question. What is growth for if it is for overproducing, overconsuming, wasting, getting sick? All of that paid by more money. Furthermore, as the Asia Times columnist Henry C.K. Liu writes, is growth based on "*excess money*", credit overcapacity, and so-called "structured" finance not simply "*illusory*" growth?[7]

Infinite progress, but finite resources

Growth is also too often confused with progress. Growing would mean progressing, and vice versa. "*Without continual growth and progress, such words as improvement, achievement and success have no meaning,*" said Benjamin Franklin. Still, progress seems to happen more as Goethe describes it: "*Progress has not followed a straight ascending line, but a spiral with rhythms of progress and retrogression, of evolution*

---

5 Cited in the Financial Times (January 28, 2009). That humorous macroeconomic statement is a bit in line with the more serious analysis of "*Selfish capitalism*", carried out by Oliver James, a former clinical child psychologist and now a Guardian columnist, about the toll taken on populations' mental illness. Read: "*Selfish capitalism is bad for our mental health*" (The Guardian, January 2, 2008), or go to www.selfishcapitalist.com.

6 Kaevan Gazdar: "*Reporting Nonfinancials*" (Wiley, 2007).

7 "*Monetarism enters bankruptcy*", a brilliant analysis of the roots and consequences of the late-2000s financial crisis, by Henry C.K. Liu in Asia Times Online (January 6, 2009, www.atimes.com).

and dissolution." Experiencing the side-effects of progress, or simply bad progress, the words from Aldous Huxley come to mind: "*Technological progress has merely provided us with more efficient means to go backwards.*"

Reality checks sometimes show inconvenient truths. A lot of oil has been burnt since Malthus's predictions about finite resources at the end of the 18th century, the Club of Rome's warning in 1972 (a couple of years before the first oil crash and... forty years ago), Al Gore's "*Inconvenient Truth,*" the 700-page "*Stern Review,*" the 2009 Copenhagen summit, and the 2011 Durban talks. More oil burnt than the resources that could have helped to shift from a growth-for-growth's sake - call it a "Standard Oil" carbon-driven - model to a more sustainable pattern.[8]

8 In chronological order: Thomas Robert Malthus: "*An Essay on the Principle of Population*" (1798. Republished by Penguin, 1976); "*The Limits to Growth*", by D.H. Meadows, D. L. Meadows, J. Randers, W.W. Behrens III for The Club of Rome, founded in 1968 (Universe Books, 1972); Albert Gore, Jr.: "*An Inconvenient Truth: The Planetary Emergency of Global Warming and What We Can Do About It*" (book based on the documentary film, Rodale Press, 2006); "*Stern Review on the Economics of Climate Change*", by Nicholas Stern (Cambridge University Press, 2007); www.copenhagenclimatecouncil.com; www.foei.org ("UN climate talks 2011: Durban").

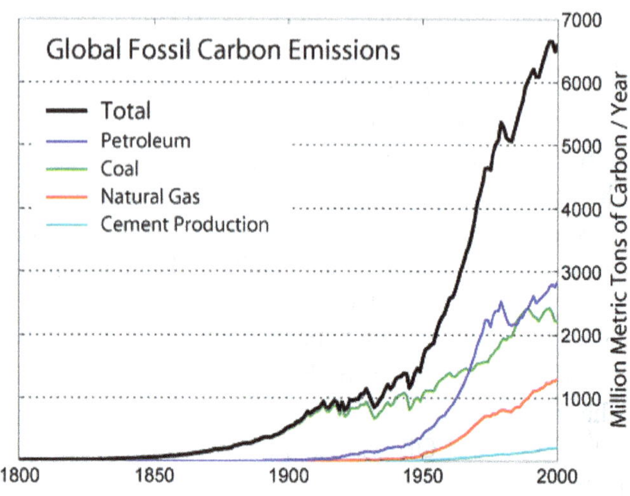

Source: Wikipedia and "Global, Regional, and National CO2 Emissions"[9]

Hold your breath: if the entire planet emitted CO_2 at today's U.S. rate, global emissions would already be five times higher. China is quickly getting there. So little has been achieved, so many bad habits have been created and bad examples followed that we are now in a situation of planetary emergency. Jeffrey Sachs contends: "*The world's current ecological, demographic, and economic trajectory is unsustainable, meaning that if we continue with "business as usual" we will hit... crises with calamitous results.*"[10] Though the oil, automotive and transportation sectors and their lobbies are in denial (yet some now admit that times are changing), and millions of vehicle drivers keep on burning the midday oil, noted experts now recognize

9 "*Global, Regional, and National CO2 Emissions*" by G. Martland, T.A. Boden, R.J. Andres; Carbon Dioxide Information Analysis Center, Oak Ridge, U.S.A. Watch also "*CO2 emissions since 1820*", an animated graph at www.gapminder.org/world.

10 Jeffrey D. Sachs: "*Common Wealth: Economics for a Crowded Planet*" (Penguin Press, 2008).

that "peak oil" is now, or already behind us. To keep on dealing (a suitable word) with oil as if it was a "normal market" of renewed resources regulated by short-term demand and supply-side is certainly not the best thing that capitalism has done these last decades. The trouble is there are many people not ready to change their habits. Arthur is a gardener (who also claims to provide organic agricultural solutions), he owns a station wagon for weekend use and mostly for short-distance shopping, and drives his truck the rest of the week. He lives next to his parents, who own three cars, of which the wife's one rides once every two months at best, and a SUV sometimes leaves the garage for a countryside ride. Recently, the father was heard complaining about oil prices! His sister lives around the corner with her boyfriend, and always drives to see the family in one of their two cars. That makes seven cars for six adults living next to each other (a last detail: three of the car owners are unemployed). This is now commonplace in Western countries.

Is that really a model for the future? Some doubt it. GIFT founder Chandran Nair warns Asians not to follow the Western growth and consumption model based on "*global privilege*" and "*access to unlimited resources*" – unlimited at least at first glance and for a relatively short period in history. Encouraging Asians to consume as westerners have been doing is "*the height of irresponsibility.*"[11] In case you would have not noticed, this responsible statement comes from an Asian. David Loy, a professor of philosophy, remarks about the "progress" achieved: "*How ingenious we have been to devise an economic system that allows us to steal from the future assets of our descendants!*"[12]

11 "*Growing consumption a bane for India*" (interview with the Economic Times in the India Times, May 16, 2011); "*We should stop talking of our Asian century*" (Financial Times, March 7, 2012).

12 David R. Loy: "*The Religion of the Market*", in the Journal of the American Academy of Religion (Summer 1997).

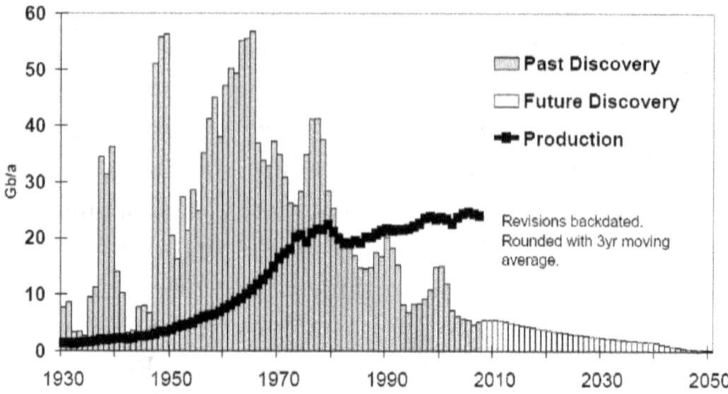

Source: Association for the Study of Peak Oil

Amid crises and their subsequent growth, jobs and income cuts; and facing the increasing role of the... faster growing economies of China, India and other (non-)BRIC areas; questioning growth and progress might not be well received in some places.[13] This is a mistake. The seriousness of the climate and energy situations requires both long- and short-term measures – and these include changes in behavior. The costs of not acting, or acting too slowly, against climate change, which is by far the biggest challenge now affecting the whole world, could be astronomical. In fact, we are already bearing part of those costs in our daily life. Matthew Simmons, an investment banker (yes), wrote in the year 2000 that "*We simply wasted 30 important years by ignoring the work*" of the Club of Rome.[14]

Switching to another less car- and carbon-intensive growth model and progress pattern would not only be beneficial to both the developed and the developing economies. It would

13 China was self-sufficient until 1993 and now buys more than half of its oil from abroad.

14 Read, among others: Matthew Simmons, on www.energybulletin.net; "*The Politics of Climate Change*", by Anthony Giddens (Polity Press, 2009); "*Blueprint for a Safer Planet*", by Nicholas Stern (The Bodley Head, 2009).

also create millions of jobs in various sectors. To take but one example, renewable energies are labor-intensive: to meet its target of producing 30 percent of UK's electricity by 2020, a workforce of 400,000 will be required.[15] Sadly, only a minority of policymakers (Nordic countries and Germany standing among these), market players and entrepreneurs are now betting on the "*transition to a low-carbon economy*" that would bring "*opportunities for growth*" (words in italics as used in the "*Stern Review*") and not just threats to current competitiveness. Cautious estimates show that inefficient energy systems and distorting energy subsidies cost around €200 billion a year, while markets for low-carbon energy products could reach €400 billion per year in the next twenty years. With the costs of global warming projected around €7,000 billion by 2050, is that not worth a switch? "*Many clean energy technologies are available but they are not deployed quickly enough to avert potentially disastrous consequences,*" said the executive director of IEA.[16] If the cost of a move to less carbon-driven economies is estimated between 1 and 3 percent of GDP – i.e. not that much, for what GDP still means (and less than many useless expenses and costly bailouts) – is it not worth the effort?

What is the drive?

Could any system other than capitalism have created, invented, developed, and marketed so many products and services? History does not show any equivalent. To name but a few, what would be life without penicillin and hundreds of other

15 Figures from www.businessgreen.com ("*Skills 'time bomb' threatens renewables growth*", April 25, 2012).

16 The quotation comes from Maria van der Hoeven, executive director of the International Energy Agency, in The Guardian: "*Governments failing to avert catastrophic climate change*" (April 25, 2012).

useful drugs,[17] paper, pens, blue jeans, light bulbs, telecommunications, refrigerators, radio, Post-it notes, discs, cameras, computers, the Web and the Internet (and related dotcoms), Google,[18] Amazon, YouTube, LinkedIn, blogs, and so on? Great stuff, isn't it? Readers can make their own list. However, mind some meaningful omissions. For all those inventions, progress and real growth benefits, capitalism has also brought us years of consuming oil, months spent watching television, days at shopping, hours of driving, minutes eating fast food. Some of those changes were once measures of growth and marks of progress: digging for oil, watching a bit (but not too much) of TV, going to the shop, using a car, enjoying a burger are not bad per se. It is the overconsumption and abuse of those capitalist symbols that indicate a declining economic model.

Everybody knows at least one neighbor like Gail the hairdresser, who, although broke these days, jumps (well, not really, because she is a more than a few pounds overweight) into her Mini Cooper to go to the bank and buy a pizza 200 meters away from the salon for lunch. Later in the day, Gail will drive back home and watch TV (or at least switch it on) for five hours. Note that all these movements are good for GDP, while just walking and turning off the screen would not be accounted! One may indeed question the good and the bad in progress and growth. The words absurd, nonsensical, or simply crazy would often come to mind. Among other thinkers and analysts, Ivan Illich, André Gorz and Jean-Pierre Dupuy have

17 For the skeptics, one of the places where the benefits of all forms of progress can be checked is the hospital. I wrote some parts of this book's first edition during an unforeseen hospital stay. For better and worse (including some side effects), I had the opportunity to check the virtues of progress at that time.

18 Not everything is perfect in Google's world. Search engines are, er, searching for you in all meanings, and Streetview clearly constitutes a dangerous intrusion into people's privacy. "Big Brother"-style totalitarianism is looming here (read e.g. "*Google must remember our right to be forgotten*" in the Financial Times, February 16, 2012).

conducted important research on counterproductive effects of "progress" on the economy and society.[19]

Here are a few examples:

- As a result of both private capitalist processes and production-first public subsidization, intensive farming is based on an extensive use of chemical inputs: the more there is the less soil and product quality increases. What is good for growth translates into bad results.
- Never before in history has so much information been available via different media and the Internet. However, many users now do not find sufficient time to deal with the overflow, and an increasing number suffer from attention span or ADD (attention deficit disorders, which can be made more serious by the "*Twitterization of culture*"). Worse, infotainment rules the media, turning – and selling – disasters, wars, and other news items into shows; and running high on emotions. We might turn into news consumers with "*no time to think*."[20]
- Medicalization and the psychologization of almost everything tends to view social problems as primarily medical or as disorders, and can sometimes turn people into "lifelong patients". Do so many people really need sleeping pills, tranquilizers and antidepressants for so long? Should the cure for obesity only consist of anti-obesity pills or should individuals be pushed to get

19 "*Tools for Conviviality*" (Harper, 1973) stands among the most notable works published by the multilingual Vienna-born philosopher (and once a Catholic priest) Ivan Illich, whose works were introduced in France by André Gorz (aka Michel Bosquet), and elaborated by the French engineer and philosopher Jean-Pierre Dupuy, a member of Collegium International.

20 The word "*Twitterization*" was used by Sharon Begley in Newsweek (March 1, 2011). "*No Time To Think*" is a book written by two former CNN and Los Angeles Times journalists (Continuum, 2008). About the role of media as a component of the "soft monster", read Raffaele Simone: "*Le Monstre doux. L'Occident vire-t-il à droite?*" (Gallimard, 2010), on which an entrancing interview in Le Monde Magazine was based ("*Pourquoi l'Europe s'enracine à droite*", 12 septembre 2010).

more exercise? Should we necessarily need psychological assistance for a minor flood caused by a small water overflow? And so on.

- "Gadgetization" is another worrying trend. Consider the number of not always very useful objects surrounding us. Why do so many people use a mobile phone so much? The answer is often: to look busy, to feel important, or just to occupy their time. Do we really need giant TV screens that rule the rooms? Is air conditioning needed under certain temperature levels? Are video games really good for the children? Does everybody really need satellite navigation (or GPS), which may be useful in some businesses, but which distracts the driver and turns people completely ignorant of geography?[21] Which real extras do iPad 4G and other "smart" devices really bring? Do they make us smarter? "*We die not wishing we owned more gadgets, Apple or otherwise. We die wishing we had more time for the people we loved,*" wrote Neal Lawson in The Guardian.[22]
- The last example is about mobility, or the lack of it, due to the number of automobiles on the roads. The number of vehicles has been multiplied by 25 over the last 80 years and is expected to be three times bigger still, before 2030, when over 2.3 billion vehicles are expected on the roads. A carmaker, Ford's chairman Bill Ford himself, points to the short-term risk of a "*world gridlock*."[23] This growth will simply be unmanageable… and destructive.

21 See e.g.: "*Hi-tech cars: Driver distraction warning in US*" (www.bbc.com/news, February 17, 2012); "*Greater Manchester road deaths up by 42%*" (www.bbc.co.uk/news, April 2, 2012).

22 In "*Steve Jobs: a stylist for a consumer society*" (The Guardian, October 7, 2011). Neal Lawson is chair of Compass, an influential UK democratic left pressure group (www.compassonline.org.uk).

23 "*Ford head warns rise to 4bn cars risks world gridlock*" and "*Drive to keep the industry moving*" (Financial Times, February 27, 2012).

> Every day, the traffic jams around and inside Brussels – often considered the most congested city in Europe – are about 200 km long. In 2010, China recorded the worst traffic jam in history when a traffic standstill lasted 11 (eleven!) days in the Hebei province. At its longest, the jam stretched for 100 km. By the/on your way, have you ever asked yourself what would happen if everyone in the world who could drive actually did drive? Could everyone still move, park, fill the tank, and simply breathe?[24] The world would be motionless, and the situation disastrous. Reducing the number of vehicles – and not only their size and consumption – as well as the huge amount of time wasted on means of transportation should be on the agenda of any responsible politician, conservative or progressive. Instead, most keep on subsidizing an automotive industry with overcapacity, give "cash for clunkers", reduce taxes on supposedly less carbon-emitting cars, promote driving classes at a lower age, do not devote sufficient resources for public transportation, etc.

Getting rid of growth for growth's sake; and shifting towards a less carbon-, consumption-, car-, calorific- and credit-driven capitalism is the biggest challenge of our times – and perhaps the only chance of capitalism's survival as an economic system and of our societies as a whole. Being aware of this and acting on that would be real progress. "*True progress is to know more, and be more, and do more,*" wrote Oscar Wilde. LSE professor Richard Layard sums it up: "*despite massive wealth creation, happiness has not risen in years or decades*" in most developed economies.[25]

24 It is estimated that nearly half of populations in industrialized countries and areas are breathing unhealthy air, mainly due to pollution from transportation.

25 Richard Layard, professor at the London School of Economics: "*Now is the time for a less selfish capitalism*" (Financial Times, March 12, 2009).

SIN NO. 9: RATIONAL ECONOMIC AGENTS ARE (OFTEN) CRAZY

"The modern world of business and politics is plagued by spurious rationality and bogus quantification."

JOHN KAY

Emotions and herd instinct

Source: Kevin 'Kal' Kallaugher cover of The Economist (November 1, 1997)

Keynes said: "*Investing is trying to predict how other investors will behave.*" As far as financial and stock markets are concerned, the herd instinct is the law of the land. Years spent in investor-related affairs have taught me how conventional and repetitive the (not so) average investor's (and IR officer) behavior is, as an individual or in a company. Forget the allegedly "sophisticated" economic models and the growing – and even more worrying – weight of algorithmic trading. At the end of the day – perhaps should we write at the beginning – the so-called rationality of market agents is mainly about human assumptions, decisions, actions, and… emotions. Société Générale's rogue trader Jérôme Kerviel, accused in January 2008 of "unauthorized" trading for amounts as large as the bank's total market value, said about his behavior: "*You lose your sense of the sums involved when you are in this kind of work. It's disembodied.*" Traders' hormones seem to rule their behavior more than occasionally.[1] Are we still in rational territory? Writing about the financial "*storm*," Vince Cable reminds that John Stuart Mill had already analyzed the "*frenzy of over-trading*" in the 18th and 19th centuries.[2] Daniel Kahneman, a Nobel Prize winner and one of the most famous founders of the behavioral school of economics, notes: "*Emotions constantly inform our judgments.*" Moreover, "*Professional investors fail a basic test of skill, persistent achievement*" and suffer from "*cognitive illusions*" which lead to failures such as the total lack of anticipation of financial crashes.[3]

Why should a Dow Jones, Nasdaq, or any other index's sneeze lead to fever and a cold on other exchanges, and impact on companies' stock (and beyond) which have no direct relation? It is not an investment manager who says: "*Investors should also insulate themselves as much as possible from Wall Street's propaganda machine.*"[4] It is baffling to watch how a craze for a stock can artificially influence the market perception, create bias in company real fundamentals analysis, and result in wrong investment decisions. In July 2000, when the dot-com bubble was deflating, Fortune magazine pointed out that over a recent period "*of the 33,169 buy, sell and hold recommendations made by stock analysts... only 125 were pure sells.*

---

1 A financial website writes without joking: "*How to profit from hormonal markets*" (www.moneyweek.com, March 16, 2012). While FT columnist Gillian Tett says that "*Regulators must get grip on traders' hormones*" (Financial Times, March 15, 2012).

2 Vince Cable: "*The Storm: The World Economic Crisis and What it Means*" (Atlantic Books, 2009).

3 Daniel Kahneman: "*Thinking, Fast and Slow*" (Farrar, Straus and Giroux, 2011).

4 Edward Chancellor, GMO investment manager, commenting on the work of Daniel Kahneman, in: "*Humans are naturally bad investors,*" in the Financial Times fm supplement ("*The Last Word*", January 9, 2012).

That's 0.3 percent... Just over a third of the ratings... were strong buys..." Eight years and millions of buys later, a New York Times article noted that, among others, Merrill Lynch analysts were finally learning to say "sell".[5] Learning, really? The New York Times wrote this at a time when most financial sector stocks were overpriced and a few weeks or months before their fall in the worst financial crisis since World War II or before. Some shareholders might remember that RBS's share price was 600 pence in April 2007 – and most analysts' tip was to buy more stock. It was still at 500 pence in October 2007, before the planned acquisition, jointly with two other European banks, of the Holland-based ABN Amro (a move then applauded by the ever-rational (buy-side?) financial analysts, and backed by a large majority of – mostly institutional – shareholders). One year later, share price had fallen to 175 pence, before further falling by almost 50 percent in a few weeks. In January 2009, shares had fallen below 15 (fifteen!) pence.[6]

This is another paradox of capitalism: a system that stresses individualism as a main virtue relies heavily on going with the crowd. In a highly perceptive comment on the role of human behavior in financial crises, Shahin Kamadolin, an economist at the Dutch Rabobank asks: "*Are we all herd animals?*" He goes on: "*The history of financial crises shows that the herd can very often head in the wrong direction and we decide to follow them regardless. The reason... is that we regularly suffer from information cascades – we make choices based on the observations of choices made by others... even if our information differs.*"[7] This contradicts the entrepreneurial and innovative behavior, summed up e.g. by Alan Kay: "*Don't worry about what anybody*

5 Fortune magazine, July 24, 2000; The New York Times, May 21, 2008.

6 "*RBS timeline: where it all went wrong*" (Daily Telegraph, December 2, 2010).

7 "*Asset bubbles, financial crises and the role of human behaviour*" by Shahin Kamalodin, Rabobank Economic Research Department (January 2011).

else is going to do... The best way to predict the future is to invent it."[8] Investors and analysts rarely behave that way.

Me-tooism

Disguised or not as creativity or rationality, "me-tooism" affects many businesses and institutions, and not only stock markets.

Why do those supposedly creative branding agencies mimic each other so often?

Why do radio and TV channels use the same formats all over the planet?

Why are so many post-merger corporate identities simply built on a copy-and-paste of two or more names? Daimler Chrysler was probably among the pioneers, then imitated by a string of dedicated followers of the branding fashion. The list includes the unpalatable Anheuser-Busch InBev (see above), as well as ArcelorMittal, AstraZeneca, Bank of New York Mellon (imitated by the even longer Bank of America Merrill Lynch), BNP Paribas, ConocoPhillips, ExxonMobil, GlaxoSmithKline, Repsol YPF, Thomson Reuters, and more. If it may occasionally reflect a respect for the two merging parties, the trend also clearly shows a deficiency in imagination, and perhaps in some cases a lack of sense of corporate direction. Oh, pardon us, we had forgotten that branding should be (mainly?) emotional and not (always that) rational!

Why have so many banks opted for IBM-style acronyms in recent times? BMO (for Bank of Montreal), BBVA (for Banco Bilbao Vizcaya Argentaria), CIBC (for Canadian Imperial Bank of Commerce), SEB (for Skandinaviska Enskilda Banken), ING and UBS (both after a merger), etc. Admittedly, some names are too long, difficult to pronounce, or hard to travel with (looking less national is a clear motive in some cases, but why are so many just following suit?). The banking and insurance sectors

8 Those words have often been attributed to Alan Kay, a computer scientist at Palo Alto Research Center.

are top-drawer me-tooists. They seem to behave like drivers on highways, overtaking others just to follow the others who are doing it. Why are so many bank branches located next to each other? Why are so many bankers jumping onto ABS (asset-backed securities), CDOs (collateralized debt obligations), derivatives, and other so-called "sophisticated" schemes and pyramids?[9] Some answer: if others do it, why should not we follow? Following the crowd is here synonymous with following the money.

Financial weapons of mass destruction?

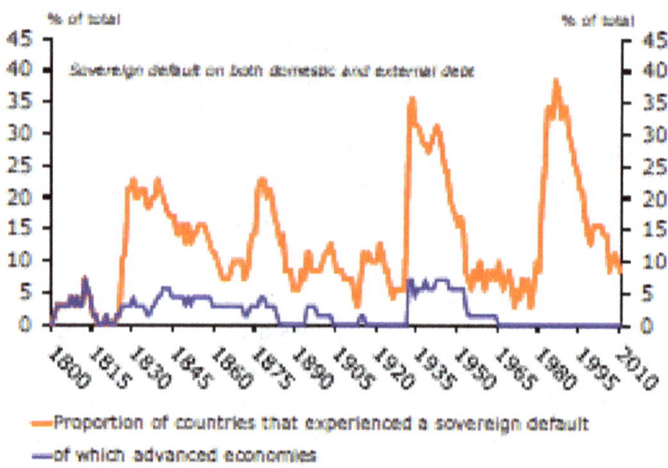

Source: Reinhart and Rogoff (2010), Rabobank

9 In his statement for Berkshire Hathaway annual report 2002 Warren Buffett wrote: "*The range of derivatives contracts is limited only by the imagination of man (or sometimes, so it seems, madmen).*"

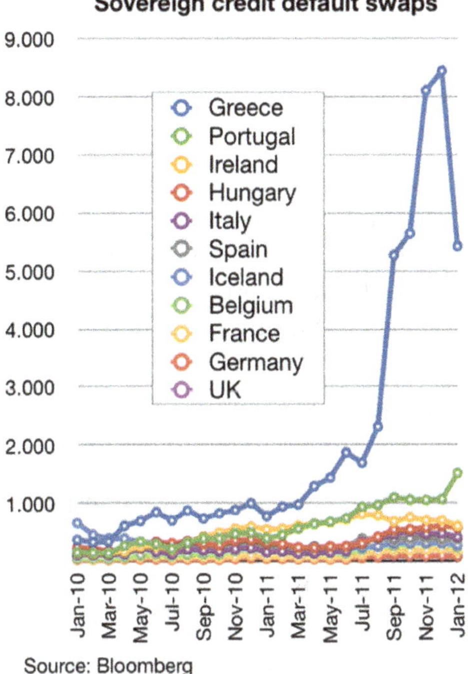

A CDS (credit default swap) is an agreement between a seller and a buyer. The former has to compensate the latter in the event of a loan (or sovereign) default, an event that happens more than once (see chart). The buyer makes a series of payments (named "fee" or "spread") to the seller and, in exchange, receives a payoff if the loan defaults. In case of default the buyer is compensated with the whole amount of insurance bought (this may be a problem already) and the seller takes possession of the loan. This sounds very rational, yet the word "swap" might already hints at a degree of irrationality. Though far from most transparent (which is another issue), those default swaps have been much analyzed, commented and criticized in the wake of the two latest financial crises, i.e. the (mainly) American subprime one and the (mainly) European sovereign debt one (see the chart for a two-year period). New York Times columnist Gretchen Morgenson referred to "CDS cowboys" while Warren Buffett himself named them named the CDS "*financial weapons of mass destruction*."[10]

Consider the following points:

- Anyone (well, almost) can purchase a CDS, even without holding loan instruments or having insurable interest, while sellers do not have to be regulated entities. "Naked" – what a lovely word! – CDS purchase means that one takes out insurance on bonds without actually owning them.
- Face value payments prove theoretical, i.e. much lower.
- Reference entities can include SPEs (special purpose entities) or ABS (which are often not most transparent).
- CDS are used by investors for speculative purpose, sometimes extending to the overall credit quality or accelerating crises (as it was reported about Bear Stearns and Lehman Brothers collapses), "*a purely speculative gamble*" with "*not one social or economic benefit*," wrote FT columnist Wolfgang Münchau.[11] Manipulation is looming (Goldman Sachs – again – has been accused of this more than once).[12] "*We all knew that Greece was heading for a credit event. It would have made sense to*

10 Wikipedia provides a rather good description of CDS. See also: "Credit default swap market under scrutiny" by Gretchen Morgenson, in the New York Times (August 10, 2008); "Credit default swaps: What are they good for?" on www.salon.com (April 20, 2010); "Credit Default Swaps" (http://topics.nytimes.com, March 1, 2012).

11 Wolfgang Münchau: "Time to outlaw naked credit default swaps" (Financial Times, February 28, 2010).

12 "Annals of CDS manipulation, Goldman Sachs edition" by Felix Salmon on http://blogs.reuters.com/felix-salmon (December 10, 2010).

have it happen earlier," declared a senior CDS trader quoted by the FT.[13]

- As for other derivatives, hedging and counterparty practices are far from most transparent (some are "*like saying that a bank robbery brings benefits to the robber,*" adds Münchau).
- Analysts and media are increasingly viewing CDS as a major risk measure, both at corporate or government level. Using CDS to destabilize governments is (sic) "*counter-productive,*" said U.S. Federal Reserve chairman Ben Bernanke in February 2010. A couple of years later, the Eurozone crisis showed how supposedly rational instruments can turn crazy at market speed.

Is Homo economicus a rating agent?

The crises and bubble bursts experienced in the last decades should have taught us how Homo economicus, aka the rational economic agent (still praised by noted economists), behaves and where the supposed market "rationality" can lead. "*If investors are freed from a belief in perfectly efficient markets, they will also be free to use their brains to question market values and to treat accounting numbers as evidence, not answers,*" wrote Jane Fuller, chair of the Accounting Advocacy Committee of CFA.[14] At best, markets work with "*bounded rationality*" and in the worst case, market agents can act sinfully, e.g. with pure greedy motives (see the related sin).[15] Increasing the role of robot, algo and high-frequency trading will just bring more problems and add more risks, despite the apparent neutrality of machines.

---

13 "*Sovereign credit swaps pass first test with Greece*" (Financial Times, March 20, 2012).

14 In the Financial Times Accountancy column (October 29, 2009).

15 The concept of "*bounded rationality*" was developed by the American psychologist Herbert Simon. For a summary, see "*Theories of Bounded Rationality,*" in "*Decision and Organization*" (North-Holland Publishing, 1972).

It always returns to business as usual, and Homo economicus is still at work. An explanation may lie in the way products – especially financial products – are packaged. After all, acronyms such as ABS, CDS, CDO, CPFF, SPE, SIV, Repo, or the lovely BISTRO, give every appearance of well-conceived, rational, and thus reassuring things, even more when they are presented as "structured", "securitized", "(de)leveraged", and, of course, rated AAA or A+. The more sophisticated, the better. Mind out for the traps: "*The next time you read that a financial advisor or hedge fund manager is a "sophisticated investor", take it with a grain of salt,*" writes Peter J. Henning.[16] Commenting on the corporate scandals of the early 2000s (Enron, Worldcom, et al.), the authors of "*Freakonomics*" *wrote: "Though extraordinarily diverse, those crimes all have a common trait: they were sins of information...; in each case the experts were trying to keep the information asymmetry as asymmetrical as possible.*"[17] In other words, some get the means to act, supposedly, more rationally than others, and these "others" constitute the vast majority.

Enron's rating was still at "investment" grade four days before the company went bankrupt. Two months before Lehman Brothers filing for bankruptcy, Morgan Stanley recommended investors to buy stock, based on its excellent ratings. A few days before the final crash, Lehman Brothers financial products were still rated AAA by Fitch. In March 2009, Bank of America's long-term debt was just downgraded from A+ to A by Standard & Poor's despite the heavy Merrill Lynch load of losses to carry. Regardless of the consequences of bank management's tinkering with its subprime-related

---

16 Peter J. Henning is a professor at Wayne State University. Cited in "*The Myth of the Sophisticated Investor*", in "*The Deal Professor*" blog, managed by Steven M. Davidoff for The New York Times (http://dealbook.blogs.nytimes.com, February 2, 2009).

17 "*Freakonomics*", by Steven D. Levitt and Stephen J. Dubner (Penguin Books, 2005).

involvement and a bet on Greek debt, Belgian-French Dexia was still rated A only a few weeks prior to its second bailout in October 2011.

A long list of similar stories – and errors – could be reported, both for the private sector and public debt, not least regarding the Eurozone crisis. As the Leuven-based economist Paul De Grauwe writes: "*Having made systematic type I errors (i.e. "excessive faith in the soundness of private companies"), they are now more likely to make type II errors – finding risks where few exist. In the past, they were over-optimistic; they now react by being over-pessimistic.*"[18] In addition to the bad effects of an oligopolistic rating market, agencies suffer from vested interests (who pays the bill, and for what?), strong bias (analytical, but also political: companies and countries outside America are not as fairly treated as others), and a number of troubles which have little to do with rationality. Republican Senator Jim Bunning did not give the worst definition of a ratings agency's' job: "*That is like a movie studio paying a critic to review a movie, and then using a quote from his review in the commercials.*"[19] If the so-called rational Homo economicus is a rating agent, he is often moody and his standards are, on balance, quite poor.

---

18 "*Warning: rating agencies can do you harm*", in the Financial Times (January 22, 2009). For those who would have forgotten, Paul De Grauwe reminds in his article that in statistics, a type I error occurs when a hypothesis is rejected (e.g. "a company is risky") when it should have been accepted; a type II error occurs when a hypothesis is accepted (e.g. "a company is risky") when it should have been rejected. Read the good summary made by Rebecca Marston on BBC News website: "*What is a rating agency?*" (www.bbc.co.uk/news, December 6, 2011), from which we drew inspiration for the tag line.

19 Quoted on http://marketplace.publicradio.org.

SIN NO. 10:
INTERCONNECTED AND OVEREXPOSED

"Invisible threads are the strongest ties."
FRIEDRICH NIETZSCHE

"Happy" globalization...

Free trade, trade liberalization, and the unprecedented globalization trend of the last century are widely discussed. On the whole, there are more pros than cons for open markets and a globalized economy. However, these words have different meanings. Convincingly argued by Smith, Ricardo and their likes, "free" trade still has its hard-line defenders like N. Gregory Mankiw, who writes: "*Few propositions command as much consensus among professional economists as that open world trade increases economic growth and raises living standards.*"[1] A classical overview that the world is more open for the powerful than for others, that global trading is based on and has created inequities, that growth for the sake of growth generates increasing externalities, and that living standards are far from rising everywhere. Another ardent supporter of free trade, Columbia University professor Jagdish Bhagwati, admits that globalization has a human face, "*but we need to make that face more agreeable.*"[2] Jeffrey Sachs contends: "*Our challenge is not so much to invent global cooperation as it is to rejuvenate, modernize, and extend it.*"[3]

That sounds as if cosmetic reforms and a bit of makeup would make it less painful and thus more acceptable. Joseph Stiglitz, also a Columbia professor as well as a former World Bank chief economist, goes one step further: "*The problem is not with globalization itself but in the way (it) has been managed.*" He questions the supposed efficiency of markets and the free-market "fundamentalists", before making out a

1 N. Gregory Mankiw: "*Outsourcing Redux*" on http://gregmankiw.blogspot.com (May 7, 2006). Mankiw was chairman of the Council of Economic Advisers for President George W. Bush and was appointed as an economic adviser to Mitt Romney in 2012.

2 Jagdish Bhagwati, an Indian-born Professor at Columbia University: "*In Defense of Globalization*" (Oxford University Press, 2005).

3 Jeffrey D. Sachs: "*Common Wealth: Economics for a Crowded Planet*" (Penguin Press, 2008).

strong case against uneven or illusory benefits, and the obvious inequities of the globalization process. Those lead to growing "*discontent.*"[4] The former Dutch finance minister Wouter Bos declared that the late-2000s financial crisis had "*killed the myth of happy globalization.*" The myth was killed not least by showing how companies and economies, big or small, were increasingly exposed to events or policies taking place very far, and sometimes totally unrelated.[5]

… also means interlocking fragility

Growing interdependence and multiple interconnections are at the heart of globalization. "*We've been having the wrong discussion about globalization,*" wrote Robert J. Samuelson in the Washington Post. He added that "*the harder questions... lie elsewhere. Is an increasingly interconnected world economy basically stable? Or does it generate periodic crises that harm everyone and spawn international conflict?*"[6] From what we have witnessed and lived these last decades, the answer is clearly no to the first question, and most often yes to the second. If any, apparent short-term stability is indeed based on hourly or daily highs and lows that result from and move billions of dollars, euros, yen, pounds... in a split second. This hardly qualifies as stability. Markets – especially financial markets – are thriving on instability, very often to the detriment of the real economy. Moreover, the fine-tuning in national macroeconomic policies has become very difficult, due to those increased interconnections. While market players need political and economic stability to prosper – the old saying from Colbert times was "Laissez faire et laissez passer" – their interconnections and a growing interdependence (not to mention other sins such as

4 "*Globalization and Its Discontents*", "Making Globalization Work", two books by Joseph E. Stiglitz (W. W. Norton, 2003 and 2007).

5 Words reported by John Thornhill in the Financial Times (March 12, 2009).

6 Robert J. Samuelson, op-ed columnist: "*A Baffling Global Economy*", in The Washington Post (July 16, 2008).

short-termism) are disrupting factors or a hindrance to more stability.

A former financial derivatives specialist now working on epistemology, Nassim Nicholas Taleb writes that "*Globalization creates interlocking fragility,*" and points to the growth of giant banks that, while giving the appearance of stability, in reality, raised the risk of a systemic collapse: "*when one fails, they all fail.*"[7] A recent study of the relationships between 43,000 transnational corporations conducted by complex systems theorists at the Zurich-based Swiss Federal Institute of Technology shows a core of less than 1,500 firms with interlocking ownerships and explains that 1 percent of the companies are able to control 40 percent of the total wealth in the network.[8] Concentration of power has always existed, but the problem now lies in the core's tight interconnections: "*If one suffers distress, this propagates,*" says researcher James Glattfelder.

That was the starting point of the late-2000s financial crisis. A number of giants fell (e.g. Lehman Brothers), some stumbled (e.g. Citigroup), some were absorbed (e.g. Merrill Lynch), some took advantage to grow bigger (e.g. Goldman Sachs), and others were nationalized, at least temporarily. Talking about the rescue of the mortgage finance groups Fannie Mae and Freddie Mac, the then U.S. Treasury Secretary Hank Paulson said in September 2008 that the companies were not only so "*large*" but also so "*interwoven*" to the whole U.S. financial system that their failure would cause too much turmoil everywhere.[9] AIG

7 Nassim Nicholas Taleb: "*The Black Swan: The Impact of the Highly Improbable*" (Random House, 2007); a book that stands among the ones that "helped change the world," wrote a bit too optimistically, the Sunday Times (November 2, 2008). See also David Brooks: "*The behavioral revolution*" (Herald Tribune, October 29, 2008).

8 "*Revealed – the capitalist network that runs the world*", a summary of that very interesting research published in New Scientist (October 24, 2011: www.newscientist.com).

9 Words reported by www.reuters.com and the New York Times (September 8, 9, 2008). Paulson was later accused to have used his… connections, e.g. with his former Goldman Sachs partners, to give them insights into the coming disasters.

was not rescued only because it was too big to fail (revenues were at $110 billion and assets were worth $1,000,000 million in 2008), but because it was too interconnected to fail.

Iceland went virtually bankrupt because the country's financial institutions suffered from too much interdependence and could not live and survive, even to a lesser extent, in a world of their own – they could have, but chose to follow the herd of banks. In addition to home-made political mistakes (all to real estate and financial assets, nothing for education and entrepreneurship), Dubai's property sector crashed in the wake of the international mortgage-based crisis due to a mishmash of local and international, political, financial and celebrity interconnections from RBS and HSBC to David Beckham, Brad Pitt, and others![10] Fragile is an apt word for the economies of the Baltic, Central and Eastern Europe, which suffered much more from the late-2000s financial crisis owing to excessive dependency on Austrian, German and Swiss banks. Bank loans to eastern Europe economies by Austrian banks in 2009 was equivalent of 70 percent of Austria's GDP. One Hungarian out of three has contracted loans in Swiss francs.[11] Ireland is the (weak) link in the chain reaction between the American-originated mortgage crisis and the Eurozone sovereign debt meltdown. The mix and the sequence are explosive – or is it implosive? A huge real estate bubble, excessive dependence on the financial sector (with a very important foreign contribution), astronomical debt levels (at corporate, household and government levels) as a cause and consequence (the perfect vicious circle), a huge banking bailout, the squeezing effect of the euro, subsequent

---

10 See e.g. the chart published on http://ftalphaville.ft.com/blog (November 26, 2009) and "*Dubai's financial crisis: a Q&A*" in the Daily Telegraph (November 27, 2009).

11 In March 2009, the EU convened a special summit focused only on Eastern Europe's financial crisis (see report on www.time.com: "*As the Crisis Bites, Splits open Up in Europe*", March 2, 2009). Read also: "*Fiddling while eastern Europe burns*" (The Guardian, February 24, 2009); "*Hungary dug itself into a debt hole, now it pays the piper*" (www.reuters.com, November 29, 2011), etc.

austerity programs, and an economic recession to cap it all, naturally. Ireland represents the mother of all crises, as well as a perfect example of the fragility of an interconnected global economy.[12]

Connected – for better or worse

Nonetheless, being "connected" is trendy and often regarded as a positive word today, and rightly so in some cases. Think of the Internet, intranet, social networks, virtual communities… which, besides their benefits, can also give a positive meaning to exposure. In an opinion column titled "*Interconnected we prosper*" the then CEO of Lenovo stated: "*Once something in one part of the world becomes a best practice, it is almost magically adopted everywhere...*"[13] If only this idealistic view could be real!

Reality checks show a very different picture.

The manufacturing and service sectors of most economies are now entangled in a global supply-chain, which is the backbone of multinational and transnational companies. It is to such an extent that a just-in-time not on time or a network bug can break down a company or industry in a few hours or minutes. It also prevents employees and management from buying out a division when a plant closure is taking place. Risk factors increasingly relate to interconnections, and dealing with them is thus a much more arduous work than in the past. Despite the trend, in many organizations, the risk manager is still "*too far removed from action to feel genuine responsibility*," say two professors

12 Read e.g.: "*Ireland debt crisis: European banks' exposure*" and "*How the Irish crisis unfolded: timeline*" (Daily Telegraph, November 15 and 22, 2010); "Eurozone debt web: Who owes what to whom?" (at www.bbc.co.uk/news, November 18, 2011); "*Debt Crisis: Ireland likely to need second bailout warns rating agency Moody's*" (www.independent.ie/business, March 5, 2012).

13 Opinion by William J. Amelio, published in the Herald Tribune (June 25, 2008).

at the London Business School.[14] "*One of the ironies of the last few years is how often risk management tools amplify risk rather than reduce it,*" wrote Henny Sender.[15] And not just at company level. Among the lessons of recent crises, states and governments often seem even less equipped than companies to manage risks in an interconnected economy.

Goldman Sachs's investment banking business is heavily based on interconnections – and connections, tout court.[16] The top 50 of the 147 "*superconnected*" companies listed in the Swiss Federal Institute of Technology research (mentioned above) almost entirely consists of financial sector companies, with Barclays, AXA, JP Morgan Chase, UBS in the top ten (China Petrochemical Group is the only non-financial group in top 50). Do these make the world a better and safer place? Malpractice can be emulated as much as best practice. Madoff's folly is not only another crazy dishonest Ponzi scheme but also a highly interconnected mechanism sold as better and ending as worse: "*Roughly half the estimated losses from Bernard Madoff's... are being borne by non-US investors, underscoring the global scope of the carnage.*" A financial carnage that hit a 162-page list of 13,567 customer accounts, and possibly 3 million direct and indirect victims connected worldwide![17]

Connectivity is useful, but risky too. One of the causes of the Asian market crash of 1997 was certainly the excessive dependence both on exports and on capital inflows that made countries such as Indonesia, Thailand and the Philippines much more exposed to currency and capital markets movements. The fact that Malaysia and Thailand managed to weather the crisis by

14 Julian Birkinshaw and Huw Jenkins, professors at the London Business School, in "*Britain in 2010*", annual magazine of the UK Economic and Social Research Council.

15 "*On Wall Street*" column, in the Financial Times (November 12, 2011).

16 Read "*Diving in Search of the Great Vampire Squid*" by Janet Maslin, in the New York Times (April 11, 2011).

17 Financial Times and Herald Tribune (January 11, 12; March 12, 2009), www.reuters.com, http://rawstory.com/news, etc.

sustaining import substitution and local value-added policies is a home truth for globalization hardliners, because the exit went through decreased exposure. Peter Newman says: "*Power tends to connect; absolute power connects absolutely.*" A capability – and the courage – to disconnect, at individual, company or political level, may be part of the solution to crises.

SIN NO. 11:
AMERICAN CREDIT (SHOT IN HOLLYWOOD)

"Money is nothing to us; it is merely the symbol of our success. We are the greatest idealists in the world; I happen to think that we have set our ideal on the wrong objects."

LARRY DARRELL, in "*The Razor's Edge*" by W. Somerset Maugham

"One for the money. Two for the show"

Though unintentionally, the first verses of Carl Perkins's rock'n'roll number provide a real snatch of American-style capitalism.[1] Capitalism was invented in Britain, but America put the money in it. An acute observer of the American society, Alexis de Tocqueville wrote in 1835: "*As one digs deeper into the national character of the Americans, one sees that they have sought the value of everything in this world only in the answer to this single question: how much money will it bring in?*"[2] Didn't Calvin Coolidge, the 30th President, say: "*The chief business of the American people is business?*" The sequence that wraps up the U.S. model goes as follows:

- Being > Having > Amassing > Buying > Consuming > Owning > Showing.

How many Hollywood movies and TV series have been based on that script over the last sixty years? Marx (Groucho, and perhaps Karl too) would certainly have made fun of a society stuck at the bottom of Maslow's pyramid![3] For the many kind words he wrote about America in the 19th century, Tocqueville also pointed to serious flaws, of which a majority of people living "*in the perpetual utterance of self-applause*", the "*tyranny of the majority*", and the "*exceedingly wearisome*" pursuit of wealth.[4] Anyway, the model was exported with great success – and occasional resistance – to many places and

1 "*Blue Suede Shoes*", written and first recorded by Carl Perkins (Sun Records, 1956), best known in Elvis Presley's cover.

2 Alexis de Tocqueville: "*De la démocratie en Amérique*" (first published in 1835-1840, Folio, 1986), or "*Democracy in America*" (republished by Chicago University Press, 2002). The very good www.tocqueville.culture.fr/en website is worth a visit.

3 Abraham Maslow was an American professor of psychology, who theorized about the hierarchy of needs, often depicted in a pyramid. His "*Theory of Human Motivation*" was published in 1943.

4 Snippets picked by Ted Widmer in "*Tocqueville on the Bush years*" (New York Times, January 2, 2009).

throughout the 20th century, especially after World War II. Various degrees of imperialism (from soft to hard power), the Cold War, Hollywood, business schools, management techniques (Fordism and business schools' prescriptions not being the least influential) also helped, sometimes more than a little, gaining such a widespread adoption and acceptance of capitalism "Made in USA".

There were some good reasons for that. Innovation, entrepreneurship, an upward social ladder, productivity, and plentiful money supply are (were?) among the major ingredients and key success factors of American capitalism and society. Note that the two terms are often synonymous to American ears and eyes, probably due to the coincidence of the creation of the U.S. and the rise of a free-market economy. Equating America with capitalism and liberties with economic freedom first has been a trademark of U.S. mainstream politicians, businesspeople, and the media, especially on the right side of the aisle. To be honest, the equation is probably shared by a majority of citizens (remember Tocqueville's words cited above). When the subprime mortgage crisis had reached its peak and President Obama was coming up with a not particularly radical agenda, Mitt Romney declared that "*we're going to have to fight... to make sure that America stays America*" while the Indiana Republican Representative Mike Pence said the U.S. should fear "*European-style socialism.*"[5] Despite what Tea Party goers (today's ones, not the original insurgents) would say, it is not absolutely certain that the Founding Fathers had this in mind at least to that extent. In their eyes, the be-all was then more important than the have-all. The "Liberty Bell" was ringing for common responsibility and not for corporate irresponsibility.[6]

5 Quoted in "*Advice for the U.S. spender*", by David Leonhardt in the Herald Tribune (February 12, 2009) and in The Economist: "*More nonsense about Europe and America*" (Lexington column, March 1, 2009).

6 "*Liberty Bell*" is one of the symbols of America's independence and a military march composed by John Philip Sousa.

It was one of them, Thomas Jefferson, who already warned in 1802: "*I believe that banking institutions are more dangerous to our liberties than standing armies. If the American people ever allow private banks to control the issue of their currency, first by inflation, then by deflation, the banks and corporations... will deprive the people of all property...*"

From the American dream to the credit nightmare

Benjamin Franklin referred to the American dream in its autobiography. Historian James Truslow Adams summed it up in his "*Epic of America*" *(1931) as a "dream of a land in which life should be better and richer and fuller for everyone, with opportunity for each...*". Note that Adams added: "*It is not a dream of ... merely material plenty, motor cars and high wages.*"[7] In "*Death of a Salesman*" Arthur Miller's major character is on a journey for the "American Dream". Over the decades, the spiritual content of the dream has diminished while material components have kept on rising. Freedom of choice is mainly synonymous with a wide variety of shopping options, a better life is reduced to "*material plenty.*" In "*Born to Run*" Bruce Springsteen talks of a "*runaway American dream*", while Randy Newman sings ironically about "*great big things*" that show "*It's money that matters in the USA*".[8]

Herman Daly, an economist, John Cobb, a theologian, and David Loy, a professor of philosophy, write that "*our shift to consumption values has revolutionized the way we relate to each other. Shopping has become the great national pastime... On the basis of massive borrowing and massive sales of national assets, Americans have been squandering their heritage and*

7 James Truslow Adams: "*The Epic of America*" (1931, Simon Publications, 2001).

8 Bruce Springsteen: "*Born to Run*" (Columbia, 1975). Randy Newman: "*It's Money that Matters*", from "*Land of Dreams*" (WEA-Reprise, 1988).

impoverishing their children. So much for their patrimony..."[9] The New York Times columnist Joe Nocera rightly puts much of the blame on credit as a whole.[10]

U.S. Federal debt (publicly held)

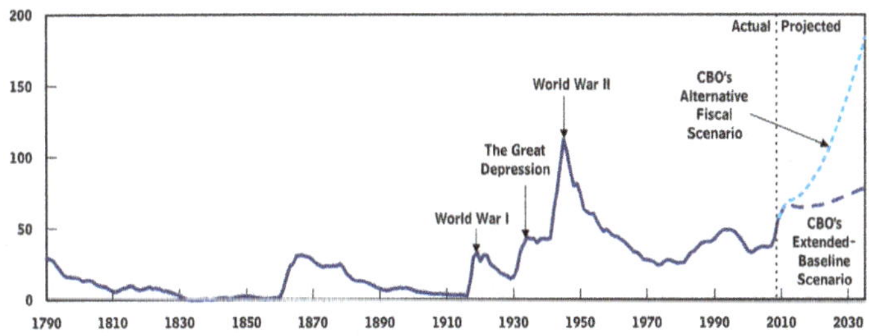

Source: Congressional Budget Office (July 2010)

Before the 1929 crash, the U.S. debt level was already way above 100 percent of GDP and surged in the 1930s; the debt problem – and its cost – has kept on worsening ever since. Before the late-2000s financial crisis, U.S. total debt reached 230 percent, excluding financial institutions. Including these, the percentage jumped to 350 percent of GDP (or to about 300 percent having removed asset-backed securities). In recent years, some firms borrowed up to $30 for every $1 they owned. Skyrocketing debt levels are/were of course not exclusive to the U.S. But the easy-money game was by far the most advanced in America. At first glance, it looked like a win-win, both for borrowers and lenders. Lending standards had been lowered, adjustable-rate mortgages had become the rule, but as most Americans want to have, buy and own, the roundabout kept on turning. At the end of 2007, the ratio of debt to disposable

9 Herman E. Daly, and John B. Cobb, Jr.: "*For the Common Good*" (Beacon Press, 1994), cited in "*The Religion of the Market*", by David R. Loy, in the Journal of the American Academy of Religion (Summer 1997).

10 "*A Piece of the Action: How the Middle Class Joined the Money Class*", by Joseph Nocera (Touchstone, 1995).

personal income had risen to 127 percent, from 80 percent in the nineties, with much of it related to mortgage costs. One of the results is that one out of every two Americans now lives on a low income or below the poverty line. On top of that, financial institutions issued large amounts of debt in the mid-2000s: the top five investment banks (of which a number have now disappeared) reported $4.1 trillion in debt in 2007, the equivalent of 30 percenr of U.S. GDP. To cap it all, government debt kept on increasing, with large amounts borrowed from Asian lenders. Note that, contrary to popular belief and right-wing propaganda, public debt increase is not only a left-leaning inclination: "*By the Treasury Department's count, Congress has acted 78 times since 1960 to raise, extend or alter the definition of the debt limit – 49 times under Republican presidents, and 29 times under Democratic presidents.*"[11]

Households, banks and the government had (have) already spent some (or much) of their future earnings: "*The current crisis marks the point at which the bills begin to get paid.*"[12] Eric Zencey thinks that all crises that have beset the U.S. economy in recent years are "*crises of debt repudiation. And we are unlikely to avoid more... until we stop allowing claims on income to grow faster than income.*"[13] Before copying a largely outdated U.S. model, one should reflect on the explanations and the implications of the late-2000s financial crisis and the huge bailout that followed. A Silicon Valley venture capitalist nailed it: "*You can bail out the economy, but you cannot bail out the environment. America has been borrowing money from China to buy oil from the Middle East. This 'borrow, buy, burn' model has*

11 "*Charting the American Debt Crisis*" (New York Times, July 28, 2011).

12 As written by David Leonhardt in the Herald Tribune ("*Debt is whittling away at U.S. economic power*", October 13, 2008).

13 "*A living, breathing economy*", by Eric Zencey, Professor at the Empire State College (Herald Tribune, April 15, 2009).

to change."[14] The buying, owning, housing, borrowing and burning model helped to define an "American way of life", regarded and preached by some as "my way or the highway". It is now running out of steam and has become purely and simply unsustainable. Claiming like Mitt Romney that his administration would "*permit drilling wherever it can be done safely*" is both pure demagogy and sheer irresponsibility. Tax-inclusive gasoline (or petrol) costs a Norwegian more than twice as much as for an American. Does that make the former's life less good than the latter's? One may doubt it, as the Norwegian state prefers to use oil revenues for funding arts and culture rather than for lowering fuel price for big drivers in big cars leaving big profits for big oil. The future oil shocks will be a rude awakening for many, and a reminder that the American dream now lives mostly in… Hollywood. "*It's called the American dream because you have to be asleep to believe it,*" said the satirist George Carlin.

So much for the American century

Mr. Romney's watch is slow. Calling for a new "*American century*" (with muscular foreign policy) is about turning the clock back.[15] That would be a rerun of the 20th century. What America is this now? John Wayne is long gone, "top gun" sunglasses are made in Italy, pink Cadillacs are replaced with imported autos, defense spending is largely covered by bonds owed to Chinese lenders, and, naturally (?), the fuel still comes from the Middle East. As to muscles, obesity statistics speak for themselves. Robert Kagan may assert that the U.S. had "*roughly a quarter*" of the world's income in 1969, and "*still produces roughly a quarter*" in the early-2010s, more accurate

14 Words of John Doerr at the Harvard Business School centennial summit held in October 2008, quoted by the Financial Times (October 21, 2008).

15 "*This century must be an American century… America leads the free world and the free world leads the entire world*", cited in "*Mitt Romney calls for new 'American century' with muscular foreign policy*" in the Washington Post (October 7, 2011). A real 20th century statement indeed.

measures show a different picture. According to the IMF's World Economic Outlook, in 1969 the U.S. accounted for 36 percent of global income at market prices, falling to 31 percent in 2000, and to 23 percent in 2010. "*Another decade like that and America's pre-eminence will look very shaky,*" writes Edward Luce.[16] Large segments of the U.S. establishment look determined to keep the illusion of power – both hard and soft – by using "*the military, economic and political tools that helped it so well in the 20th century.*"[17] Andrew Bacevich, a West Point graduate and Vietnam veteran, rejects that illusion, and says bluntly: "*The American Century Is Over – Good Riddance*".[18]

Many of the features that characterize modern capitalism were invented, made in U.S.A., and then exported abroad – like Hollywood movies. From blue jeans (and zippers) to electric dental drills, from bottle caps to offset printing, from the supercomputer to the PC, from Benjamin Franklin (one of the Founding Fathers was also the inventor of bifocals and the lightning rod) to Thomas Edison to Steve Jobs, to name but a few, American-style capitalism has a number of pluses to its credit. An unmatched entrepreneurial spirit, excellent research capabilities, and a capacity for innovating and developing new products have been at the heart of the American model.

But bookkeeping is double-entry and thus has its debit sides – and there are many in "*The World America Made.*"[19] Fast food, soft drinks, streets filled with cars and emptied of

---

16 Edward Luce: "*The reality of American decline*" (Financial Times, February 6, 2012).

17 In the words of Chandran Nair: "*We should stop talking of our Asian century*" (Financial Times, March 7, 2012). Lest some forget, dominance was also marked at macroeconomic level. For the benefits of the Marshall Plan and the dollar, the misbehavior resulting from malign effects of "Benign neglect" inspired policies should not be forgotten either. Remember the words "*The dollar is our currency, but your problem,*" said by Nixon's Treasury Secretary John Connally in 1971.

18 "*The American Century Is Over –Good Riddance*" by Andrew J. Bacevich on http://chronicle.com (February 19, 2012).

19 Title of a book written by Robert Kagan (Knopf, 2012).

pedestrians, (overused) credit cards, casino mentality (from Las Vegas to Wall Street), mindless and round-the-clock TV,[20] the MIC-derived Hummer and other gas guzzlers (then copied by most carmakers), obesity, waste (one quarter of world's waste for less than 5 percent of world's population), etc. To paraphrase FT's Martin Wolf, what is/was good for Wall Street is/was deemed as good for the world markets.[21] "*What has been going on may well not be the globalisation of world markets, but their Americanisation*," wrote WPP chief executive Martin Sorrell in an analysis of market trends written in his company's annual report.[22] There are visible signs of this "soft power", such as The Wall Street Journal, published in Europe and Asia under the same name as its New York-based parent yet there is no Wall Street elsewhere![23] In a similar vein, it is still mystifying to see the Hollywood Oscars advertised as "the" international movie competition, with one single category in twenty-plus for the (sic) "best foreign language film." All other major film festivals are much more international, just less hyped.

In his statement (quoted above), Martin Sorrell added: "*We may now be witnessing a change from Americanisation to globalisation*", because, "a*t times in history, when a country or empire seemed to have total political, social or economic hegemony, things changed and the vacuum was filled...*" Even an advocate of American exceptionalism like Robert Kagan has to admit that history shows that "*world orders, including our own, are transient. They rise and fall.*"[24] The first big financial crisis of the 21st century did not mark "*the end of American*

20 Well described in Bruce Springsteen's "*57 Channels (And Nothin' On)*" (on "*Human Touch*", Columbia, 1992).

21 Martin Wolf:: "*Cutting back financial capitalism is America's big test*" (Financial Times, April 15, 2009).

22 "*What we think*", in WPP annual report and accounts 2006.

23 The U.S. business daily has also increasingly shifted from an information newspaper and website to a vehicle for a (neo)conservative ideological agenda, courtesy of the Murdoch dynasty.

24 Robert Kagan: "*The World America Made*" (Knopf, 2012).

capitalism," as Anthony Fajola was asking in the Washington Post at the peak of the late-2000s financial crisis; and as the return to business, finance, consumption and credit as usual (well, almost) has illustrated it. However, for LSE professor Willem Buiter, it was at least "*the end of American capitalism as we knew it.*"[25] According to David Rothkopf, the U.S. approach is now "*discredited by abuse, shriveling opportunities and a shrinking middle class.*"[26] Although less sharp, Newsweek editor Fareed Zakaria also stresses the move towards a "post-American" world. His book is "*not about the decline of America but rather about the rise of everyone else*" (it is both, actually) and refers to three "tectonic" power shifts over the last 500 years: first, the rise of the Western world; second, the dominance of the U.S.; third, "*the rise of the rest,*" which is happening now.[27] The rest? This sounds very ethnocentric, although ironically, or is it not, most of the examples listed by Zakaria in his first chapter are defined by American yardsticks, from the tallest buildings to the casinos (?) and movie studios.

"*Three to get ready*" for a post-American capitalism.

25 Anthony Fajola in The Washington Post (October 10, 2008); Willem Buiter in the Financial Times (September 17, 2008).

26 David Rothkopf: "*Free-market evangelists face a lonely fate*" in the Financial Times, February 1, 2012. He is the author of "*Superclass: The Global Power Elite and the World They are Making*" (Farrar, Strauss and Giroux, 2008).

27 "*The Post-American World*", by Newsweek Editor Fareed Zakaria (W. W. Norton & Co, 2008).

SIN NO. 12:
WHAT DO WE BUY, ACTUALLY?

"To have little is to possess. To have plenty is to be perplexed."
LAO TZU

Supermarket capitalism

"*There is so much you can find in stores here!*" My Polish aunt (whose family had moved to Western Europe years before) was always surprised to hear those words from her relatives who were paying a rare visit to her place after a long ride to the western side of the Iron Curtain. That was in the years before the fall of the Berlin Wall, and Polish stores were not that well stocked. Capitalism has much in store, literally. And it has performed way better than communism and other alternatives on this matter too. Is it a perfect world? Daly and Cobb, an economist and a theologian, note: "*With the breakdown of community at all levels, human beings have become more like what the traditional model of Homo economicus described... Shopping has become the great national pastime....*"[1] And this is now the case in Poland, too. The oversupply economy and overconsumption society meet in supermarkets, department stores, shopping centers and malls, and other specially designed places. Before or after having filled your shopping cart, have you ever considered the number of products you never look at, and you would certainly never buy? Others might do it, but it is not 100 percent sure. Take the example of food waste: every year, one-third of food produced in the world, or 1.3 billion tonnes, is wasted. The average European or North American consumer wastes 95-115kg of food a year.[2] Much of the waste begins at the store, and originates in bad consumption habits, stimulated by irresponsible advertising and promotion: larger "family" portions, buffet service, "3 for the price of 2", etc.

---

1 Herman E. Daly, and John B. Cobb, Jr.: "*For the Common Good*" (Beacon Press, 1994).

2 In contrast, the average consumer in sub-Saharan Africa, South and East Asia wastes only 6kg-11kg. Read: "*One-third of the world food goes to waste, says FAO*" (The Guardian, May 12, 2011); "*1,3 milliard de tonnes de nourriture gaspillées chaque année dans le monde*" (Le Monde, 11 mai 2011, 14 février 2012).

Appearances can be deceptive

The rise of private, or white-label, goods and services as alternatives to often more expensive branded products naturally reflects consumption trends. It may also look weird when one knows that some of the makers of premium brands are the same as the ones producing lower-priced ones. And the winner is... It would not be an exaggeration to say that in some cases, the main value added for a company consists of sticking a brand on NPH (Not Produced Here) products.[3] Think of clothes, computers, shoes. The bulk of Nike products are manufactured in China, Thailand, Indonesia, and Vietnam, in facilities often controlled by South Korean and Taiwanese companies that are under contract with the Oregon-based firm, which just puts its brand on them. In the best cases, R&D, manufacturing, distribution, and social responsibility and externalities are under control, enabling customers to buy at a well-deserved (?) premium. In a less favorable light, purchasing is not really WYSIWYG (What you see is what you get) but more like WYGINRWYS (What you get is not, really, what you see – or think). In the 1970s, 70 to 80 percent of vehicles were produced at the manufacturers' factories. Now the amount lies between 20 and 30 percent, with the rest, i.e. the main part, outsourced, then assembled, and finally branded. Even to a casual observer, only the differences between visible exterior NIH components make cars distinct from each other, yet any automobile specialist will note that those differences are smaller than in the past. And now for the invisible parts. Europe's biggest automaker, Volkswagen is an example of cross-selling and cross-producing at large scale. Besides its home brand, the group controls Porsche, Audi, Seat, Skoda, Bentley, Lamborghini, Bugatti, the Swedish truck maker Scania, and, more recently, the Italian motorcycle maker Ducati. What is the difference between a

3 The term refers to the better-known NIH (Not Invented Here) syndrome (see below).

VW Cayenne and a Porsche Touareg (model swap intended)? The engine, the interior, the radiator grille, the brand, and... the price (here we are). The platform, and a significant percentage of assembly features are exactly the same (as the same goes for the Audi Q7, by the way). What is the USP for each of those SUVs? We leave it up to the reader (and buyer), but the question about what is really bought – and at what price – should be asked. The group wins as a supplier, perhaps the buyers are a bit duped but they do not seem to care that much. In the same industry, let us remember the ludicrous rebranding of Daewoo to Chevrolet by GM, as if changing a name could convince buyers that, overnight, their car had turned into a Chevy by waving a magic wand! In a recent survey among U.S. university students, 50 percent thought that Volvo was German, 56 percent that Hyundai was Japanese, and 34 percent that Lexus was an American brand. Even direct descendants of John Bull still think that Jaguar is as English as it was. Differentiation, so much hyped by carmakers, is often more about appearance than about realities.

On the debit side of the road

"*America began to change on a mid-September day in 1958, when the Bank of America dropped its first 60,000 credit cards on the unassuming city of Fresno, California.*" That is how Joe Nocera introduces one of his books, adding: "*... the Fresno drop also marked the beginning of something larger... A money revolution, you might call it... this is when the middle class began to change the way it thought about, and dealt with, its money.*"[4] James Carroll says: "*Capitalism is founded on an illusion. It is not only the delayed pain of the credit card bill that comes later, but the inevitable regret when, once home, the purchase disappoints.*"[5]

4 "*A Piece of the Action: How the Middle Class Joined the Money Class*", by Joseph Nocera (Touchstone, 1995).

5 James Carroll: "*Surviving the dark winter solstice*" (The Boston Globe, December 8, 2008).

How we buy matters as much as *what* we buy, or almost. About 20 percent of U.S. consumers have more than ten credit cards. A growing number of North American startups and SMEs are funded via credit cards, which is of course not the most orthodox way of financing a business. Note that on the other side of the border the average Canadian has two. Do you really need more than one? "*Probably not*," says Jeffrey Schwartz, a director of a Toronto-based credit counseling service. He adds that the danger comes when people view their credit limit as "free money" and start using a credit card to pay off the other, one of the quickest ways "*to spiral downwards in your financial situation*."[6] Easy money seems to have replaced hard cash and debt under control, or the use of one's own money "*as a store of wealth*," as Keynes put it.[7] Easy money comes at a price, and it starts with lender's control. "*Everything is good for you, if it doesn't kill you*."[8] Or the difference between good and bad debt. The addiction goes so deep and hits so many that the fix is long and costly. Fortunately, not everyone is following the credit (card)-addicted crowd. The more prudent Asian people, especially in the Buddhist cultures in China, Japan and elsewhere, put an emphasis on saving and preparing for the long term. However, there are some warning signs. The news that Citigroup is the first Western bank to offer own-brand cards in China might mean that less credit-based Asian capitalism's days are numbered.[9] What to think when a former World Bank director advises China to fall into the same trap as Western economies, and advocates for "*less frugality*" through saving less and buying more?[10]

---

6 Quoted in "*How many credit cards is too many?*" (www.theglobeandmail.com/globe-investor, January 24, 2012).

7 John Maynard Keynes: "*The General Theory of Employment, Interest and Money*" (first published in 1936. Prometheus Books, 1997).

8 Chorus of a Crowded House song, on "*Recurring Dream*" (Capitol, 1996).

9 "*Citigroup to issue China credit cards*" (Financial Times, February 7, 2012).

10 "*China's new challenge: less frugality*" by Yukon Huang, a former World Bank country director for China, on www.ft.com (The A-List, January 18, 2012).

Developed economies are excessively reliant on credit; at individual, corporate and government levels. That dependency has proved particularly damaging in triple D (for triple debt) economies such America, Britain and Ireland, much more addicted to credit cards than other countries. It came as no surprise to see those three countries hit more seriously by the subprime mortgage crisis in the late 2000s. That was a rude awakening. The disastrous results of irresponsible indebtedness, encouraged by the financial sector and nurtured by an individual greed for possession of home and other "assets" were exposed. Many seem to have forgotten – and keep on forgetting – the bottom line: you are the real owner of a house, apartment, car, and any other asset, when the last installment is paid, period.

The ownership society has always been a cornerstone of the conservative ideology. In June 2002, George W. Bush said: "*Part of economic security is owning your own home.*"[11] In October 2004, a couple of years before the biggest mortgage crisis in American history, he repeated: "*America is a stronger country every single time a family moves into a home of their own.*"[12] Following in Margaret Thatcher's footsteps, the British Conservatives still "*instinctively believe in creating an ownership society.*"[13] In his 2007 and 2012 presidential campaigns, Nicolas Sarkozy used "*Une France de propriétaires*" as one of his slogans. As another sign of a TINA-style consensus, the ownership theme has progressively (?) been adopted by segments of the Left, in the "third way" – Tony Blair took over on that, too – and beyond. Only a few months after the beginning of the subprime crisis, Jacques Attali, a socialist ideologue and former advisor to President Mitterrand, declared that, thanks to lower rates and estate prices, easier access to home

11 Quoted by the Herald Tribune (December 22, 2008).

12 Cited in "*End of the Ownership Society*" in Newsweek (October 10, 2008).

13 In the words of David Cameron, in "*From central power to people power*" (speech on February 22, 2010, available at: www.conservatives.com).

ownership would be one of the positive aspects in the ongoing crisis.[14] This is about going full circle, and thus getting ready for a new round of credits, and another potential crisis. Once again, the left has bought some of the major illusions sold by the capitalist supermarket.

Do not misread this. Ownership and private property are among the essential components of free markets and democracy. They can even bring solutions to some problems, such as poverty, maintenance, employee control over their business (e.g. via ESOP).[15] But why should buying property be the be-all and end-all of everything? Jean-Jacques Servan-Schreiber, the famous French journalist, centrist politician and author of "*The American Challenge*" used to say: "*Never own too much*."[16] The chart below shows the ownership rates in selected countries: Spain, Ireland and Greece – three countries among the most seriously hit by the latest financial crises (is it a coincidence?) – lead the pack, while France and Germany are lagging (far) behind. Note that home ownership in Singapore and Taiwan compare with Spain, while Thailand, Hong Kong and Japan are in the same bracket as France and Germany.[17] Are the Germans, the French or the Japanese less economically secure, less strong, and less happy than the "big" owners?

14 Jacques Attali, at a conference based on his book "*La crise, et après?*" (Fayard, 2008) in Brussels in January 2009. To be (un)fair, in the meantime, he had been entrusted with various reports by the then president Sarkozy.

15 Read e.g. "*Curing World Poverty. The New Role of Property*", published by Saint Louis, Missouri-based Catholic Social Justice Review (1994).

16 "*Le Défi Américain*" was published in 1967 in French (Denoel) and translated as "*The American Challenge*" (Avon Books, 1969). For those not familiar with French politics, JJSS (as he was nicknamed) was not a socialist, but a centrist liberal, thus supposedly less on the left wing than Mr. Attali.

17 Source: Modus RICS magazine, September 2011, April 2012.

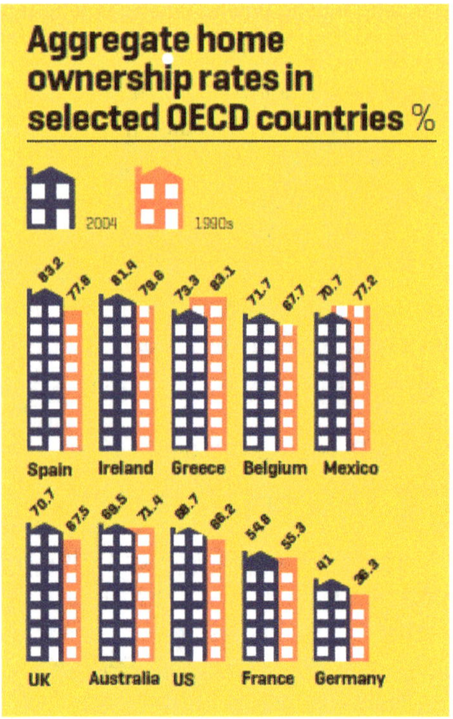

Source: Modus RICS magazine (September 2011)

Do we really need all that stuff?

"*Is it possible that the present economic crisis is a final reckoning with the lie that happiness can be purchased?*" wrote James Carroll in The Boston Globe.[18] Does that not bring us back to Abraham Maslow's hierarchy of needs?[19] Maslow wrote: "*Classic economic theory, based as it is on an inadequate theory of human motivation, could be revolutionized by accepting the reality of higher human needs, including the impulse to self actualization and the*

18 James P. Carroll : "*Surviving the dark winter solstice*" (The Boston Globe, December 8, 2008).

19 Abraham Maslow's "*Theory of Human Motivation*" was published in 1943.

love for the highest values." Overconsumption and dependency on credit tend to fulfill our "wants" instead of our "needs". Some might not like to hear that home truth, but status symbols are a perfect illustration of this. What are the big, expensive and luxury item purchases about? Are luxury watches about telling time, or about telling people who are... watching you about your status and wealth? This can sometimes border on ridiculous. In August 2011, the Sultan of Brunei decided to sell 21 cars (whose total number once reached 2,000) he had never driven! Back to earth with a bang. A significant part of purchases is about possession, perception and recognition, nothing else. Why are so many people reluctant to switch off their mobile phone and use it so heavily? This is less about a real need than about killing time, a fake sense of urgency, showing off, or just addiction (nomophobia). Desmond Tutu and Bettina Gronblom are right in saying that "*We cannot worship money and our self-interest alone – it leaves us with a hunger that can never be satisfied by acquiring more goods.*"[20] Bad news then: Homo economicus would not be a very advanced stage of Homo sapiens. As Polish sociologist Zygmunt Bauman stated, in today's world, freedom to purchase and to consume too often seems to matter more than freedom to enjoy life.[21] Something that cannot be bought...

20 "*Camels can pass through the eye of a needle*" by Desmond Tutu and Bettina Gronblom (Financial Times, April 5, 2012).

21 Zygmunt Bauman lives in Britain. Read e.g. "*Liquid Times: Living in an Age of Uncertainty*" (Polity, 2007).

SIN NO. 13:
IS SERVICE INCLUDED?

"I awoke and understood that life was about service, I served and realized that service is joy."
RABINDRANATH TAGORE

Service economies...

Many of us are now supposed to live in service economies.

A recent U.S. survey showed that 75 percent of CEOs believed that their company was providing (sic) "*above-average*" customer service. Really? The same survey pointed out that 59 percent of consumers were dissatisfied with their most recent service experience.[1] Research in other parts of the world supports this trend, yet probably with higher satisfaction rates in Japan and Southeast Asia, and lower service ratings in Germany, Nordic countries, Russia... Other studies have showed that only one-third of buyers of cars or domestic appliances would be ready to go back to their dealers or stores after having experienced poor service on after-sales and maintenance. As Frederick F. Reichheld, a specialist in customer satisfaction issues, puts it, the ultimate question for the seller is: "*On a scale of 1 to 10, how likely is it that you would recommend our company to a friend or colleague?*"[2] Peter Drucker often said that creating a customer is one thing, but keeping them is something else. Service is the best way to achieve this.

Phrases such as "*May I help you?*", "*How can I help you?*", "*What can I do for you?*", "24/7 assistance" abound everywhere. However, and paradoxically, the more we hear or read about service, the less we are effectively and efficiently served.

... are not always well served

- An increasing number of products or services are marketed as all-inclusive. Some are, but some are bogus, making the request for other options more difficult, or providing a ready-made menu that is not at all à la carte.

---

1 Mentioned by Bill Price, former VP for customer service at Amazon.com, and now President of Driva Solutions at a Stanford Breakfast Briefing on "*The Best Service Is No Service*" (available from http://breakfastbriefings.stanford.edu/).

2 Frederick F. Reichheld: "*The One Number You Need to Know*" in "*Increasing Customer Loyalty*" (Harvard Business Review Press, April 2011).

When it comes to service, the price to pay for extras makes them very exclusive indeed (some car brands are quite (in)famous for that.)

- "Buy it!" (and shut up) was the prevailing attitude among U.S. carmakers and dealers for years. "*The answer is that Detroit never really researched customers' wants. It only researched their preferences between the kinds of things it had already decided to offer them... The areas of the greatest unsatisfied needs are ignored...*"[3] Who wrote that? Theodore Levitt, about the American automobile industry. When? In 1960 (nineteen sixty)! It took Motown giants more than 40 (forty) years to listen, and to (re)start buying cars meeting customer expectations. Meanwhile, that short-sightedness cost market shares, sales, and profits, and benefited the Japanese carmakers, who proved to be better watchers and listeners. Listening before selling is marketing basics 1-O-1.
- "*Best service is no service*". Nobody knows who coined the expression. Anyway, that can be a very positive thing. When a product is so good that after-sales, maintenance or repair costs are down to zero or not much, service matters less significantly, if it ever does. Regrettably, some companies misinterpret the message and apply it literally. That is how, bar a few exceptions, the retail banking sector has almost become a no-service business in developed economies. Most airlines have lost their service edge, under the pressure of low-cost (and zero-service) carriers. Train service performance has much decreased these last years in many countries (chalk this up to liberalization and the lack of investment, too).

3 In his seminal article "*Marketing Myopia*", published in the Harvard Business Review (1960).

- DIY is what IKEA furniture stores are all about. If the whole service is in the hands of the clients, they may not serve any complaints about poor service, service that is clearly not used as a sales argument by the Swedish company. The rules are clear and there is nothing (well, almost) to complain about. The IT service industry also uses this model (with the little "help" buttons). Many problems can be self-fixed by the user. When there is no major trouble, that works fine. The limits of DIY appear when there is one, and one needs to find a reliable service provider, or simply someone to talk to at a nearby shop. A product is a flow of services. Marketing masters such as Kotler, Levitt, Peters and Davidson have taught this to thousands of students, managers, readers.[4] Unfortunately, millions of business people seem to ignore this every day. The marketing guru Philip Kotler himself once declared: "*Who has read my books? The students and the Japanese.*" Experiencing the decreasing quality of service and comparing good and bad performers, often vindicates that statement. As Rosabeth Moss Kanter wrote, too many manufacturers view what they make as a product, while customers buy it as a service.[5] There is something happening before, during, around and after any purchase. That "something" can weigh a lot in the buying decision, but also impacts on sales and profits. Most often, the service starts… or finishes with a "help" touch, an answering machine, a voicemail, or a robot-sounding voice saying "*Hold the line*"... According to some surveys, half of bad experiences that

4 Read, among others: Philip Kotler: "*Principles of Marketing*" (Prentice-Hall, 1980); Theodore Levitt: "*Marketing success through differentiation of anything*" (Harvard Business Review, 1980); Thomas J. Peters and Robert H. Waterman: "*In Search of Excellence*" (Harper & Row, 1982); Hugh Davidson: "*Offensive Marketing*" (Penguin Business, 1987).

5 Rosabeth Moss Kanter: "*Think Like the Customer: The Global Business Logic*" (Harvard Business Review, July-August 1992).

cause a customer to drop a supplier happen in call centers.[6] Fortunately, some butchers, bakers and grocers (but fewer brewers) still serve that "something" on top of their products. "*Old Fashioned Service Never Gets Old... Or Out of Fashion*," says Tom Peters.[7]

- Some studies have showed that firms obsessed with market share (and its increase) are distracted from their existing customer base and lose clients at the end of the day – and profits at the end of the year.[8] One may draw the same conclusion about an excessive priority given to cost reduction or to short-term profits. Likewise, excessive employee turnover is certainly a hindrance to sustainable customer service. Those trends often clash with service quality. A service charge has a cost – and requires investment.
- Social, cultural, education and health care related services are underdeveloped in many... developed economies. And free-market forces do not constitute the most suitable providers at best, or do not favor public services in the worst case. The list of unmet needs is long. Queuing up for medical care is now common in many Western countries. Illiteracy is rising in America and other places. Parents cannot find day care centers (nurseries) for their small children while they are at work. Schools lack teachers and maintenance. Retirement and old people's homes are full. Etc. A few economists, such as the French Julia Cagé, boldly state that it is not worth fighting deindustrialization and it is instead preferable to develop a comparative

6 MarketingWeek: "*Customer is king*", by Michael Barnett (November 3, 2011).

7 On www.tompters.com/blogs/main/service.

8 Read e.g. J. Scott Armstrong: "*Companies should focus on quality, not market share*" (Wharton School, "Executive Issues", Summer 1992).

> advantage based on education, culture, nursing, hospitals, and other public and private services.[9]

Services are labor-intensive and can generate thousands or millions of jobs not only in the private sector, but also in the third and fourth sectors. The late Alfred Sauvy used to say that an economy and a society based on unmet needs would reach permanent full employment.

9 "*Pourquoi la France doit continuer à se désindustrialiser*" (interview with Julia Cagé, in La Tribune, 5 mars 2011), and "*Une division mondiale du travail*" (L'Expansion, mars 2012). An interesting viewpoint, yet it overlooks the financing aspects, both upstream – wealth must be created – and downstream – users have to afford the cost.

SIN NO. 14:
WHITE AND BIG LIES

"A lie would have no sense unless the truth were felt dangerous."
ALFRED ADLER

Big shots, bigger lies

Yes, capitalism can be synonymous with free market and democracy. History teaches us that they have often reinforced each other, that free markets have been a prerequisite to political liberties, that democracy and free enterprise are intertwined. No, capitalism and democracy are not necessarily synonymous with each other. At best, the synonymy files under oversimplification. At worst, it is pure ideological falsehood. Chris Patten, a British Conservative, writes: "*Capitalism does not for me supersede democracy, nor guarantee it.*"[1] Still, mixing up both has been common practice from conservatives for some time, to make capitalism more acceptable; and from Communists, Fascists, Islamists et al., to reject both free market and democracy. As its deadly and other sins addressed in this book show, capitalism itself is not as "free-market" based and as democratic as it is claimed by its faithful supporters. After all, as the brilliant French liberal-conservative political scientist Raymond Aron wrote (cynically), democracies have remained, to some extent, softer forms of oligarchies.[2] As the U.S. case illustrates, oligarchy may even border on plutocracy. Inequalities, corporate greed, the power of lobbies, corruption, political donations et al. should restrain U.S. leaders from lecturing other countries about democracy. Even Warren Buffett recognized that "*we have moved in my lifetime towards a plutocracy... the distribution of wealth and the influence of wealth have moved in that direction.*"[3] Jeffrey Sachs puts it more bluntly: "*It's more accurate to say that the Republicans are for Big Oil while the Democrats are for Big Banks.*"[4]

---

1 Chris Patten: "*Not Quite the Diplomat. Home Truths about World Affairs*" (Penguin Books, 2006).

2 Raymond Aron: "*Démocratie et totalitarisme*" (Gallimard, Idées, 1965).

3 Quoted on Pragmatic Capitalism website (http://pragcap.com, March 29, 2011).

4 Jeffrey Sachs: "*Budgetary Deceit and America's Decline*" (www.huffingtonpost.com, July 23, 2011).

Various forms of capitalism have coexisted with and prospered under non-democratic systems. Without engaging in China-bashing – why should democracy or capitalism as defined in Western terms be the best recipe everywhere? – it is fair to say that China is a mix of entrepreneurial spirit, state-controlled capitalism, and limited democratic areas. The relationship between Nazi Germany and big business was far from clear. Or perhaps was it too clear after all, as "National Socialism" might as well been more aptly named state-guided capitalism. Hitler reportedly said: "*I absolutely insist on protecting private property... we must encourage private initiatives.*"[5] Despite their (very expensive) PR efforts, Middle-East oil-producing regimes are still leaning towards feudalism, yet their monetary resources are mostly invested in a pure capitalistic fashion. Chile, Argentina, and other Latin American "experiences" stood among the best (we mean worst) examples of unbridled capitalism imposed thanks to the suppression of democracy and heavy-handed repression methods. On the other side, it was easier to buy a small enterprise in the last years of Hungary's market socialism than to create one in the first years of post-Franco statist – and real-estatish – Spain. For conservatives and the Right, the Cold War was as much about defending a capitalist system and the wealth and privilege of a minority as about promoting democracy for the majority. Admittedly, the wealth was trickling down to the middle and working classes, perhaps owing to redistribution policies as to free markets themselves. Ask the Latin Americans, the Greeks and the Italians, among others, how they lived the democracy-free market mix, made of a strong invisible market hand helped with political arms.[6]

---

5 Cited in "*Hitler's Secret Conversations*", by N. Cameron and R.H. Stevens ((Farrar, Straus and Young, 1953).

6 No need to remind the role played by the CIA and other MIC connections in Gladio and other "stay-behind" operations supposed to fight against communism after World War II.

When the Great Depression was just about at its worst, the U.S. president Herbert Hoover said to a group of businessmen: "*Prosperity is just around the corner.*"[7] It took more than ten years, a "New Deal", and a war to get America out of the woods. Nevertheless, Milton Friedman wrote forty years later: "*The Great Depression, like most other periods of severe unemployment, was produced by government mismanagement rather than by any inherent instability of the private economy.*"[8] We know that the leader of the Chicago School was self-opinionated…

Daniel Kahneman, a founder of the behavioral school of economics, writes: "*A reliable way to make people believe in falsehoods is frequent repetition, because familiarity is not easily distinguished from truth. Authoritarian institutions and marketers have always known this fact.*"[9] Big shots from Big Oil boards and their followers – and there are many in an oil-addicted world – have repeatedly denied the scientific evidence of human-caused climate change. Any unbiased gardener or farmer would tell you the opposite? Never mind! All means (and not always most legal) have been used to keep on burning oil and polluting.[10] In the same vein, until recently, the oil peak has been denied, while there are clear indicators that future discovery will not replace past discovery, and production cannot pick up and follow the increasing demand (as the chart below shows). Still, the Saudi minister of petroleum dares to state: "*Yet fundamentally the market remains balanced. It is the perceived potential shortage of oil keeping prices high*

7 In the same vein, the then French president Sarkozy declared in March 2012: "*Nous sommes sortis de la crise financière… la confiance revient… nous sommes en phase de reprise économique*" (cited on www.lepoint.fr, March 27, 2012).

8 "*A Monetary History of the United States, 1867-1960*", by Milton Friedman and Anna J. Schwartz (Princeton University Press, 1971).

9 Daniel Kahneman: "*Thinking, Fast and Slow*" (Farrar, Straus and Giroux, 2011).

10 Lobbying is one of those means: according to the Center for American Progress, the energy sector has at times enjoyed returns of 3,000 percent on its lobbying investment (mentioned by Gillian Tett in "*Down with lobbyists! Or not?*", Financial Times, March 3, 2012).

-not the reality on the ground..."[11] The "perceived" potential shortage! Despite that, ExxonMobil's public tune goes: "*A peak in petroleum liquids production, resulting solely from resource limitations, is unlikely in the next 25 years.*" Careful readers of ExxonMobil reports could point out that those optimistic views contradict even the company's own research. The chart below is excerpted from an ExxonMobil report published in 2004. As noted by a Peak Oil Center commentator, it is "*very disturbing as it comes from an oil producer itself.*"[12]

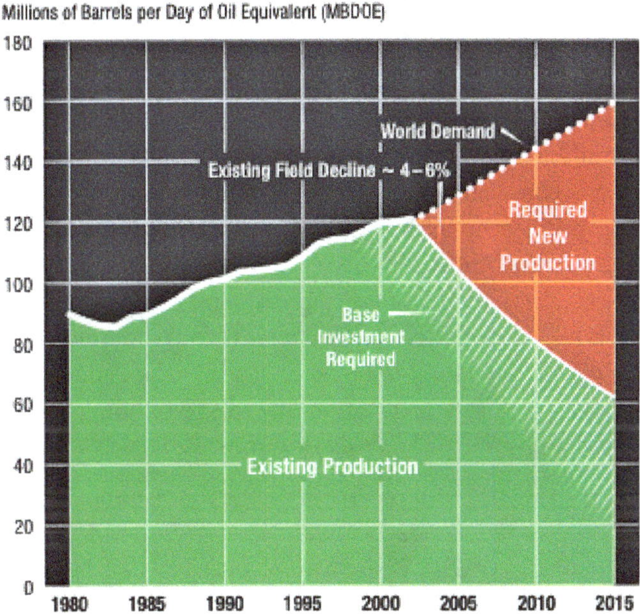

Source: ExxonMobil yearly report on energy 2004, Peak Oil Center

11 "*Saudi Arabia will act to bring down oil prices*" by Ali Naimi, in the Financial Times (March 29, 2012). Read, and compare with: "*How much oil does Saudi Arabia actually have?*" (The Guardian Environmental Blog, February 15, 2011).

12 "*Exxon Mobil Says Peak Oil Unlikely in the Next 25 Years*" (www.dailyreckoning.com.au, May 3, 2007). Read also the repeated statements in meetings, (good) annual reports, and the worth-reading "*Outlook for Energy*", published yearly by the Texas-based oil giant. Visits to http://members.home.nl/peakoil are recommended.

General Motors' vice chairman Bob Lutz said in February 2008 that hybrids like the Toyota Prius "*make no economic sense*" and that global warming (sic) "*is a total crock of s...*"[13] That was nine months before begging for taxpayers' money to help produce… hybrid vehicles, among others. In February 2009, Lutz announced that he would retire, declaring that the firm was "*designing what people want*", and complaining about the "*increase in regulation*" related to the production of less polluting and gas-guzzling models. Early in 2011, GM finally launched an electric hybrid car![14]

Bank statements

Yes, we know, Lord Hanson said: "*Always be nice to bankers.*" How could we? Apart from never missing a trick, the financial sector has come up with a rare number of "misses" in the last decade: misinforming, misjudging, misleading, misspeaking, misrepresenting, misstating…

A selection of these last years' greatest hits:

- Bank of America annual report 2007 boasted of "*A mortgage without the worries*" (p 19). The Federal bail-out in January 2009 amounted to $20 billion, plus $118 billion worth of "*guarantees against bad assets*".
- Fortis board of directors' message in the annual report 2007 was: "*We believe that our acquisition of selected activities of ABN Amro can be described as truly transformational.*" Nine months later, the group had to drop the case and was split into two government-owned companies plus a hollow holding after having been on the verge of bankruptcy.

13 Quoted by Thomas L. Friedman, asking "*How could America's big automakers be so bad for so long?*", in "*How to Fix a Flat*" in The New York Times (November 12, 2008).

14 "*GM's Latest Challenge: Losing Lutz*" (BusinessWeek, February 9, 2009), "*General Motors launches new electric hybrid car in US*" (The Guardian, December 19, 2010).

- Credit Suisse corporate citizenship report (2008) stressed that "*In the financial services industry, professionalism, trustworthiness, diligence... are more than just catchwords*" (p 12). A few months later, some traders were suspended in connection with a $2.85 billion over-evaluation of assets.
- HSBC half-year interim report 2008 stated: "*Our US-based consumer finance business will now be focused mainly on cards and consumer lending.*" Less than six months later, the bank was planning "*to quit US consumer lending.*"[15]
- In April 2008, UBS's then chairman Marcel Ospel declared: "*The storm is passing,*" A few months before, a Singapore government-owned institution had become Swiss group's main shareholder. A few months later, in the wake of further losses, the Swiss government was called to the rescue. Fiscal year 2008 result was a €13 billion loss.
- Lehman Brothers went bust on September 15, 2008. A few months before, a senior executive told a newspaper: "*From a risk management perspective, we continued to operate in our disciplined manner we're known for.*"[16]
- Bernard Madoff said: "*In today's regulatory environment, it's virtually impossible to violate rules.*" One year later, Madoff, a former Nasdaq chairman, was charged for what one of the largest financial frauds ever (well, at least until the next one is uncovered). A fraud for which the culprit later said that "*there was no innocent explanation*".[17]

15 Excerpt from the "*Group Chief Executive's Review*" in the Interim Report 2008. Financial Times, March 2, 2009.

16 Cited in the Herald Tribune (December 12, 2008).

17 Madoff's quote from Money Manager (October 20, 2007). "*Questions remain in Madoff drama*", by Joanna Chung and Brooke Masters in the Financial Times (March 11, 2009).

- Hypo Real Estate's chief executive said in January 2008: "*The management has done a fantastic job. We have not made any mistakes.*" Through the last six months of 2008, the German lending firm went through several bailouts by the Bundesbank, totaling around €100 billion. In January 2009, the company announced it would cut 40 percent of its workforce. In October 2009, the Munich-based group, also much involved in the Irish real estate market, was nationalized.[18] No mistake, he said!
- In 2011, RBS, Barclays, Credit Suisse, Goldman Sachs, et al. increased fixed pay by between 50 and 100 percent to offset bonus cuts.[19]
- Early in February 2012, Deutsche Bank's chief executive Josef Ackermann stated: "*The fact that we have never taken any money from the government has made us, from a reputational point of view, so attractive to so many clients in the world that we would be very reluctant to give that up.*" Just a few weeks later, Deutsche Bank took €10 billion of European Central Bank LTRO.[20]
- In March 2012, the head of credit trading at Credit Suisse was fined £210,000 by the UK Financial Services Authority (FSA) for disclosure about a forthcoming bond. The smooth-talking comment from Credit Suisse was: "*We deeply regret that one of our employees was sanctioned... Credit Suisse fully supports the FSA's actions to ensure information is properly controlled.*" In spite of

18 Reported in the Financial Times (January 16, December 31, 2008), FAZ Net ("*Der Hypo Real Estate droht die Insolvenz*", September 29, 2008), on www.reuters.com (February 18, 19, 2009; October 13, 2009).

19 "*RBS bonus cuts offset by big salary increases*" (www.ft.com, February 22, 2012).

20 "*Deutsche Bank taps ECB cash for Italy, Spain ops*" (Guardian, March 9, 2012).

an internal penalty, the bank continued to employ the trader.[21]

In the financial sector – or close to it – let us not forget the role of rating agencies. According to some, one of the sources of the problem dates back to the year 2000, when Standard & Poor's decided that credit "piggyback" was not riskier than a "normal" debt. According to some estimates, 60 percent of structured (you read right, structured) issues were rated AAA. Many went bust in the late-2000s financial turmoil. The total amount retrieved after default would be around 5 (five!) percent.[22] Too slow, too late, agencies made a mea culpa (before lending a hand in the following crisis): "*The assumption that we made about how these assets would perform in the future turned out to be incorrect*," said a Standard & Poor's manager in London, early in 2009.[23] Paul De Grauwe sums it perfectly: "*Is S&P still in the business of producing risk analyses? How can these agencies, which were systematically wrong in the past, have any credibility in whatever risk analysis they make?*"[24]

"A business of words"

That is how David Ogilvy defined advertising. He also stated: "*The enemies of advertising are the enemies of freedom.*" This sounds too much like a judge and party verdict, and is grossly exaggerated. In this world invaded by hyper-advertising and overconsumption (are these two not perhaps connected?), some might be in search of ad-free spaces and moments. This is

21 "*Credit Suisse trader fined after game of charades*" (Financial Times, March 14, 2012), from where the quotation is excerpted.

22 Mentioned by Olivier Pastré and Jean-Marc Sylvestre: "*Le roman vrai de la crise financière*" (Perrin, 2008). Amount cited by Tony Jackson: "*Is the writing on the wall for regulatory role of the ratings agencies?*" (Financial Times, March 2, 2009).

23 Standard & Poor's Ian Bell quoted on http://news.bbc.co.uk/: "*Ratings agencies admit mistakes*" (January 28, 2009).

24 "*Warning: rating agencies can do you harm*", in the Financial Times (January 22, 2009), by Paul De Grauwe, Professor of economics at the University of Leuven.

not about disputing the role of advertising to promote products and services. Nor is it to pretend that all ads are lies. Some ads help convey a message and inform the customers. A number of them may even be considered useful – and sometimes smartly done – communication vehicles. However, it would be fair to say that the number of half-truths – to put it mildly – is significant. The American comedian Fred Allen joked: "*Advertising is 85 percent confusion and 15 percent commission*," and F. Scott Fitzgerald even said: "*Advertising is a racket*."

A few examples to illustrate the list of advertising abuses:

- Low-cost airlines' tricks, which are purely and simply deceitful, such as advertising for a minimum price for a one-way ticket (who doesn't come back?) to a destination that will finally cost the customers many times more minimum (distance from and to airport, taxi, etc.), even before the return flight.

- Under pressure from consumerist and environmentalist groups, advertising and PR agencies and their clients have made efforts to look whiter than white. Well, sort of. Greenwashing is still trendy. BP spent $200 million to wear a greener badge to show it wanted to go "Beyond petroleum" (no, really?). McDonald's also put a coat of green paint on its European logo. Beyond appearances, carmakers advertise CO2 emissions per km, which is far from making sense (especially for powerful engines).[25]

- The same trend sometimes produces amusing oxymorons, such as "clean coal" or "hybrid-diesel";or hilarious messages, such as one inviting people to eat "responsible meat".[26]

---

25 A cleverly written book by two French engineers demonstrate the vacuity of those measures: "*Le plein, s'il vous plait*" by Jean-Marc Jancovici and Alain Grandjean (Seuil, 2006).

26 Heard in a radio campaign on the Belgian Flemish channels in the first quarter of 2012.

According to Carl Hausman, advertising practices mostly consist of "*lying with numbers, lying with words, and lying with images.*" Each category comprises "*about a half-dozen techniques.*"[27] We guess that the reader can easily spot more than a half-dozen examples for each kind of lie. The different degrees in lying techniques go beyond advertising. They have now spread to business and politics, not least courtesy of the increasing number of lobbyists, spin doctors, spokespersons, and talking heads whose role is to relay "home truths" that should be read between the lines and not taken for granted. Peter Drucker's words "*The most important thing in communication is to hear what isn't being said*" often come to mind when one hears or reads their statements, press releases, communiqués…

Corporate ethics are a serious matter, but this can be packaged for cosmetic use. "*True ethics begin where the use of language ceases,*" said Albert Schweitzer. Believe it or not, since post-Enron days most major U.S. companies, including Goldman Sachs, have an ethics officer, and a CCO or chief compliance officer (we do not know about rating agencies).[28] Although they may not qualify as lies, some of the lovely acronyms or names invented in the wake of the latest crises clearly belong to the business of words. The "Made in USA" TARP (Troubled Assets Relief Program) and the "Made in EU" LTRO (Longer Term Refinancing Operations), are two politically correct euphemisms for what mainly refers to a financial sector bailout (the dirtier "toxic assets" and "bad banks" have also been created for that purpose, probably implying there were still some good and nontoxic ones).

Ralph Waldo Emerson said: "*Truth is beautiful, without doubt, but so are lies.*"

---

27 Carl Hausman, Professor at the Rowan University (New Jersey): "*Lies We Live By. Defeating Doubletalk and Deception in Advertising, Politics, and the Media*" (Routledge, 2000).

28 As reported by Claudia Parsons on Reuters (January 29, 2009), cited on www.globalcompliance.com.

PART 3
REINVENTING A MODEL FOR THE ECONOMY, SOCIETY AND WELFARE

"A pessimist because of intelligence, an optimist because of will."
ANTONIO GRAMSCI

"The dogmas of the quiet past are inadequate to the stormy present... As our case is new, so we must think anew and act anew."
ABRAHAM LINCOLN

BUSINESS AS USUAL – OR NOT

"Those who manage their way into a crisis are not necessarily the right people to manage their way out of a crisis."

Albert Einstein

Down but not out

With such a load of sins to bear, will capitalism die from one or more of its seven deadly sins, or from other more or less serious ones? *"Some say the world will end in fire. Some say in ice,"* wrote the American poet Robert Frost. To use a religious reference that would please its true-blue evangelists, the same can be said about capitalism's future: heaven or hell? *"In the long run we are all dead,"* famously said Keynes.

In the meantime. The system has gone through many crises and its ability to adapt – its resilience, in the buzzword du jour – is not its least strength. To borrow from Mark Twain via the famous sociologist Zygmunt Bauman (himself not an ardent defender of capitalism), "*the news of the capitalism's demise is somewhat exaggerated.*"[1] However, the repeated crises since the late nineties have knocked the system off its pedestal, at least as an ideology. Anatol Lieven wrote about the subprime crisis: "*The latest crisis has dealt the coup de grâce to the Anglo-American economic model – summed up in the "Washington Consensus" that was preached with near-religious fervour and dogmatism in the 1990s.*"[2] A well-known supporter of capitalism, Samuel Brittan writes: "*market fundamentalism... is now well and truly dead.*"[3] Dead? Not sure. From Chicago to Bangalore, from the Hudson Institute, the Hoover Institution and other think tanks (and there are many), you will still hear distinguished economists and preachers of free-market capitalism extolling the virtues of the system, no matter what emerges. When the worst financial crisis since the Great Depression was raging, Gary Becker and Kevin Murphy, two noted Chicago professors, probably a bit scared of bold reform

1 Zygmunt Bauman: "On the Nature of Capitalism" on www.social-europe.eu (October 17, 2011).

2 "*Europe has to guard democracy amid crisis*" (Financial Times, December 11, 2008).

3 Samuel Brittan: "*A credo for a revived capitalism*" (Financial Times, May 7, 2010).

projects (abandoned since), advocated for a "*cure*" that should not "*destroy*" the system. Actually, they said that no major change was required because, "*given the losses, actors in these markets have a strong incentive to correct their mistakes the next time.*"[4] Belief, ideology or naivety?

Anyway, the pro-capitalists' task is made easier thanks to globalization (who is still out of it? Cuba? North Korea? Zimbabwe?), the lack of credible alternatives, and due to the vanishing camp of opponents. That seems to vindicate Fukuyama's thesis.[5] Where have all the alternatives – and radical doomsayers – gone? Communist Russia and China have embraced oligarch-led and state-controlled capitalism, respectively. Hard-line communists are an endangered species. Even if they support Robin Hood taxes and other tough measures, the "Occupy" movement and other "Indignados" protest against inequality but do not want to get rid of free markets as such. Though alter-globalists (with ATTAC as one of its most prominent movements) include a more radical segment, many among them fight for more economic justice and climate protection within market economies.[6] Some regimes are leaning towards Middle Ages-style feudalism, yet with mobile phones and other gimmicks invented by otherwise despised market economies. Outside America – where nationalism, populism and capitalism go hand in hand – many ultra-right

4 "*Do no let the 'cure' destroy capitalism*", by Gary Becker and Kevin Murphy (Financial Times, March 20, 2009).

5 "*The End of History and the Last Man*", by Francis Fukuyama (The National Interest, 1989; expanded book in Free Press, 1992). Beyond that apparent vindication, the ethnocentric Western model, and the claim that it would be an end point may be strongly disputed.

6 The term alter-globalization is a translation from the French word "altermondialisation". These gather annually at the World Social Forum and are active in a number of circles and publications. ATTAC defines itself as "*an international movement working towards social, environmental and democratic alternatives in the globalization process.*" (more information at www.attac.org/en/ or at Brussels-based GRESEA: www.gresea.be).

parties and right-wing populists have now included (forms of) capitalism as one of their basic tenets.

On a broader scale, social-democratic and other progressive parties have embarked on "Third Way" options whose ingredients, instead of going beyond left and right, too often look like a softer replica of capitalism. This functioned in times of prosperity, e.g. for redistribution policies, but often lacks the boldness required in difficult times.[7] It is strange that a new "Third Way", radical or progressive agenda has not emerged from the latest crises. One that would not throw the liberal baby and its virtues out with the capitalist bathwater (and sins) yet would boldly embark on a radical overhaul.[8] Instead, conservative austerity policies have prevailed, with some stimulus measures; and "*the third way (has) degenerated into platitude and vacuity*"[9] (and this goes beneath the surface, Tony Blair having sold his soul and cozying up to Rupert Murdoch). In 2011, a Spanish movement called Universidad Nomada stated: "*Here we have a social left which does not coincide with the political left. The latter has been absorbed by economic elites to such an extent that it is difficult to distinguish between the recommendations of big business groups and the decisions of the politicians.*" As Paul Mason commented in The Guardian, the remark can extend to large parts of the Left establishment in many countries. The French journalist Jacques Julliard says that the modern Left

7 See Anthony Giddens: "*Beyond Left and Right – The Future of Radical Politics*" (Polity Press, 1994).

8 The plural form might be used for "Third Way" as a generic term. It may refer to the convergence of capitalism and socialism; a mix between Keynesianism and liberal economics; a compromise between free-market liberalism and democratic socialism (or social democrats and liberals); the ideology claimed by Christian democratic parties (see e.g. the Dutch "Polder Model"); and, more recently, was revisited as a way to go beyond old-fashioned social democracy, uncontrolled markets, and to manage modern societies. Read "*The Third Way: The Renewal of Social Democracy*", by Anthony Giddens (Polity, 1999), and remember the good sides -there were some- of Clinton, Blair and Brown's policies.

9 Words used by John Kay in "*Obama is right to put pragmatism at the core of politics*" (Financial Times, November 19, 2008).

has not only adopted the market economy - which is not bad - but has also increasingly been fascinated by money and finance - which is questionable. Philip Stephens rightly points out that "*What's missing... is a model for social democracy that fits its aspirations to the new economic realities.*"[10]

Response to crises: plus çà change...

"*Why did no one see it coming?*" asked Queen Elizabeth II at a visit to the LSE. That was indeed the first question to ask about the biggest financial crisis since World War II. Professor Garicano answered: "*At every stage, someone was relying on somebody else and everyone thought they were doing the right thing.*"[11] No, really? Perhaps many economists are conformists, and the mainstream media and the establishment do not listen to dissenters. More broadly, large parts of business and financial sectors (populated by economists) have no interest in sending warning signals.

The Chinese definition of crisis means both "Threat" and "Opportunity." For all their threats, crises are also an opportunity to depart from business as usual, to try something else, and reinvent economic and societal models. Especially when these are broken. Paul Krugman comments: "*When depression economics prevails, the usual rules of economic policy no longer apply: Virtue becomes vice, caution is risky and prudence is folly.*"[12] Unfortunately, to paraphrase Keynes, the difficulty

10 Source: www.universidadnomada.net. Paul Mason: "*The European dream is in danger: prepare for another rude awakening*" (The Guardian, May 24, 2011). Philip Stephens: "*I told you so is not enough to save a left in crisis*" (Financial Times, September 29, 2011).

11 "*The Queen asks why no one saw the credit crunch coming*" (Daily Telegraph, November 5, 2008).

12 "*Depression Economics Returns*": column in the New York Times (November 14, 2008). Read also the updated version of his simply put yet witty book "*The Return of Depression Economics and the Crisis of 2008*" (Penguin, 2009). A few months later, Krugman also regretted "*The big dither*" of Obama's administration (New York Times, March 6, 2009). A couple of years later, he lambasted Eurozone austerity policies.

is not so much in developing new ideas as in escaping old ones – at least the ones that have not worked. What we have witnessed in the wake of the biggest financial and economic crisis in decades is not encouraging. The time was ripe for seizing opportunities to REFORM the system. Unfortunately, in many cases, it has been a relief for the ones who wanted to maintain the status quo. A missed opportunity, as even some among the conservatives were ready – or forced to – change their mindset. It was amusing to read a former Reagan Treasury Secretary arguing in support of at least temporary nationalization of banks.[13] Talking about the TARP he had to put in place, the then U.S. Treasury Secretary – and former Goldman Sachs CEO – Hank Paulson admitted: "*We did things that under normal circumstances would have been and are objectionable but are better than the alternative.*"[14] The then newly elected French president made a U-turn contrasting with his pro-business agenda and started ranting (not for long, though) on the abuses of financiers. How ironic it was then to see The Economist asking "*what should governments do?*" to face the looming "*misery of mass employment*" instead of its more usual call for market forces.[15]

Seven examples, each of them referring directly to a deadly sin, picked among dozens these last years, show piecemeal changes here and (the return to) business as usual there:

- The financial sector, and investment banking in particular, is now much more concentrated than before the subprime crisis. Bear Stearns and Lehman Brothers have disappeared, and Merrill Lynch was acquired by Bank of America, but in recent years the top ten investment banks

13 James Baker: "*How Washington can prevent 'zombie banks'*" (Financial Times, March 2, 2009).

14 "*Paulson rues shortage of firepower as battle raged*": interview with Krishna Guha in the Financial Times (December 31, 2008).

15 In: "*The jobs crisis*" (March 14, 2009). We write ironic because of the usual free-market and conservative leanings of the ever-smart London weekly.

(of which five are from the U.S.) have remained the same, and concentrate unprecedented financial power. Even in France, rather less affected by the mortgage crisis, one of the first consequences of the turmoil was the merger of Banque Populaire with Caisse d'Epargne. This was a bit surprising as both had avoided risky financial bets.[16] The benefits of this consolidation for shareholders, customers, and other stakeholders are not obvious.

- In 2011, German banks were the most exposed among foreign ones to the sovereign debt of Greece, Ireland, Portugal, and Spain, second only to the banks from the countries of origin. Germany's exposure was less serious in the case of Italy, yet it still ranked in the top three of foreign banks. One-third of the Irish debt and one-quarter of the Portuguese was in the hands of German banks.[17] Some may ask what they have been doing so far from the banks of the Main river. And some still wonder why Frau Merkel wants to rescue the Eurozone and the euro at all cost.
- Basel III is now on its way to help better regulate banks' capital adequacy and risk management. That is good news.[18] Besides the fact that it took some time to come to agreement (not least due to lobbying efforts from financiers who left – with golden handshakes – and then returned to business), enforcement will take some time, and some loopholes might already open doors for future crises. For example, Karel Lannoo, chief execu-

16 See tables, diagrams and comments about the banks' fate before and after the crisis in the Financial Times: "*Bank rankings. The fearsome become the fallen*" (March 23, 2009); and The Guardian: "*Questions of trust at the heart of a banking revival*" (March 25, 2009). For updates, use e.g. investment banking league tables, published by Thomson Reuters and http://markets.ft.com/investmentBanking.

17 Source: "*Goldman Sachs publishes list of banks exposed to PIIGS*" on www.investmenteurope.net (July 14, 2011).

18 By the way, let us point out that the U.S. has never implemented Basel II.

tive of CEPS, points to the limited role of the leverage ratio designed to limit banks' risk-taking, the reliance on credit ratings, and excessively positive bias towards real estate exposure, among other weaknesses.[19] We are not far from the causes of the first great financial crisis in the 21st century, which were precisely the reason for setting up Basel III.

- "*Is Facebook a Bubble?*" asked Fast Company magazine in January 2011, one year prior to the company's planned IPO. The social media company was valued at $50 billion (with a little help from Goldman Sachs). "*More than a bubble, Facebook is a manifestation of the rational excesses that only the financial markets are capable of when confronted with something without precedents and more importantly unexpected,*" says Luigi La Ferla, of an investment advisory services company, referring more than implicitly to the dot-com bubble.[20]
- In 2010, 3,100 of the largest companies were producing sustainability or corporate responsibility reports, compared with about 300 in 1996.[21] That makes a welcome change. Now back to business as usual. In April 2010, Walmart's chairman declared: "*What Walmart has done is approach (sustainability) from a business standpoint and not from a point of altruism.*" One cannot reproach a company management for putting business – and profit – at the top. But what happens when citizen responsibility clashes with the (single) bottom

19 Karel Lannoo: "*Rulemakers in Europe must flex muscles on Basel III*" (Financial Times, January 31, 2012). CEPS is the Centre for European Policy Studies (www.ceps.eu).

20 "*Is Facebook a Bubble?*" (Fast Company, January 28, 2011).

21 Figures provided by Patrick Eastwood, managing partner at Further (London), in the Financial Times (October 4, 2010).

line?[22] While the company's 2011 "*Global Responsibility Report*" emphasizes that it has met 15 of its sustainability commitments, its greenhouse gas emissions and its waste disposal have kept on increasing over the last two years. Making money comes first.

- Originally located in Anglo-Saxon economies and the financial sector, the extravagant bonuses – heavily criticized in the post-Enron and late-2000s crisis – are not only still alive out there, but have now spread to other countries and industries. Even the more egalitarian cultures are succumbing to bonus culture: for 2011, Volkswagen's CEO earned a total of €17.5 million, while the head of the French advertising group Publicis was entitled to a €16 million bonus. Twenty years ago, such announcements would have raised a storm of protest on both sides of the Rhine. And stock options, which epitomize short-termism, selfishness and greed altogether have remained a key compensation component across large corporations.
- To avoid deeper recession, stimulate growth, and decrease unemployment, many policymakers have gone for subsidizing industries of the past, instead of orienting economic and social policies towards sustainable development, the climate challenge, and planet conservation.[23] One of the best-worst examples is the subsidization of automakers and users, e.g. "Cash for Clunkers" in the U.S. or "Bonus-Malus" in France. In the latter case, from early in 2008, cars with carbon emissions above certain target are taxed more. A well-

22 "*Walmart Says Environmental Initiatives About Money, Not Brand Image*" (April 13, 2010), and "*Walmart Accused of Greenwashing*" (March 8, 2012), on www.environmentalleader.com.

23 As it was advocated by Joseph Stiglitz and Nicholas Stern in the Financial Times: "*Obama's chance to lead the green recovery*" (March 2, 2009).

> intentioned measure which has resulted in… an increase of CO2 emissions! Carmakers produced – and polluted – more, people bought more cars (mainly more-polluting diesel cars), and used their car more often because it was more economical.[24] Hardly green growth. More trivially, one of Formula One's major sponsors in 2007 was the Dutch financial group ING, which withdrew in the wake of the financial crisis and its bailout by the government. In 2012, two of the main sponsors are Allianz, the German insurance group, and Santander, the Spanish bank. Responsible driving, probably.

Piecemeal changes are necessary but not sufficient. Capitalism needs to be reformed, and that goes beyond the usual fine-tuning and mitigation measures. Even some of its enthusiastic supporters now admit that the system in its current form no longer fits this world. As the head of a Danish pharmaceutical company puts it in his annual letter: "*It seems more like a crisis of confidence – confidence in our financial systems, in our democracies' ability to agree on long-term solutions, and in ourselves and each other.*"[25] Even a Conservative prime minister, David Cameron, now refers to "*moral capitalism*" and pleads for "*rebalancing*" the economy towards less financial activities, while Barack Obama called for "*making stuff*" instead of "*phoney financial profits.*" Klaus Schwab, the founder of Davos World Economic Forum, said in January 2012: "*We must recognize that solving problems in the context of outdated and crumbling models will only dig us deeper into the hole.*"[26] You read correctly, this statement does not come from a disciple of Karl Marx or Antonio Gramsci! Radical changes

24 A good summary of the unintended consequences was made in the French monthly L'Expansion (mars 2012), which mentions an increase of CO^2 emissions by 170 kilotonnes per quarter in 2008 only.

25 Novo Nordisk annual report 2011.

26 Cited on "*Capitalism in current form no longer fits world: WEF's Schwab*" on http://news.xinhuanet.com (January 18, 2012).

and a major overhaul should be on the agenda of policymakers, businesspeople, and all stakeholders involved.

The economic system must be reinvented. New models of society have to be invented. It is about going BACK to the roots; going AGAINST and bucking the system where and when necessary; going BEYOND capitalism (exploring alternatives towards more diverse economies); and getting OUT of it, when possible.

Back to the roots

In spite of all its insufficiencies, flaws, and... sins, it would be ill-advised to throw the free market baby out with the capitalist bathwater. Capitalism has showed more than once that it could reinvent itself. Mikhail Gorbachev was right in saying: "*The market is not an invention of capitalism. It has existed for centuries. It is an invention of civilization.*"[27] The primary component of a free market is entrepreneurship. In mature and, to a lesser extent, in emerging economies, grass-roots entrepreneurs and firms find it increasingly hard to blossom and prosper in a world dominated by financiers, traders, megastores, mergers, oligopolies, private corpocrats, and public bureaucrats for whom the motto often seems to be "bigger is better." Size has become a goal as such. This proves wrong in a certain percentage of cases, to put it mildly. Worse, the entrepreneur (i.e. the butcher, brewer, baker et al.), the customer, the shareowner, are often the losers in that game. Today's corporate capitalism is too financially driven and asset-based. It should get back to more objective- and result-based entrepreneurial economies. Small-scale production, distribution and services are key to a renewed economic model, making financial performance a

27 That view echoes what the French historian Fernand Braudel analyzed brilliantly in his broad-scale account of the origins of civilization and capitalism: "*Civilisation matérielle, économie et capitalisme*" (1967-1979). I never find enough time to read those hefty books entirely, but perhaps Gorbachev did.

result and not an objective. Various means towards that end exist and are provided in the toolbox (see below).

Another major sickness of today's capitalism is short-termism. A long-term investor par excellence, Warren Buffett summed it up perfectly: "*Someone's sitting in the shade today because someone planted a tree a long time ago.*" The average entrepreneur cares about the business and lives with a long-term perspective, not just for making a quick buck. Today, short-term price and earnings matter more than long-term return and dividends. Despite all the hype about sustainable growth, in many cases (fortunately, there are still some exceptions from Stockholm to Tokyo), making the quarter for analysts and investors has in fact become a substitute for building a long-term strategy for customers and stakeholders.

Although not entirely bad as such, free-trade globalization often happens to the detriment of local economic fabrics that have always been the sources of economic and social progress – and political independence (see below). "*We cannot maintain global integration if it is seen as a source of domestic disintegration. This tension – that between the global economy and domestic politics – is a central challenge of our time,*" writes former U.S. Treasury Secretary Lawrence Summers.[28] As Cambridge professor Ha-Joon Chang shows, Britain, the home of free-trade policy, used varying degrees of protection measures in its development. It reduced manufacturing protection when its competitive advantage was highest. From 1820 to 1980, the average tariffs on manufactured goods in major industrial countries varied from 11 to 32 percent.[29] In another case of double historical standards, is it not that protectionism for which China is blamed now? Free trade is, on the whole, a good thing – but it is also about rich nations' hypocrisy.

---

28 Quoted by Martin Wolf in "*Will the will to take on difficult issues disappear?*" (Business blog, http://blogs.ft.com/businessblog, January 29, 2010).

29 Ha-Joon Chang: "*Kicking Away the Ladder: Development Strategy in Historical Perspective*" (Anthem Press, 2002).

As much market as possible, as much regulation as necessary

Markets cannot regulate themselves. Unfettered free markets require permanent adjustments and regulations. As Martin Wolf puts it: "*I have now lost faith in the view in giving the markets what we think they may want... should be the ruling idea in policy.*"[30] States, governments, policymakers have a role to play to manage macroeconomic policies, oversee markets, preserve a level playing field, correct the excesses, fine-tune, redistribute (markets are definitely not good at doing this), etc. "*A good many of the economic ills of each country are domestic. Much of the remedy must be what the nations do themselves,*" declared Roosevelt in 1933. Today, even if many of the "*ills*" are imported – and exported – those words still sound true. States – preferably democratically-controlled ones, of course – should have sufficient means to keep markets in check. Furthermore, the state has another key role to play when it comes to guarantee political independence and the minimum control on key resources against the ever-growing economic and financial dependence. The way Southeast Asian countries and Argentina weathered their crises in the late 1990s offers a better model than Eurozone management of the Greek and other "PIIGS" problem in this regard.

The slogan "*Government is not the answer. It is the problem,*" probably coined somewhere in Chicago, and then extensively used by Ronald Reagan, Maggie Thatcher and other disciples, is another motto of market fundamentalism. Like Samuel Brittan, I would like to say: "*Unless you are a sincere anarchist, you cannot believe that; and I hope that I never said it, even in my most anti-statist moments.*" This is not to say that government and the public sector can provide solutions to all problems. "*By definition, a government has no conscience. Sometimes it has a policy, but nothing more,*" wrote Albert Camus. That is even

30 Martin Wolf: "*Spare Britain the policy hair shirt*" (Financial Times, May 28, 2010).

less to claim that they are always best equipped for managing economies (mind the red tape, and see below for alternatives). But it is too easy to take the economy off governments' hands in good times and to call them to the rescue in bad times. Nevertheless, privatization of gains and socialization of losses have characterized, at various scales, the before and after stages of many crises – not least the first two crises of the 21st century.

To paraphrase the words used by the German Social Democrats in their Godesberger Programm, the answer is: "*As much market as possible, as much regulation as necessary.*"[31] Consider public goods, for which, as GIFT founder Chandran Nair writes, states have to "*take the lead in shaping incentives under which companies and individuals make decisions. Using taxes and fees, resources – be they energy, fisheries, forests, water or land – must be made more expensive.*"[32] A bold statement that departs from business and politics as usual. A series of actions and policies shown in the toolbox are clearly inspired by those principles. Indeed, both in good times and through crises, various forms of mixed economies and strong welfare states have clearly outperformed big, far, short, selfish, greedy, and wild variants of capitalism. Consider for example the Nordic and Rhine models, Argentina's debt and default management, Singapore's success, and even Saint-Simon-style Chinese socialism. Free markets without regulation would be comparable to roads without signs, traffic lights and policemen.

"*Control your destiny or someone else will do.*" Strangely, these words, attributed to various authors, seem to be more acceptable in the private sector than in politics. Governments and policymakers are no longer the masters of their own

31 Named after the town of Bad Godesberg, the program, adopted in 1959, dropped a more Marxist orientation for a social-market economic policy. The original phrase goes as "*As much market as possible, as much planning as necessary.*"

32 From "*We should stop talking of our Asian century*" (Financial Times, March 7, 2012). A Malaysian citizen of Indian descent, Chandran Nair is the founder of Asia-based GIFT (Global Institute For Tomorrow).

destiny and are submissive to markets. That is political liberalism defeated by market neoliberalism. If nation has always had wide currency, nationalism is often labeled as a bad word, and rightly so due to its historical record. Why does this rule not apply to protection as compared with protectionism? Chalk it up to the all-to-market ideology. Reducing exposure factors is viewed as a useful job at company level. Somewhat unfairly, it is not the case at macroeconomic and political level. Why should it not be a necessity, or at least temporary solution, at economic and political levels, too? The policies followed by countries such as Malaysia, Singapore, Thailand, a few Latin American nations, and… China have created a mix of open markets and protection through tariffs as well as the promotion of local value added and manufacturing. That is what the Canadian author John Ralston Saul calls "*positive nationalism.*"[33] Well, why not? Karel Williams, a professor at Manchester University, rightly says that policymakers should throw off their obsession with exports, "*and focus instead on import substitution.*"[34] Isolation is virtually impossible today, but temporary or local insulation and an ability to disconnect might be part of the response, as it was in the first stages of capitalism, whatever the country.

A more diverse economic model

The market does not have the answer to all problems. On the other hand, state-controlled sectors and nationalizations do not always show the most favorable track record in history. That said, there were hardly many alternatives to rescue the financial sector from a bankruptcy created by its excesses (to

33 John Ralston Saul: "*The Collapse of Globalism and the Reinvention of the World*" (Penguin Books, 2005). Catalonian and Scottish nationalism certainly fall into that category, but we would not say the same about Hungarian or other Eastern European nationalist parties.

34 Quoted by Tony Jackson in "*We need new thinking to bring home the UK bacon*" in the Financial Times (February 27, 2012).

use a polite word) in the late-2000s crisis.[35] The Washington Consensus (or is it the Wall Street Dogma?) was (?) mostly about liberalization and privatization. While the need for better management and service, increased resources (through private shareholders) was (and is) indisputable in a number of cases, all-to-market solutions are not the be-all and end-all. Sometimes they go wrong, or even prove harmful to the economy, society, and people. It is time to get out of that dualistic approach, in which the Left automatically means state and the Right represents markets. The answer lies in more diverse economies and societies.

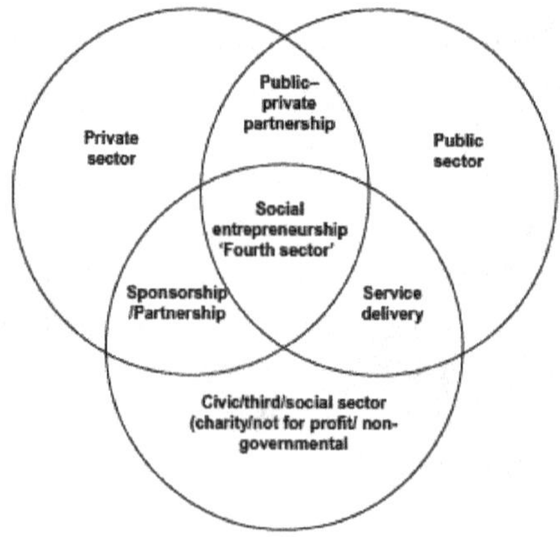

Source: Tania Ellis: "The New Pioneers"

The above diagram shows how a diversity of solutions can more effectively deliver the diversity of needs in our economies and societies. In many cases, policymakers promoting or involved in privatization programs do not even explore possible alternatives. This may of course result from subservience to market and financial players' interests, ideology, or from a need for cash to finance other expenses. Anyway, that can lead

35 As regards the pros and cons of banks' nationalizations, read "*To nationalise or not to nationalise is the question*", by Martin Wolf in the Financial Times (March 4, 2009).

to selling the family silver, as Harold Macmillan said about Margaret Thatcher's large-scale privatizations.[36] More fundamentally, as Richard Murphy writes: "*We cannot afford markets in some essential services*" where they "*do not meet needs*."[37] Should air, earth, water, food, health, education, energy, electricity, waste, science, justice, art, sports... be wholly left to market forces? The answer is a straight NO. The transition to "green growth" and a low-carbon economy requires a mix of resources and market and off-market players, e.g. to build or renovate energy-efficient housing, manage renewable energies, bring in cogeneration and smart-grid systems, contribute to "circular" economic processes (an alternative to the "Take. Make. Dispose" model based on recycling or using product components twice), etc.[38]

There are at least six alternatives to pure private sector companies: public utilities, partial ownership, PPP or public-private partnership (the BOT concession schemes, as developed in Asian economies and elsewhere, offer an interesting pattern, e.g. for infrastructure and energy projects),[39] non-profit institutions, municipalization, and sub-contracting or outsourcing. At small-scale and grass-roots level, the third and fourth sectors, made up of cultural associations, social enterprises, non-profit organizations, workers' cooperatives (and ESOP) et al. are often best equipped to meet market, environmental, and people's needs. A country like Denmark stands among the

36 For those who are not familiar with British politics, Harold Macmillan was also a Conservative prime minister from 1957 to 1963.

37 Richard Murphy: "*The Courageous State: Rethinking Economics, Society and the Role of Government*" (Searching Finance, 2011).

38 According to McKinsey, circular economy at large scale could save €288 billion annually for European companies.

39 BOT stands for Build-Operate-Transfer, or a concession received by one or more private investors to operate facilities for a period of time before being transferred (partly or wholly) to regional or national authorities.

champions in social innovation and entrepreneurship.[40] India has nurtured a strong cooperative tradition. Even in the U.S., the homeland of wild capitalism, things are changing. Gar Alperovitz notes: "*just below the surface of media attention literally thousands of grass roots institution-changing, wealth-democratizing efforts have been quietly developing throughout the nation for the last several decades.*"[41] Some figures substantiate this statement: roughly 4,500 not-for-profit community development corporations are devoted to housing manage day-to-day operations in cities. There are also now more than 11,000 businesses owned in whole or part by their employees, and 130 million Americans "*are members of various urban, agricultural, and credit union cooperatives.*" In Europe, FEBEA (the European Federation of Ethical and Alternative Banks) counts 25 financial institutions that claim to provide "ethical" and "alternative" banking services to 528,000 clients.

Today's definition of David Ricardo's comparative advantage should be as much about economic diversification and diversity as it was about excessive specialization and private sector monomania.

Free markets, but also market-free

Markets and money are present everywhere in our daily life. Free markets may be the most efficient economic systems (yet far from perfect, as we have seen), but spreading the market logic to all dimensions of society and social life is not a solution and should be fought against. Of course, money is required for exchange – that is one of the basics of modern economies – but exchange may not be reduced to monetary issues. However,

40 No wonder then that a good book about the topic has been written by a Dane. Tania Ellis: "*The New Pioneers - Sustainable business success through social innovation and social entrepreneurship*" (Wiley, 2010).

41 Gar Alperovitz: "*America Beyond Capitalism: Reclaiming Our Wealth, Our Liberty, and Our Democracy*" (Democracy Collaborative, 2nd edition, 2011).

that is what is increasingly happening. It looks as if financialization and privatization were extending to minds too.

Market intrusion threatens the very fabric of society. Remember the communist utopia according to Karl Marx, a world in which people would be free to "*do one thing today, and another tomorrow, hunt in the morning, fish in the afternoon, and discuss philosophy in the evening.*"[42] The real-life communist version turned that into oppressive regimes. Nevertheless, the fact remains that we all need, and enjoy, taking a breather – the longer the better. Another German fond of philosophy, Chancellor Helmut Schmidt, once said that people should stop watching TV for a minimum of two days a week to enjoy life (and, incidentally, help repopulate the country) – that "*TV screen (that) makes you feel small*"[43]. Would any politician dare to advise the same about the Internet today, for example?[44] For doing what? Going out, making new and meeting old friends, instead of just socializing only via social networks – where they are turned into advertising targets. And moving a bit: remember that walking is healthy even if it does not increase GDP! Or just... breaking free. We might as well enjoy car-free, fat-free, carbon-free, ad-free spaces and moments. Those choices – that can be encouraged by responsible businesspeople and policymakers – can help to escape from the tyranny of the market.[45] More importantly, some can contribute to save on energy,

42 From "*The German Ideology*" (published in 1845. Excerpts available at www.marxists.org/archive).

43 In the words of Iggy Pop and Goran Bregovic, from the soundtrack of "*Arizona Dream*" movie (Mercury, 1994). The whole verse goes as: "*TV screen (that) makes you feel small. No life at all.*"

44 A French poll showed that one person out of three would drop plans to go out because they do not have friends to do so. What use do they make of their 130 to 160 so-called "friends" on Facebook? ("*Tant d'amis sur les réseaux... mais si seul(e) le soir*", Le Monde, April 3, 2012).

45 Title of a book written by Wharton professor Joel Waldfogel: "*The Tyranny of the Market: Why You Can't Always Get What You Want*" (Harvard University Press, 2007).

protect the environment, reinforce safety and security, mitigate climate change effects, improve health, etc.

Michel Rocard, another great social democrat and a former French prime minister, said that when one looks back at what really makes you happy in a lifetime, very few moments or circumstances can be measured by economic and market standards. Those are: falling in love, having children, meeting friends, sharing some time with your family, achieving professional projects, performing in arts or in sports, traveling…[46]

The English poet John Ruskin wrote: "*There is no wealth but life*."

46 Michel Rocard: "*La société de demain sera moins marchande et moins cupide*" (entretien avec Françoise Fressoz, Le Monde, February 26, 2012).

POSSIBLE ACTIONS AND REINVENTION POLICIES: A TOOLBOX

Forget TINA, there is always an alternative – or more than one.

In the following pages, the reader will find more than one hundred principles, ideas, possible actions and reinvention policies presented as alternatives to current trends or classical answers from left, right, or center; from the states and from the markets. Each of them addresses – and tries to go against or at least mitigate the effects of – a deadly sin of capitalism as defined in this book. In the last section, seven alternative values to the related not that venial sins are also proposed.

Some ideas are about basic principles, or just common sense, or have already been raised by other distinguished voices. Some suggestions are about going back to the roots – the point is not to throw the good sides of free markets out with wicked capitalist practices. A number of recommendations come from my background and experience in the private sector, the corporate world, and investor-related matters. Some actions should happen at grass-roots business and microeconomic level; while others depend on macroeconomic policies – provided the will exists, there is still room for fine-tuning and a bit more out there. Some prescriptions are referred to more than once because they provide answers to more than one sin. Some contradictions may of course appear – remember the "Uneasy Square" in economic policy. The pendulum must swing from time to time: some measures may prove right in good times and wrong in bad times, and vice versa. Same about short-term vs. long-term, etc. Nothing is eternal – even capitalism! A significant part of the proposals clearly refer to a progressive agenda that reflects my philosophical, economic and political views and are therefore more radical – because profound changes are needed!

We must think and act anew.

The sin: Too big

CURRENT TRENDS OR CLASSICAL ANSWERS	POSSIBLE ACTIONS AND REINVENTION POLICIES
• Resource-driven or asset-based corporate capitalism.	• Objective- and result-based entrepreneurial market economies.
• Buying outside: external growth plays a major role.	• Developing inside: organic growth is a primary means.
• Market domination, consolidation, mergers, takeovers, acquisitions virtually unregulated or approved without many conditions.	• Consolidation, mergers, takeovers, acquisitions inevitable but regulated, and broken up if necessary (Sherman Act-inspired policies).
• "Too big to fail." Size matters.	• "Small is beautiful." Flexibility matters.
• Tough competition, hostile takeovers (also allowed by high levels of free-floating equities).	• Fair competition, friendly bids (can be encouraged with multiple-voting schemes, stable holders, shark repellents, etc).
• Wholly-owned or fully controlled subsidiaries.	• Joint ventures, corporation breakups, spinoffs, partnerships, buyouts.
• Right: private sector oligopolies and market domination in a number of sectors.	• Dominant positions fought, fined, and broken up if necessary to promote healthy competition.
• Left: state-controlled monopolies.	• Regionally regulated bodies and/or coordinated competition.
• Economies of scale. Lack of innovation. Slow market response.	• Economies of scope. R&D productivity. Responsiveness.
• Market shares a major goal.	• Market niches. Product leadership.
• Total assets, market value, ROC(E) become key indicators.	• ROE, ROS, ROA as key indicators (keep a close watch on others too!).
• Big international financial institutions rule the game. Capital markets as main financing source.	• Small regional banks play a more active role. Deposits and interests as main financing source.
• Low capital requirements for financial sector.	• Tighter capital requirements for financial sector.
• Risks spread across and off banks balance sheet.	• Split up banks.
• Costly short-term credit.	• Affordable long-term loans.
• Large listed stock markets.	• Regional unlisted bourses.
• International private equity.	• Local venture capital. Microcredits.
• Imitation.	• Innovation.

The sin: Too far

CURRENT TRENDS OR CLASSICAL ANSWERS	POSSIBLE ACTIONS AND REINVENTION POLICIES
• Economic and financial dependence. • Think global – first or only. • Centralization. • Export as a main priority. • Left: state-led protectionism. • Right: free trade at any cost. • Attract international investors (sometimes with big subsidies). • Remote, anonymous, institutional investors. • Up to one hundred percent free float. • Cross-border shareholdings. • Remote decision centers and HQs. • Inflated financial sector meeting international markets' demands. • International private equity. • Transnational stock exchanges listed and controlled by other institutions. • Hedge funds. • A global marketplace. Products from everywhere come to your supermarkets (out of season).	• Political and social independence. • Act local – or "glocalize." • Decentralization. • More focus on import substitution. • Insulation when/where necessary. Local value added. • Free and fair trade (possibly including tariffs and taxes). • Encourage local entrepreneurs (with incentives), attract international investors, develop regional interconnections/subcontracting. • Individual shareholders informed and committed about their investments. • Mix of free float and core stable stockholders. • Neighborhood investments. • Keep and attract decision centers. • More balanced industrial fabric oriented towards local needs. • Local venture capital. Microcredits. • Unlisted stock exchanges structured as cooperative institutions managed by constituents' representatives. • Sovereign and pension funds. • Back to the market square. Go to – and buy on – local markets (in season) too.

The sin: Too short

CURRENT TRENDS OR CLASSICAL ANSWERS	POSSIBLE ACTIONS AND REINVENTION POLICIES
• Bottom-line "shareholder value": priority to year/quarter earnings and dividends.	• Top-line company value: the bottom line is a result of revenue (growth), margin, earnings, return (in descending order).
• Share price as a financial policy goal, among other stock exchange so-called "fundamentals" (P/E et al.)	• Share price as an expected result from other real fundamental performance indicators.
• Market value fetishism.	• Market capitalization a short-term indicator, weighing less than revenues, profits, margins, ratios.
• Short-term earnings and dividends.	• Long-term returns and dividends.
• Making the quarter.	• Medium-term strategic agenda.
• Quarterly/interim reports made compulsory.	• Quarterly/interim reports not mandatory.
• High-interest short-term credits.	• Low-interest long-term loans.
• Off-balance sheet.	• On-balance sheet.
• Investor relations and "guidance" pulled by analysts' expectations and large shareholders and funds' demands.	• Investor relations pushed by internal variables, market trends, and investors' expectations (analysts welcome too!).
• Free float leads to volatility.	• Core shareholders mean stability.
• Variations on EBIT.	• Managing operating income and cash flows.
• Quick ROI.	• Medium-term ROE and ROC.
• Invisible risk pyramids.	• Risk mapped and managed.
• Short-term driven hedge funds.	• Long-term investing sovereign and pension funds.
• Excessively complex derivatives.	• Complex derivatives tracked – or prohibited.
• "Casino" finance.	• "Boring" banks.
• Derivatives excesses.	• Naked derivatives banned.
• Ratings (agencies) rule.	• Ratings are indicative.
• Fair/market value.	• Book value.

The sin: Too selfish

CURRENT TRENDS OR CLASSICAL ANSWERS	POSSIBLE ACTIONS AND REINVENTION POLICIES
• Self-interest.	• Business in a community.
• Externalities often left to the outside world.	• Externalities' management: company social responsibility.
• Disposable.	• Sustainable.
• CSR as add-on.	• CSR part of strategy.
• CO2 emissions markets.	• CO2 emissions control, taxes and incentives.
• Reactive crisis management.	• Proactive collective bargaining.
• Privatization of profits and socialization of losses: e.g. bail-out, (pre)retirement measures, assets relief, nationalizations...	• Shared responsibility: e.g. (non-) controlling stakes, voluntary flexible career ending, assets freeze, granted concessions...
• Privatization policies defined in shareholders and large investors' interests.	• Privatizations policies defined first in individual owners and benefits for society.
• Chairman = chief executive.	• Chairman # chief executive.
• Market-based private pension schemes. Pension funds at company level.	• Publicly guaranteed minimum pension with voluntary supplementing schemes. Mixed pension funds.
• Big bonuses, mainly for executives.	• Cap on bonuses. Shared bonuses.
• "Golden parachutes" granted for executives.	• Executives' termination schemes and amounts approved by shareholders.
• Right: layoff benefits, small or no unemployment benefits.	• Layoff benefits guaranteed for all workers.
• Left: open-ended or long-term unemployment benefits.	• Time-limited unemployment benefits (training and reinsertion schemes).
• Hire and fire.	• Long-term employee relationships.
• Corruption. Lobbying.	• Clearer boundaries between private and public sector.

The sin: Too greedy

CURRENT TRENDS OR CLASSICAL ANSWERS	POSSIBLE ACTIONS AND REINVENTION POLICIES
• Big gap between executive and worker pay.	• Set limits to possible highest-lowest income gap (in the form of brackets).
• Labor income is overtaxed while capital income is undertaxed.	• Labor income should always be proportionally less taxed than capital income.
• Ownership society promoted.	• Promote a mix of coexisting owning, leasing and renting formulas.
• Credit heavily encouraged.	• Savings effectively stimulated.
• Speculative short-term profits.	• Long-term investments.
• "Sophisticated" or "complex" financial products.	• Simple, clear and intelligible financial services.
• Credit card as a major payment means.	• A mix between cash, debit and credit cards and safe bank transfers.
• Bonuses paid whatever the results.	• Bonus paid only for positive results. Penalty for negative ones.
• Short-term price-based stock options.	• Long-term earnings-based stock ownership.
• Stock options as an important remuneration component.	• Stock options banned as compensation means.
• Corporate deception and fraud cases becoming system ingredients often solved with... money.	• Corporate deception and fraud cases tracked and treated with the highest severity.
• Buying and credit incentives.	• Saving and investment incentives.
• Too much off-balance sheet.	• Much on-balance sheet.
• Debt-based economies.	• Savings-based economies.
• "Casino" finance.	• "Boring" banks.
• "Bad" and "Zombie" banks after crises. Quick return to private sector.	• Write off toxic assets. Banks in public ownership then gradual return to private or mixed control.

The sin: Too wild

CURRENT TRENDS OR CLASSICAL ANSWERS	POSSIBLE ACTIONS AND REINVENTION POLICIES
• Laissez faire: unfettered free markets.	• Faire passer: regulated free markets.
• Capitalism creates wealth and enlarges the pie.	• States and policymakers take care of redistribution.
• Booms and busts come and go.	• Pro- and contra-cyclical policies.
• Speculative bubbles.	• Measures against speculation.
• Destructive creation.	• Creative destruction.
• "Cowardly State."	• "Courageous State."
• Low inflation as priority.	• High employment as priority.
• Income and other inequalities fuel capitalism.	• Income and other inequalities threaten (life in) society.
• Right: tax cuts for wealthy and trickle-down effects. • Left: progressive (high) tax levels and possible impact on trickle-up.	• Wealth disparities mitigated through progressive and/or proportional taxing schemes, with fair thresholds (e.g. to allow entrance into labor markets) and ceilings (e.g. not to penalize hard-working executives, risk-taking and responsibilities).
• Increasing gap between executive and worker pay.	• Set bracket limits to possible highest-lowest income gap.
• Right: "Hire and fire", temporary employment. • Left: fixed jobs, (mainly) open-ended contracts.	• "Flexisecurity" and employment diversity: full-time, fixed, part-time, job-sharing plans, voluntary retirement, outplacement, temporary schemes.
• Market-based private pension schemes. Pension funds at company level.	• Publicly guaranteed minimum pension with voluntary supplementing schemes. Mixed pension funds.
• Shock therapies (e.g. Chile, Greece).	• Managed exit strategies (e.g. Southeast Asia, Argentina).
• Trade wars.	• Free trade as a peace-keeping instrument.
• Military-industrial complex and wars for control and/or resources.	• Multilateral and national resource management.

The sin: Too much

CURRENT TRENDS OR CLASSICAL ANSWERS	POSSIBLE ACTIONS AND REINVENTION POLICIES
• Invisible hand dogmatism.	• Visible hands pragmatism.
• "Cowardly State."	• "Courageous State."
• Top-down politics.	• Bottom-up policy-making.
• Debt-based economies.	• Savings-based economies.
• Balanced budget dogma.	• Deficit spending.
• Right: laissez-faire, all-to-market.	• Highway codes, regulation.
• Left: dirigisme, all/much to public sector and/or state control.	• Third and fourth sectors, social enterprises, cooperatives.
• Irreversible liberalization and privatization process.	• Progressive, reversible and partial liberalization schemes.
• Right: market-managed natural resources and public policies. • Left: bureaucratic government-owned resources.	• Public-interest aimed and governed natural resources and policies (PPP, BOT, municipalization, concessions, cooperatives...).
• Private or privatized health care.	• Managed health care (public, social, public-private partnerships).
• Commodities.	• Common goods.
• Energy and finite resources prices based on a blend of markets and cartels pursuing short-term interests.	• Energy and finite resources prices based on medium-term collective price and volume agreements.
• Consumption and credit incentives: e.g. to drink sodas, buy cars, own homes, dispose, etc.	• Saving and investment incentives: e.g. to learn, practice sports, renovate, recycle, use a transportation mix, etc.
• Have-eat-drive-watch.	• Be-do-enjoy-share.
• Low fuel taxes or subsidized prices.	• High fuel taxes used for new energy sources funding and alternative transportation.
• 24/7 TV, Internet, advertising.	• TV-free, Internet-free, ad-free moments.
• Disposable.	• Sustainable.
• Virtual social networks.	• Real-life socializing.
• Egomania.	• Conviviality.
• Market society.	• Out-of-market times and places.

Versus consensus – Seven alternative values

THE SIN	CONSENSUS	ALTERNATIVE
Good and bad.	• Growth = progress.	• Progress # growth.

THE SIN	CONSENSUS	ALTERNATIVE
Crazy.	• Keep up with the Joneses.	• You can go your own way.

THE SIN	CONSENSUS	ALTERNATIVE
Exposed.	• "Interlocking fragility."	• Insulated areas and havens.

THE SIN	CONSENSUS	ALTERNATIVE
Credit.	• Bad debt. Short-term credit.	• Good debt. Long-term loans.

THE SIN	CONSENSUS	ALTERNATIVE
Buying.	• Selling (much) more.	• Buying (a bit) less.

THE SIN	CONSENSUS	ALTERNATIVE
Not served.	• Standardized products.	• Client service and respect.

THE SIN	CONSENSUS	ALTERNATIVE
Lies.	• "The market is always right."	• If it is broke, fix it.

ACKNOWLEDGMENTS

In the first weeks of 2009, the financial crisis was raging through the whole world (or at least many parts of it). I was sitting in a hotel bar in Brussels with my old (not every inch a) Flemish friend Marc Honnay. He told me: "*You have a good vantage point to watch the economy, so why don't you write a book.*" I was just working on it! A couple of years later, sitting in a pub in London, my old (every inch an) English friend Reg Pauffley asked me if the sins – and my views – had developed over time and, in that event, if I should not update the book. Thanks to Ashwin Rattan, from Searching Finance, this book is now in your hands or on your screen. Although the sins have all remained the same, the new edition is very different from the first self-published book, which was written in a hurry and with a sense of urgency. I hope this revised, entirely updated and expanded, yet still concise edition is up to the publisher's and readers' expectations.

My views and principles have been defined thanks to a liberal education. I owe this to my mother (a nurse), my father (a painter) and my grandfather (a carpenter). (My grandmother was not exactly a liberal but taught me about the seven deadly sins.) This book is written in memory of them. I owe a special debt, one that cannot be measured by any capitalist metrics, in good and bad times, and much more to Veronique Escarmelle, who is often there even when she is not there, and who has relentlessly encouraged me to write from the first day on. Jean

Janssens was the first professor who taught me economics, and I will always remember him, as well as Stéphane Bernard and Pierre Wathelet, among a few others as my most demanding teachers – the ones you always thank for what you learned from them, no matter their toughness. The first made me love economics (the hard way, and the net result is here!), the second pushed me to work on macroeconomic models (and discover their limits), and the third always reminded me that economics is primarily a social science, not more than that. Henri Le Marois, Yves de Wasseige and Guy de Faramond helped me discover that bigger was not always better and that more egalitarian forms of market economy could often outperform wild capitalism. This book is also written in memory of Catherine Beccarelli, who died while I was writing the first edition and with whom I will never have the opportunity to talk again about capitalism, la France, and Greece. I really valued the comments made about the first "draft" edition of this book, especially from Walter Coscia (who is also my best friend), Sergio Arzeni, Claude Thayse, Christine Robinson, Jean-Charles Drabs, Marsja Hall-Green, Francis Baudoux, Silvia Holgado-Gomez, José Syne, Norman Kurland, Bernard Lacroix, Louise König, Henk van Dijke, and Hisashi Ota.

Throughout my professional life and in business I have had opportunities to meet and work with clients, partners, employees, trainees, suppliers who have proved to be more than just "business contacts", and also act as real people in the society – some having been sidekicks, others soul mates, others just themselves. This book is dedicated to my relatives and friends' children, who will live in another world that will, hopefully, be a better place. My gratitude also goes to the people, known or unknown, in my region of origin and from other places on the planet, who help to remind me that most of real life happens outside capitalism.

INDEX

THE SEVEN DEADLY SINS OF CAPITALISM

REINVENTING A MODEL FOR THE ECONOMY, SOCIETY AND WELFARE

The book

Many books have been, and will be, written about capitalism. With a wealth of information –footnotes abound – and a vast store of knowledge – dozens of examples substantiate the subject – this concise, incisive and thought-provoking essay is one of the first that recapitulates and reviews the seven deadly sins of capitalism (plus seven other not so venial ones). Sins? The word seems appropriate, when for some all-to-market ideology has turned into a form of religion.

Recognized by many, including the author, for its unmatched economic efficiency, free-market capitalism is no longer what it used to be. Corpocrats rule, bankers have lost much of their credit, greed fuels the system, individual shareholders have no say, speculative bubbles burst regularly, financiers play casino money, daily share price targets have replaced strategies, etc. Those flaws come on top of other weaknesses (some of them being original sins): booms and busts, inequalities, selfishness, the cult of growth, supposed rationality, unfettered globalization, overconsumption, indebtedness, environmental damage…

The economic and financial system must be reinvented. That goes beyond fine-tuning, crisis mitigation and piecemeal reforms. New models of society have to be invented. The challenge is to go back to the roots, but also to buck the system when necessary, and to go beyond – and outside – capitalism and build up more diverse economies. No business as usual...

The author

Mike Guillaume is the co-founder and manager of e.com-ReportWatch, an Anglo-Euro-American London-based company that specializes in company reports assessment and benchmarking. He has been the editor of the "Annual Report on Annual Reports" since 1996. Prior to that, his track record includes extensive entrepreneurial and international management consulting experience, for local startups, SMEs and international firms, public institutions. He has consulted extensively in all industries in Europe, North and South America, and Southeast Asia. Parallel to his career path in markets, he did stints in the public sector, public-private partnerships, and academia.

That blend has given him good vantage points for watching economies and economics.

Mike has a degree in political science and international economics, and is a financial analyst and communication specialist. He has authored many articles, and contributed to various publications, courses and seminars. Mike has lived, worked and consulted in twenty-five countries on four continents.

www.ingramcontent.com/pod-product-compliance
Lightning Source LLC
Chambersburg PA
CBHW052122270326
41930CB00012B/2728

9781907720680